Male Peer Support and Violence against Women

The Northeastern Series on Gender, Crime, and Law Editor:
Claire Renzetti

For a complete list of books available in this series, please visit www.upne.com

Walter S. DeKeseredy and Martin D. Schwartz, *Male Peer Support and Violence against Women: The History and Verification of a Theory*

Chitra Raghavan and Shuki J. Cohen, editors, *Domestic Violence: Methodologies in Dialogue*

Karen G. Weiss, *Party School: Crime, Campus, and Community*

Claire M. Renzetti and Sandra Yocum, editors, *Clergy Sexual Abuse: Social Science Perspectives*

Taryn Lindhorst and Jeffrey L. Edleson, *Battered Women, Their Children, and International Law: The Unintended Consequences of the Hague Child Abduction Convention*

Edward W. Gondolf, *The Future of Batterer Programs: Reassessing Evidence-Based Practice*

Jessica P. Hodge, *Gendered Hate: Exploring Gender in Hate Crime Law*

Molly Dragiewicz, *Equality with a Vengeance: Men's Rights Groups, Battered Women, and Antifeminist Backlash*

Mary Lay Schuster and Amy D. Propen, *Victim Advocacy in the Courtroom: Persuasive Practices in Domestic Violence and Child Protection Cases*

Jana L. Jasinski, Jennifer K. Wesely, James D. Wright, and Elizabeth E. Mustaine, *Hard Lives, Mean Streets: Violence in the Lives of Homeless Women*

Merry Morash, *Women on Probation and Parole: A Feminist Critique of Community Programs and Services*

Drew Humphries, *Women, Violence, and the Media: Readings in Feminist Criminology*

Gail A. Caputo, *Out in the Storm: Drug-Addicted Women Living as Shoplifters and Sex Workers*

Michael P. Johnson, *A Typology of Domestic Violence: Intimate Terrorism, Violent Resistance, and Situational Couple Violence*

Susan L. Miller, editor, *Criminal Justice Research and Practice: Diverse Voices from the Field*

Jody Raphael, *Freeing Tammy: Women, Drugs, and Incarceration*

Kathleen J. Ferraro, *Neither Angels nor Demons: Women, Crime, and Victimization*

Michelle L. Meloy, *Sex Offenses and the Men Who Commit Them: An Assessment of Sex Offenders on Probation*

Amy Neustein and Michael Lesher, *From Madness to Mutiny: Why Mothers Are Running from the Family Courts—and What Can Be Done about It*

Jody Raphael, *Listening to Olivia: Violence, Poverty, and Prostitution*

Cynthia Siemsen, *Emotional Trials: Moral Dilemmas of Women Criminal Defense Attorneys*

Lori B. Girshick, *Woman-to-Woman Sexual Violence: Stories of Women in Prison*

publication of this book
is supported by a grant from
Jewish Federation of Greater Hartford

The History and
Verification
of a Theory

Male Peer Support and Violence against Women

Walter S. DeKeseredy
Martin D. Schwartz

Northeastern University Press   BOSTON

Northeastern University Press

An imprint of University Press of New England

www.upne.com

© 2013 Northeastern University

All rights reserved

Manufactured in the United States of America

Typeset in Minion Pro and Optima by

Integrated Publishing Solutions

Hardcover ISBN: 978-1-55553-832-3

Paperback ISBN: 978-1-55553-833-0

Ebook ISBN: 978-1-55553-834-7

For permission to reproduce any of the material in this book,
contact Permissions, University Press of New England,
One Court Street, Suite 250, Lebanon NH 03766; or visit
www.upne.com

Cataloging-in-Publication data available upon request.

5 4 3 2 1

This book is dedicated to our families and to all of our wonderful friends who supported us during good and bad times, which amazingly is pretty much the same list of names.

Contents

Acknowledgments

This book is about negative forms of social support, but it is an outcome of very strong relationships with loved ones, caring friends, and inspiring colleagues. We must first thank Claire Renzetti for encouraging us to pursue this project and for so many other wonderful things she has done for us over the past twenty-five years. She personifies social support and is a friend in the true spirit of the word. Special thanks also go to Phyllis Deutsch, editor-in-chief at the University Press of New England. Her patience and guidance are immeasurable.

When you write several dozen books, you have a tendency to think of them as your children. Of course, all of the books Walter and Marty have written together are products of a collective effort. However, just as it takes a village to raise a child, what each of us brought to the table was in part influenced by numerous fruitful exchanges, conversations, critiques, readings, and discussions with colleagues and friends. Unlike our other books, however, this one tries to bring together our work of the past twenty-five years, and therefore the colleagues who have influenced it, and to whom we owe thanks, span a wide range of time and geographic space. They include (while hoping we haven't left too many out): Rowland Atkinson, Bernie Auchter, Karen Bachar, Ronet Bachman, Gregg Barak, Ola Barnett, Raquel Bergen, Helene Berman, David Bird, Rebecca Block, Avi Brisman, Henry Brownstein, Liqun Cao, Steve Cake, Gail Caputo, Gary Cassagnol, Susan Caringella, Pat Carlen, Kerry Carrington, Meda Chesney-Lind, Ann Coker, Kimberly Cook, Terry Cox, Wesley Crichlow, Francis T. Cullen, Elliott Currie, Kathleen Daly, Juergen Dankwort, Jodie Death, Ashley Demyan, Joseph F. Donnermeyer, Molly Dragiewicz, Chrissy Eith, Desmond Ellis, Edna Erez, Danielle Fagan, Jeff Ferrell, Bonnie Fisher, William F. Flack Jr., Diane Follingstad, David O. Friedrichs, Rus Funk, Jen Gibbs, Alberto Godenzi, Edward Gondolf, Judith Grant, Carol Gregory, Steve Hall, Barbara Hart, Jen Hartman, Keith Hayward, Ronald Hinch, Russell Hogg, Sandra Huntzinger, Mark Israel, Clifford Jansen, Rita Kanarek, Victor Kappeler, David Kauzlarich,

Dorie Klein, Mary Koss, Peter Kraska, Salley Laskey, Julian Lo, Michael J. Lynch, Brian MacLean, Mason Martin, Anne Menard, James Messerschmidt, Raymond Michalowski, Jody Miller, Susan L. Miller, Dragan Milovanovic, Warren S.E. Morgan, Louise Moyer, Christopher Mullins, Kyle Mulrooney, Darlene Murphy, Stephen Muzzatti, Nancy Neylon, Patrik Olsson, Sue Osthoff, Reiko Ozaki, Sandy Ortman, Barbara Owen, Ellen Pence, Ruth Peterson, Victoria Pitts-Taylor, Lori Post, Gary Potter, Mike Presdee, James Ptacek, Callie Rennison, Robin Robinson, Jeffrey Ian Ross, Dawn Rothe, Linda Saltzman, Rick Sarre, Daniel Saunders, Donna Selman, Aysan Sev'er, Susan Sharp, Michael D. Smith, Natalie Sokoloff, Betsy Stanko, Cris Sullivan, Thomas Sutton, Jim D. Taylor, Alex Thio, Kenneth Tunnell, Jeffery Walker, Ron Weitzer, David Wiesenthal, Simon Winlow, Jock Young, and Joan Zorza. Unfortunately, many of these people disagree with one another, so it has been our job and responsibility to come up with the information and arguments presented in this book. Walter accepts full responsibility for any errors on his part. David Friedrichs, however, has agreed to accept responsibility for any of Marty's errors.

Over the years, we have greatly benefited from the assistance of many practitioners heavily involved in the constant struggle to end woman abuse. People affiliated with Luke's Place, the Ontario Women's Directorate, the Ohio Attorney General's Office, the Ohio Domestic Violence Network, the Athens County Coalition Against Sexual Assault, My Sisters Place in Athens, various social services based in Athens and other parts of Ohio, the California Coalition Against Sexual Assault, and other organizations contributed to our empirical, theoretical, and political efforts.

We are, as always, indebted to our loved ones. Carol Blum, Pat and Andrea DeKeseredy, and Eva Jantz were constantly there when we needed them. Walter's "fur children" Captain, Drew, Higgins, and Ola B. (named after feminist psychologist Ola Barnett) were also sources of inspiration and love. Ola died one week before we completed the first draft of this book. She was twenty-four years old and always sat on Walter's desk while he wrote books, articles, etc. Ola will always be in Walter's heart and mind. Drew and Eva Jantz will also be sadly missed and they both passed away a few months after Ola died.

Introduction

> In order to know how to foster change in abusive men, individuals and
> communities need to understand not only how abusive thinking works . . . ,
> but also where it comes from. Overcoming the scourge of relationship abuse
> demands attention to the root causes of the problem
> —*Lundy Bancroft, Why Does He Do That?*

Why do so many men beat, sexually assault, psychologically abuse, and otherwise harm their current and former intimate female partners in ways that
few of us can imagine? The main objective of this book is to help answer this
question. Unlike Lundy Bancroft cited above, we do not go "inside the minds of
angry and controlling men."[1] Perhaps because we are sociologists rather than psychologists, our explanations are grounded in what C. Wright Mills (1959) refers to
as the "sociological imagination." Mills never denied the angst, anguish, or problems that any individual man, woman, or family was going through. However,
he asked us to raise our sight to look at why many people act in similar ways,
and why some groups or societies have more of a particular social problem than
others. This doesn't diminish individual problems or personal pain, but it does
open our eyes to systemic issues and problems. In our case, this involves carefully examining how broader social and social psychological forces influence
men to abuse women.

Of course there is no question that men with psychological problems have
been identified as woman abusers. If we could accept arguments (e.g., Dutton,
2006, 2010) that battering is limited to a very few men with personality disorders, the problem would be simple. The problem is that while some batterers
have psychological problems, most abusive men are "less pathological than expected" (Gondolf, 1999, p. 1), with only 10 percent of all incidents of intimate
violence resulting from mental disorders (Brownridge, 2009; Gelles and Straus,
1988). Simply put, most men who abuse women physically, sexually, emotion-

ally, or economically are not identifiably different than other men in terms of their mental processing. As Bancroft (2002) notes, if a violent controlling man has an "aggressive personality," he will not be able to reserve that side of himself solely for his female partner. Rather, he will be violently aggressive in a variety of settings. That, however, is not the usual case. Although there are some men who are violent in a variety of settings, most men who abuse their current or former female partners do not have convictions for violence against other people or for actions in public places (DeKeseredy and Schwartz, 2011). These uncontrollable urges are remarkably controllable for everyone except female partners in private places.

A second reason for writing this book is that after conducting an array of studies of woman abuse in a variety of places over many years, we, and others (e.g., Miller, 2008), now have ample evidence showing that male peer support is one of the most powerful determinants of the harms covered in this book. Originally developed by Walter DeKeseredy (1988a), this concept is defined as the attachments to male peers and the resources that these men provide that encourage and legitimate woman abuse. Data scattered throughout subsequent chapters support what Lee Bowker (1983) said close to thirty years ago about all-male subcultures of violence:

> This is not a subculture that is confined to a single class, religion, occupational grouping, or race. It is spread throughout all parts of society. Men are socialized by other subculture members to accept common definitions of the situation, norms, values, and beliefs about male dominance and the necessity of keeping their wives in line. These violence-supporting social relations may occur at any time and in any place. (135–36)

Male peer pressure that legitimates the sexual objectification of women and the sexual and/or physical abuse of them is found among African American men in Chicago (Wilson, 1996), among Puerto Rican drug dealers in East Harlem and poor African American boys in parts of St. Louis (Bourgois, 1995; Miller, 2008), on Canadian college campuses and their immediate surroundings (DeKeseredy and Schwartz, 1998a), in rural Ohio and Kentucky (DeKeseredy and Schwartz, 2009; Websdale, 1998), and in rural New Zealand and rural South Africa (Campbell, 2000; Jewkes et al., 2006). There is also, as discussed in chapter 6, evidence of the emergence of pro-abuse male peer support groups in cyberspace, and many men who abuse women consume electronic forms of pornography with their male friends (DeKeseredy, in press; DeKeseredy and Olsson, 2011).

The world is, of course, multivariate and it is impossible to pick out one sociological factor and announce that it covers all cases of woman abuse at all times. Nevertheless, all of the research into variants of male peer support theory covered in this book supports the central tenets, showing that it is certainly a powerful explanation of the mechanism that contributes to much of North America's woman abuse.

Purpose of This Book

There is an argument to make that sociological insights are being pushed out of criminological study generally, but this trend is not at all apparent in the study of the abuse of women. On sociology's influence generally within criminology, Kreager, Rulison, and Moody (2011) note in the widely read and cited journal *Criminology*: "Gangs and group level processes were once central phenomena for criminological theory and research. By the mid-1970s, however . . . [this] was displaced by studies of individual behavior . . . [which] . . . removed groups from the theoretical foreground" (p. 95). Eminent criminologist Francis T. Cullen (2009) agreed with this trend: "I am equally persuaded that sociological criminology has exhausted itself as a guide for future study on the origins of crime. It is a paradigm for the previous century, not the current one" (p. xvi).

Within the field of violence against women, though, sociological theorizing is very much alive and well (Renzetti, Edelson, and Bergen, 2011a). Additionally, understanding male-to-female violence as shaped by broader social forces, such as patriarchy, is gaining increasing worldwide acceptance (Dragiewicz, 2011). In fact, although we disagree with many of their findings, it should be noted that the first group of North American scholars to conduct large-scale studies of violence against women were sociologists (e.g., Straus, Gelles, and Steinmetz, 1981).

Another sociological contribution has been the theoretical and empirical work that began twenty-five years ago when Walter DeKeseredy (1988a) first announced the development of male peer support theory in the *Journal of Family Violence*. Shortly after, he provided the first empirical evidence and support for this offering (DeKeseredy, 1988b). Within a few years, Martin Schwartz teamed up with him to create the modified male peer support model and much related work has been done since that time (DeKeseredy and Schwartz, 1993). Over the past twenty-five years, male peer support theory has proliferated in a number of ways that were never anticipated in the beginning. In fact, since 1988 we have developed seven variants of this theory and have linked our theoretical development to rigorous qualitative and quantitative data analysis. Along with other scholars who have used the theory (e.g., Dragiewicz, 2008; Franklin, 2005), we found that there are several sociological and social psychological processes by which patriarchal and/or violent peers influence men to abuse and oppress women. The key within all of this work has been the proposition that certain all-male peer groups encourage, justify, and support the abuse of women by their members.

This book chronicles how male peer support theory was created twenty-five years ago, and how it has been expanded again and again over these years to remain today a vitally alive theory. This will not be a history of where the field was in the 1980s, but rather a discussion of the development of a theory that is particularly relevant today. However, this project is not to provide the dry recitation of a literature review of our previous work. Instead, our goal is to provide a vibrant story of how and why men learn to abuse women in a variety of ways in a variety of arenas, ranging from impoverished public housing projects or elite college campuses to rural semi-isolated homes to newer online cyber communities.

The scholarly material presented in this book is punctuated with the stories and voices of survivors of woman abuse, as told to us and others over the years of work in this field. Our experience includes not only a combined sixty years of academic teaching and research, but also decades of work in the shelter movement, with nongovernmental and nonprofit organizations, and doing government research.

This book is much more than an academic enterprise. We, like our feminist activist and practitioner friends and colleagues, are deeply concerned with providing useful answers to the question "What is to be done about violence against women?" Instead of simply repeating what has been said in previous publications, we make the case for some new initiatives, such as using computer technology to help change social norms. It is necessary to create policies and practices that meet the unique needs of people in an ever-changing world, and the Internet and social media are effective means of facilitating social change and enhancing women's health and well-being (DeKeseredy and Dragiewicz, 2013).

Chapter Outline

Chapter 1 reviews several ongoing and heated debates about defining violence against women. As a first step, special attention is devoted to examining the strengths and limitations of narrow, broad, gender-neutral, and gender-specific definitions. As a related issue, Michael P. Johnson's (2008) widely discussed typology of intimate partner violence is also evaluated. Overall, a key point made in this chapter is that major definitional debates are not trivial or minor boring discussions carried out by pedants while the rest of us wait outside impatiently. Rather, these debates critically affect not only how data are gathered, but also how these data are interpreted. The resulting interpretations shape the quality and quantity of social support services for women who are beaten, sexually assaulted, and abused in other ways by intimates and acquaintances (DeKeseredy and Schwartz, 2011). While these interpretations inform the many subtle and daily judgments by decision makers, such definitions are also used politically as tools in social struggles. In many of the countries we live in, there are lively political battles over how we define such things as poverty, unemployment, and terrorism. Just as a minor example, back in the 1980s the Reagan administration tried to respond to a mandate for nutritious meals to be served to school-children by redefining ketchup on French fries as a vegetable, and therefore nutritious. Similarly, the field of violence against women is highly politicized, and definitions of male-to-female violence that are used (or not used) in social science research reflect these battles (Dragiewicz and DeKeseredy, 2012b; Ellis, 1987).

Chapter 2 shows that woman abuse is a major international social problem. Sexual assaults, beatings, stalking, and the like are not rare incidents, or limited to only certain regions, but rather are brutal events that could happen to women in any social, economic, religious, ethnic, or geographic group. On top of presenting incidence and prevalence data generated by our own studies, the World Health Organization (Garcia-Moreno, Jansen, Ellsberg, Heise, and Watts, 2005), the International Violence Against Women Survey (IVAWS) (Johnson, Ollus, and Nevala, 2008), the Centers for Disease Control and Prevention (Black et al., 2011), and survey work done by other scholars (e.g., Fisher, Daigle and Cullen, 2010), we review research on intimate relationship status variations in violence against women. For example, a large literature demonstrates that separated, divorced, and cohabiting women are at much higher risk of being beaten than are their married counterparts (Brownridge, 2009; DeKeseredy, 2011a).

It is not only marital status that differentiates between women in terms of statistical likelihood of victimization. In general, poor and minority women are at higher risk of being physically abused by men than are white and middle-class women (Basile and Black, 2011; Renzetti, 2011). We will look at the ultimate physical abuse, by examining recent research on intimate femicide, which is defined here as "the killing of females by male partners with whom they have, have had, or want to have, a sexual and/or emotional relationship (Ellis and DeKeseredy, 1997, p. 592).

Chapter 3 describes the construction of our original male peer support theories, including the personal, empirical, and theoretical rationales. These rationales are important because all theoretical explanations emerge out of particular political and economic contexts (Young, 2011). For example, at the time of crafting the first male peer support theory in 1988, the bulk of the sociological work on woman abuse in dating was fairly atheoretical. DeKeseredy's (1988a) first model helped fill this major gap in the literature.

In the first instance, male peer support theories are heavily influenced by social support theory, which is commonly used to explain the role of social support in health maintenance and disease prevention (Cohen and Wills, 1985). However, researchers interested in violence against women have reconceptualized this theory to take advantage of its value in the field (Schwartz and DeKeseredy, 1997). Other perspectives that helped shape male peer support models are briefly explained, such as Lee Bowker's (1983) standards of gratification thesis, E.J. Kanin's (1967a; 1967b) reference group theory, and Albert K. Cohen's (1955) theory of delinquent boys. Quite clearly, our own theoretical work "stands on the shoulders of giants" (Merton, 1965).

Since 2002, DeKeseredy, Schwartz, and their colleagues have crafted male peer support theories that explain violence against women inside and outside the realm of colleges and universities. The perspectives described in chapter 4 are: the gendered social bond male peer support theory of university woman abuse (Godenzi, Schwartz, and DeKeseredy, 2001); the economic exclusion/male peer support model (DeKeseredy and Schwartz, 2002); the feminist/male peer support model of separation and divorce sexual assault (DeKeseredy, Rogness, and Schwartz, 2004); the rural masculinity crisis/male peer support model of separation/divorce sexual assault (DeKeseredy, Donnermeyer, Schwartz, Tunnell, and Hall, 2007); the social and economic exclusion model of separation/divorce woman abuse in public housing (DeKeseredy, Schwartz, and Alvi, 2008); and the gendered left realist subcultural theory (DeKeseredy and Schwartz, 2010).

What do the data say? Answers to this question are provided in chapter 5, as well as suggestions for new directions in empirical and theoretical work, one of which is the study of how male peer support contributes to rape in war.[2] The research is described in a highly intelligible fashion and readers will not be inundated with boring statistical analyses.

Since the late 1990s (see DeKeseredy and Schwartz, 1998a; Schwartz and De-Keseredy, 1998), we have been interested in the use of pornography as a part of the male peer support system that facilitates violence against women. Much has changed since then with the growth of the Internet. Today, there are thousands of websites explicitly featuring adult women being degraded and abused in a myriad of ways. Actually, a common feature of new pornographic videos is painful anal penetration, as well as men slapping/choking women and/or pulling their hair while they penetrate them orally, vaginally, and anally (Bridges, Wosnitzer, Scharrer, Sun, and Liberman, 2010; Dines, 2010). The main objective of chapter 6, then, is to review the extant social scientific research on the relationship between violence against women, male peer support, and Internet pornography. Certainly, many men learn to objectify women through their exposure to cyberporn (Bridges and Jensen, 2011), and there is a growing body of qualitative and quantitative data showing that the contribution of such sexist media to woman abuse is related to male peer support (DeKeseredy, in press, 2011a).

Accompanying the mushrooming of the Internet is, as stated previously, the growth of pro-abuse cyberspace male peer support groups (DeKeseredy and Olsson, 2011). To be sure, many if not most of the men who belong to these factions do not move from consuming pornography to physically committing acts of violence against women. But, just as we found in the 1990s that men often insisted on imitating pornography to the distaste of their intimate partners, these increasingly violent scenes may be triggering acts of violence among a very large number of men. Even if only a small percentage of the very large number of men who view pornography turn to physical violence, this small percentage is at the same time a rather large group of men.

In chapter 7, we recommend progressive policies informed by male peer support theories. These include the use of new social media such as Facebook and Twitter. As stated by DeKeseredy (2011b), using computer technologies to help achieve social justice is a contemporary example of what Gregg Barak (2007) refers to as "newsmaking criminology" that attracts more and more people each day. After Facebook was commonly credited in January 2011 with facilitating the peaceful overthrow of the government of Tunisia, many people worldwide became newly interested in the social reform value of social media. Communication is vital, and Facebook, Twitter, and other media help make a large group of people become aware of violence against women (DeKeseredy and Dragiewicz, 2013). At the same time, these technologies also enable more people to voice their discontent with the prevailing status quo (Walker Rettberg, 2009), and to demand that politicians more effectively respond to the plight of thousands of women who continue to suffer in silence.

Effective ways of dealing with pornography, such as boycotting hotels that offer "adult videos," are also covered. On top of addressing the "dark side of the Internet" (DeKeseredy and Olsson, 2011), we propose ways of targeting the mainstream media. This is essential because belief in gender inequality and rape myths are promoted by elements of popular culture, such as Hollywood movies, video games, certain genres of music, advertising, and television shows. Patriarchal violent messages transmitted by the media tend to increase people's tolerance for sexist discourses and practices, including violence against women (DeKeseredy, 2011a).

No book on male peer support is complete without a section on progressive men's informal responses to abusive and sexist men. Thus, in chapter 7, we suggest practices used by the feminist men's movement, such as bystander approaches and the Fraternity Peer Rape Education Program (Banyard, Plante, and Moynihan, 2004; Wantland, 2008). Other policies and practices used by a wide range of practitioners and activists will be proposed in this chapter, given that violence against women requires a multipronged approach.

1 | Definitional Issues in Violence against Women

I think we spend a great deal of our time fighting against the notion that these assaults are logical extensions of relationship problems or dysfunctions.
—*Legal advocate cited in introduction to Pence and Shepard,* Coordinating Community Responses to Domestic Violence

Box 1.1 briefly describes the pioneering efforts of Ellen Pence, who passed away on January 6, 2012. Pence will be remembered for her kindness, compassion, scholarship, activism, and friendship, and for saving many women's lives. However, Pence also played a key role in influencing scholars, practitioners, and government agencies to use broad definitions of violence. Some of these abusive behaviors are included in the "power and control wheel" (see figure 1.1) that she both developed and popularized.[1] What is the advantage of using a broad definition of woman abuse? Is there an alternative, and why would anyone oppose using such a definition? In fact, as Kilpatrick (2004) points out, the debate about whether to define violence against women narrowly or broadly is "old, fierce, and unlikely to be resolved in the near future" (p. 1218).

Another ongoing heated definitional debate involves the very naming of what we are talking about: is it "domestic violence," "interpersonal violence," "woman abuse," or some other name? This unlikely-to-be-resolved-soon debate routinely involves feminist scholars on one side (e.g., DeKeseredy, 2011c; DeKeseredy and Dragiewicz, in press), and on the other side "family violence researchers" such as Murray Straus (2011) and Zeev Winstock (2011). The key argument in this debate is whether the main problem is that men commit violence against women or that men and women are equally violent. Everyone knows that there are *some* violent women. The key question here is whether men are the offenders in most cases, or whether women "cause" men to be violent. What we observed twenty years ago still holds true today: "Right now, there is an important battle being waged over the nature of women's behavior and its role in woman abuse" (Schwartz and DeKeseredy, 1993, p. 249).

This plays out in the definitional debate in the very terms that we use to describe what we are talking about. Thus, many feminists (like us) use terms such as "woman abuse," "violence against women," and "male-to-female violence." However, there are people who fervently oppose these terms and contend that they should be replaced with gender-neutral language such as "domestic violence," "family violence," or "intimate partner violence" (IPV). What is the difference? Quite simply, some of these labels clearly point out who is the offender and who is the victim (e.g., male-to-female violence). Others obscure that relationship, leaving it unclear who is to blame for the violence (e.g., interpersonal violence). Of course, those who claim that women are as violent as men in heterosexual intimate relationships prefer the gender-neutral terms, since they do not blame men for the violence.

Renzetti, Edleson, and Kennedy Bergen (2011b) remind us that, "these disagreements are not mere academic exercises" (p. 1). Rather, definitions "constitute a primal sociological act or decision" and have major empirical, theoretical, and political consequences (Ellis, 1987, p. 210). The main objective of this chapter, then, is to review what many people would agree are the most heated debates in the study of interpersonal violence. Defining violence against women has been a catalyst for bringing people, including researchers, together. Unfortunately, it has also created bitter divisions among social scientists and others involved in the movement to make intimate relationships safer.

In both naming the problem and the broadness of the definitions used (how many acts are covered), there are pockets of strong opposition, including antifeminist scholars and conservative fathers' rights organizations. It is common among these oppositional groups to contend that those who use broad definitions are guilty of "definitional stretching," artificially inflating the rates of abuse that do not coincide with "reasonable" women's attitudes and experiences (Gilbert, 1991). Some people feel that a reasonable woman would not define herself as abused unless she was injured badly enough to need a doctor to stitch up her wounds. Within the field, this was often termed the "stitch rule." Others feel that broad definitions are ideological inventions designed to make an antimale point.

Broad versus Narrow Definitions

So, our opening question must be: what is violence against women? That there are conflicting answers is not surprising, given that this field is one of the most

1.1 The Duluth Model Is the Mother of Innovation

Dr. Ellen Pence, who died in 2012 at age 63 of breast cancer, is widely known and respected in the violence against women community not only for her personal characteristics but because she was a true pioneer in the development of strategies to both explain and combat such abuse. The Domestic Violence Intervention Program, founded in 1980 in Duluth, MN, still operates in that city. Here her innovative work in training and theory has influenced the entire field and the way in which law enforcement, social work, and many other professions view the entire notion of violence against women and children.

The Duluth Model (as it quickly became known) has exerted several important influences on the field, but three are particularly important. In the first place, Pence developed and popularized the Power and Control Wheel (see fig. 1.1) that explained in clear and simple terms an entire theory of men's violence, based on the voices of survivors. To visually represent the cycle of control that men use to exercise power over women, the wheel includes economic abuse, physical abuse, minimizing, denying and blaming, and other tactics that are commonly used. Pence's model, which has been adopted in forty languages by trainers around the world, also serves as the basis for the Equality Wheel, which shows behaviors that facilitate egalitarian partnership, and the Creator Wheel, which identifies strategies men can adopt to achieve the goals of the Equality Wheel (see www.theduluthmodel.org/training/wheels.html for these and other relational wheels).

One place these wheels have been used is in training men to accept responsibility and to change abusive behavior. Such training, often based on curricula developed in Duluth, is found in almost every North American community today and in several other countries. Even those who prefer a different training technique are likely to find that alternatives are based largely on the concepts developed by Pence and her colleagues. Often, such training is used in conjunction with a criminal sentence of probation for men who are arrested for domestic violence.

continued

1.1 *continued*

The third far-reaching effect of Pence's work is an effort to integrate a broad variety of agencies in social services and victim services work with police and other criminal justice agencies to develop community-coordinated responses to the problem of violence against women and children. Pence's community model has served as a blueprint for local response teams across North America and the United Kingdom.

politicized topics of social inquiry (DeKeseredy and Schwartz, 2011; Ellis, 1987). Of course, any attempt to simplify definitional debates will only do injustice to the great complexities recognized by many researchers, students, and workers in the field. Still, it is important to attempt to develop a scheme that enables us to understand some of the broad contours of the ongoing debates. A debate that will inform much of the discussion in this chapter is the one between broad and narrow definitions.

Narrow Definitions

Many North American researchers, policy makers, journalists, and members of the general public focus only on physical abuse that results in visible harm or sexual assaults involving penetration. These are not the only behaviors that hurt women, but there is widespread reluctance to recognize that other behaviors, even harmful acts that are against the law, are serious crimes. One newer media device that makes this easier to see is the online mainstream news agency story. For any assault on a woman that is short of murder, in almost any city, one can count on a large number of men to post a comment pointing out that the woman wasn't substantially physically harmed, and asking why people are making such a big deal. For example, in 2007, eight male students at Smithfield Middle School in Rexdale, Ontario, Canada, were charged with sexual assault because they restrained and groped four girls on school grounds. Some were concerned that the charges were "a result of actions that may have been blown out of proportion" (Powell and Brown, 2007, p. A27). *Washington Post* columnist Paula Dvorak (2012) reported that after the District of Columbia

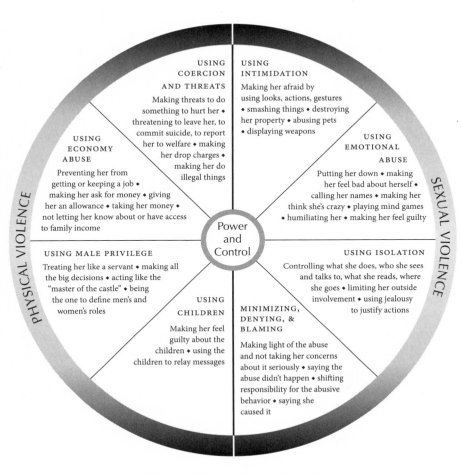

Figure 1.1 Power and control wheel.

police had taken very seriously a complaint about a bicycle rider who thrust his hand up under women's skirts to violate them and then rode off laughing, and a blog site description of the event went viral, there was a rush of similar reports from women who claimed similar victimization. Her column attracted 320 online comments, many to argue that the police should limit their inquiries to "real crimes," to attack the victim as a narcissist looking for attention, or to claim that such a crime was impossible to commit. All across the world, people are quick to go public with their belief that women who have not suffered major physical injury, even when the acts against them are clear law violations, are minor events that should be ignored. Many trivialize such behavior and label it "soft-core abuse" (Fox, 1993). Another version of this is researchers who view psychological assaults as "early warning signs" of physical and sexual attacks, rather than as abusive in and of themselves (e.g., Kelly, 1994).

Some people prefer narrow definitions for other reasons. They do not dismiss the trauma caused by psychological, verbal, spiritual, and economic abuse but claim that grouping these harms with physically injurious behaviors "muddies the water so much that it might be impossible to determine what causes abuse" (Gelles and Cornell, 1985, p. 23). The most strident proponents of narrow definitions are the researchers (e.g., Archer, 2000; Dutton, 2010), right-wing fathers' rights groups, and other antifeminists who claim that women are as violent as men. In order to reach that conclusion, they use a narrow definition of violence that of course does not include any of a variety of highly injurious nonphysical acts. Just as an example, it is possible to create a terroristic household through threats and fear, but without actually engaging in physical violence. The people trapped in such households can be completely terrorized and suffer extreme trauma but have no bruises or cuts. Further, such narrow definitions do not include homicide, stalking, sexual assaults that do not involve physical force (such as those resulting from blackmail or any other coercion), assaults that take place during or after separation or divorce, strangulation, and a host of other harms that thousands of women experience on a daily basis (DeKeseredy and Dragiewicz, 2007). More is said about this cohort's claims later in this chapter.

For some specific tasks, there are some advantages to narrow definitions. Liz Kelly and Jill Radford (1998) argue that an attempt to isolate certain specific illegal acts of abuse may, in fact, be useful and important for certain analytical tasks. R. Emerson Dobash and Russell Dobash (1998), spell out this argument:

A more "narrow" or circumscribed definition of violence, with each type examined in its own right and statistics gathered accordingly, may sometimes have the advantage of increasing clarity about the nature and context of a specific form of violence, but may simultaneously lose the prospect of generalizing across a much wider spectrum of violence(s). (p. 4)

Yet, it is essential to keep in mind the difference between analytical and experiential boundaries. For example, a researcher might choose to ignore rape for the time being and to instead devote attention to studying beatings, sexual harassment, prostitution, or sexual trafficking, such as sex tourism.[2]

However, it is impossible to make an experiential differentiation along the same lines, as forcible rape is an integral component in many episodes of each of these latter forms of violence (DeKeseredy and Schwartz, 2009; Maier and Bergen, 2012).

The limitations of narrow definitions, however, greatly outweigh the advantages. For instance, large-scale studies that are introduced to respondents as crime surveys and that exclude a broad range of hurtful behaviors that may not be illegal or are minor crimes typically generate very low rates of violence. One prime example is the National Violence Against Women Survey (VAWS), which found that 1.8 percent of the female participants reported having been victimized by one or more of these acts committed by an intimate partner in the past twelve months: rape, physical assault, rape and/or sexual assault, and stalking (Tjaden and Thoennes, 2000). Similarly, north of the border, Statistics Canada's (2011) recent General Social Surveys elicited markedly lower rates of male-to-female intimate violence for a five-year period (6.4 percent) than the incidence (past year) statistics obtained by surveys that extended their operational definitions of violence beyond the limited realm of the criminal law. Generally, these studies show that at least 11 percent of North American women in marital or cohabiting relationships are physically assaulted in any twelve-month period (DeKeseredy, 2011a).

The most important point to consider here is that unless women clearly label hurtful behaviors as "criminal" in their minds, they tend not to report them in a survey of criminal behavior. If you tell someone that you are studying criminal behavior, and then ask a question about whether you were ever hit or attacked, the typical person will only answer yes if they have in mind a hit or an attack that they think was criminal. If you have defined being hit by a spouse or a parent as normal noncriminal behavior, you will no doubt tell the interviewer that you have never been attacked, or you will only tell her about clearly criminal attacks, such as being attacked by a mugger. The problem is that in dealing with attacks by intimates, including forcible rape by partners or dates or friends, many women who experience what the law clearly defines as assault or forcible rape do not label their assaults as criminal or sometimes even as a form of victimization (DeKeseredy and Schwartz, 2011). For example, Pitts and Schwartz (1993) asked a number of women if they had ever been forced into sexual intercourse, described in a way that clearly fit their state's definition of forcible rape. As part of an interview about their experiences, they were later asked if they had ever been raped. Although only women who had just reported forced sex were asked that question, a strong majority denied that they had ever been raped. These women knew that something terrible had happened and were discussing a number of reactions to it, but they had not applied the word *rape* to their experiences. Often, this is because they believe that the word *rape* only applies to violent stranger attacks.

As a comparison, surveys that attempt to study violence by intimates but that are not presented within the context of criminal assault and victimization have found major reporting differences (Fisher, 2009). Mihalic and Elliott (1997), for example, found that up to 83 percent of the marital violence incidents reported in surveys of family behavior are not reported in contexts where the presentation emphasis is on criminal assault and victimization.

Low rates of violence uncovered by government agencies are worrisome for many researchers, practitioners, and advocates, especially in today's political economic era, where most federal, provincial, state, and local governments are actively cutting social service budgets drastically. Certainly, a figure such as 1.8 percent could easily be used by conservatives to justify limiting funds to shelters, rape crisis centers, and other service providers. After all, the argument might go, if "so few" women are victimized, there isn't much need of the funded services. The fear of this happening in Canada is certainly well founded because the federal Conservative government led by Prime Minister Stephen Harper is heavily influenced by political forces guided by fathers' rights groups and others with a vested interest in discounting or minimalizing the pain and suffering caused by violence against women. Consider that Statistics Canada (2002, 2005, 2011), which once was a highly praised source of information on the subject, no longer conducts surveys that focus primarily on violence against women.[3] Now, their surveys produce equal rates of male and female intimate violence, which is only possible when the different contexts of these behaviors are ignored (Dragiewicz and DeKeseredy, 2012b). To make matters worse, On October 3, 2006, Bev Oda, federal minister for the Status of Women Canada (swc), announced that women's organizations would no longer be eligible for funding for advocacy, government lobbying, or research projects. swc was also required to delete the word *equality* from its list of goals. A year later, Prime Minister Harper caused more damage to the women's movement by eliminating funding to the National Association of Women and the Law (nawl), a nonprofit women's group that deals with violence against women and other injurious symptoms of patriarchy.

At the time of writing this chapter, President Barak Obama had not taken similar steps, but his predecessor, President George W. Bush, definitely did. Intent on weakening the Violence Against Women Act (vawa) passed in 1994 and efforts to support it, his administration's budget for the Fiscal Year 2007 proposed funding for shelters and direct services to abused women that was $195 million below the authorized level, and Bush did not request any money for Native American and Alaskan programs (National Coalition Against Domestic Violence, 2007). The federal government also refused to allow protections for battered women in the marriage protection programs that were part of the administration's welfare proposal for the Fiscal Year 2005 (National Organization of Women, 2004). Further, due in large part to the efforts of conservative men's groups, newer versions of VAWA view women *and* men as victims of violence and sexual assault and provides for the of services to men.

One more example of the Bush administration's assault on VAWA is warranted here. Attorney General John Ashcroft appointed former Independent Women's Forum (IWF) president Nancy Ptotenhauer to the National Advisory Council on Violence Against Women, which advises the Department of Justice and the Department of Health and Human Services on implementing VAWA. IWF is an explicitly antifeminist women's organization, and as noted by Hammer (2002), it was "formed in 1992 by Republican women angered by the testimony of Anita Hill at confirmation hearings for Supreme Court Justice Clarence Thomas, and the prominent role played by the National Organization of Women and other feminist groups" (p. 28). Ptotenhauer frequently and publicly testified against VAWA, saying, "The Violence Against Women Act will do nothing to protect women from crime. It will, though, perpetuate false information, waste money, and urge vulnerable women to mistrust all men" (Independent Women's Forum, 2002, p. 1). It doesn't take much of an effort to figure out the point of appointing Ms. Ptotenhauer to the group giving advice on how to best use the funds to protect women in America.

Narrow definitions not only exacerbate the problem of underreporting and help serve the interests of antifeminist organizations and politicians, they trivialize women's real-life feelings and experiences. For example, although marital rape is now illegal in all American states, thirty states have retained measures to exempt from prosecution men who rape their wives in certain situations, such as when the victims are physically or mentally impaired (Bergen, 2006), even though marital rape is an act of extreme cruelty. Consider what this rural Ohio woman told us about her husband:

> He wanted me to have sex with a few people. Okay, like I was telling you earlier, and I didn't want to. And, uh, I finally did. And then I got beat for it because I did. I tried not to, but then when we did, I got beat. And that's not good. And then, we

was at one of his friend's house and we got drunk and I fell off a four-foot drop porch and I remember, I don't remember how I got off the porch, but I remember being put in the car and going home. I remember being put in the bed, with all my clothes on. But when I woke up, everything was off but my shirt. And I asked my husband, "Did you have sex with me last night?" He said, "Yep, while you were passed out." I said, "What encouraged you to sleep with anybody who can't even move?" He replied, "Oh, all I had to do was hold your legs for you." (Cited in De-Keseredy and Schwartz, 2009, p. 61)

Another common worry is that narrow definitions discourage abused women from seeking social support. If a survivor's male partner's hurtful behavior does not coincide with what researchers, criminal justice officials, politicians, or the general public refer to as abuse or violence, she may be left in a "twilight zone" where she knows that she has been abused but cannot define it or categorize it in a way that would allow her to seek help (DeKeseredy and Schwartz, 2011; Duffy and Momirov, 1997). As stated by a rural Ohio woman victimized by separation/divorce sexual assault, "I don't sit around and share. I keep it to myself. . . . I'm not one to sit around and talk about what's happened" (cited in DeKeseredy and Schwartz, 2009, p. 49).

Finally, narrow legalistic definitions exacerbate the problem of underreporting. For example, Koss (1996) and a host of other highly experienced survey researchers show that asking questions based on narrow legal criteria and using words like "rape" instead of behaviorally specific terms elicits data that underestimate the amount of abuse (Jacquier, Johnson, and Fisher, 2011). Consequently, in the words of the late Michael D. Smith (1994), the scientific credibility of an entire survey is "put into jeopardy, for one cannot know if those women who disclosed having been abused are representative of all victims in the sample (p. 110).

Broad Definitions

Many of us have occasionally been told, "Choose your words carefully." This statement certainly applies to defining violence against women. In fact, how one defines violence is one of the most important research decisions that a methodologist will make (Ellis, 1987). It is important to constantly question whether the words we use in our definitions and the questions we ask measure what women themselves feel. For example, as we noted earlier, many researchers view "real" battering as bruises and stitches and specifically exclude abusive, wounding words and terroristic behaviors (Schwartz, 2000). To give perhaps an extreme example, below is part of a divorce petition from an impoverished California woman many years ago. She had "gotten a few things together" for the children on Christmas Eve, including gifts and a small tree:

> Her husband arrived home late, drunk and angry, and upon entering the house and seeing the little tree, all fixed up, he became so angry that he took the tree and tore it to pieces, took all the little gifts and presents off the tree and mutilated and destroyed them. . . . Not being satisfied with this, and while cursing and defaming the plaintiff, he took all of the table linens and mattresses and sheets and quilts off the bed, took them to the kitchen and dumped them on the floor, gathered up all the food there was in the house and spilled these on the floor, put the cooking utensils on the floor and then took the stove pipe and dumped soot over the bed linen and food and everything he had put on the floor and then turned water all over this mess, then broke and tore up all the furniture. (Peterson del Mar, 1996, p. 124)

This woman is not, by most definitions currently in use, a battered woman because she was never touched. However, psychological abuse can be just as, if not more, injurious as physical violence (Adams, Sullivan, Bybee, and Greeson, 2008; DeKeseredy, 2011a). For example, Diane Follingstad and her colleagues (1990) found that 72 percent of their abused female interviewees reported that psychological abuse had a more severe effect on them than did physical abuse. People who work with battered women regularly hear stories about how bruises, cuts and even broken bones aren't the worst part of being attacked. After a time the external bruises usually heal or go away. The problem for some women, such as this rural Ohio resident we interviewed, is that she can recover completely from physical assaults, but the consequences of psychological abuse can last forever:

> And years ago, years ago when I still only had one child, he told me he knew that I wanted out of the relationship and he said, "If I can't have you, I'm gonna make it so nobody can have you." And I didn't understand what he was talking about. And it was many, many years later that I realized he meant psychologically. He was going to destroy me psychologically so I wouldn't be fit to enter into another relationship. And it's basically true; I have not had any other relationship. I'm afraid to go into a relationship. I don't trust men in general. So basically I live a solitary life, not by choice, but because I'm afraid I'm going to end up in relationship like that again. (Cited in DeKeseredy and Schwartz, 2009, p. 84)

Likewise, many women are hurt by sexual assaults that do not involve violent forcible penetration, such as unwanted sex acts when they were drunk or high or when they were unable to give consent:

> I agreed to meet with him to discuss visitation and child support for our daughter, and I wanted to go to a public place after everything he had done because it wasn't just sexual, it was mental, physical. And I showed up there. I had a couple of friends who were sitting throughout keeping an eye on me. Ordered the drink, got up to use the bathroom, drank my drink and that was pretty much the last thing I remember until the next morning when I woke up with a killer headache and my daughter crying in her crib. That's what woke me up. I looked over. He was in the bed next to me. (Cited in DeKeseredy and Joseph, 2006, p. 304)

Then there are married and cohabiting women who are "blackmailed" into having sex with their partners. There may be no threat or actual use of force, but this does not mean that such an experience is not terrifying, emotionally scarring, or highly injurious. One of Diana E. H. Russell's (1990) respondents did as it turns out label this assault by her first husband as rape, which may not be very common, although the behavior is something that many counselors have heard about:

> The worst raping occasion was in the morning I awoke in labor with my first child. The hospital I was booked into was a thirty-minute drive away, and this being the first time I had undergone childbirth, I had no idea of how close I was to giving birth, or what was to happen to me next. I labored at home for a few hours until perhaps 11:00 a.m., and then said to my ex-husband that I thought we'd better go to the hospital. The pains were acute and I was panicking that I would not be able to bear them. He looked at me and said, "Oh, all right. But we better have a screw first, because it'll be a week before you're home again." I couldn't believe it, even of him. "Please, W., take me to the hospital," I begged as another contraction stormed across my body. "Not until we have a screw," he insisted. I wept, I cried, I pleaded, but he wouldn't budge. The pleading went on until midday, by which time I was frantic to get nursing help. He stood adamant with his arms crossed, a smirk on his face, and jiggling the car keys as a bribe. In the end I submitted. It took two minutes, then we dressed and drove to the hospital. The baby was born five hours later. (p. 383)

Many women have unwanted sex out of a sense of obligation or because of partners' threats or because they are coerced into having sex for other reasons that do not involve the use of or threats of physical force (Bergen, 1996). Agnes, a woman we interviewed in southeast Ohio, explains the point of view of the survivor who has succumbed to this pressure:

> So there might be some entitlement that the husband feels. The woman feeling that it's easier to give in, especially for the kids. A lot of social norms, I guess, social pressure to where the woman takes on a passive role sexually. It's not a big deal. It'll be over soon. That's not addressing a solution other than a marriage counselor or someone that she goes to for help could address the issue of where you're going to be and how you're going to handle and come up with a plan. (Cited in DeKeseredy and Schwartz, 2009, p. 24)

Another strong reason for using broad definitions is that regardless of which behavior women find to be the most hurtful, abused women are rarely only victimized by a single type of assault. In fact, in every study of woman abuse we conducted over the past twenty-five years, we found that our respondents suffered from a variety of injurious male behaviors that include sexual assault, physical violence, psychological abuse, economic blackmail or denying them money even if they earn wages, harm to animals or possessions to which they have strong attachments, or stalking behavior. Below is a brief true story that exemplifies this point. The woman featured here is a friend of one of Walter DeKeseredy's third-year undergraduate students, and her experiences were described in an electronic message sent to him on February 10, 2012:

> A friend of mine was with her boyfriend for ten years; they share two children. He was very controlling, often interrogated the eldest child about his mother's actions when she wasn't around. He put her down and seemed to take a little bit away from her every day they were together. . . . They went out one night; he drank a lot, became aggressive, so she left for home. He came home angry. She was afraid, so she phoned a friend to come and get her. While on the phone he struck her in the face, the phone fell and he continued. This time she didn't fight back, she had learned her lesson. The friend on the phone called the police, by the time the officers and friend arrived at the home, he was gone. She was covered in blood, her face swollen, a boot print already bruised into her side. He had hit her nearly 13 times, then other places, while she laid on the ground he had kicked her.

This example does show physical violence, but it also exemplifies another extremely common form of woman abuse that is garnering much empirical and theoretical attention today, and that a growing number of scholars and practitioners assert should be added to broad definitions of violence. Referred to as *coercive control,* this involves psychologically and emotionally abusive behaviors that are often subtle and hard to detect and prove and that seem more forgivable to people unfamiliar with violence against women and its traumatic outcomes. The main goal of coercive control is to restrict a woman's liberties (Tanha, Beck, Figueredo, and Raghavan, 2010), and two prime examples are threatening looks and criticism (Kernsmith, 2008). Men also use other tactics of coercive control to suppress their female partner's personal freedom, including the types of "microregulation" described to Evan Stark (2007) by Laura, one of his clients. Her husband Nick gave her "lists" of tasks to be completed around the house, including the following he wanted done in the bedroom:

- Vacuum daily "so you can see the lines."
- Closets color-coordinated and sorted by length.
- Dressers symmetrical with only perfume, two pictures (Nick plus Poppy); and nail polish.
- Drawers in order of the way things are put on.
- Telephone, answering machine, notepad, pencil, one book, and one picture of Nick on nightstand.
- Bed made first thing every morning.
- Sheets changed every Sunday morning.
- Two upright cushions, two throw pillows, two ruffled throw pillows, and one stuffed animal from Nick on bed.
- Shoes on closet floor . . . matched, clean, and color-coordinated.
- Belts hung from closet door . . . color-coordinated.
- Everything kept clean, neat, and in its place (p. 319).

As British feminist scholar Ruth Hall (1985) discovered, just "ask any woman"[4] about her encounters with violence and other types of intimate abuse and readers will undoubtedly discover that she will call for a definition that includes many harmful nonphysical and nonsexual behaviors like those described in this chapter. Yet, especially in response to such examples as the above list, many critics accuse proponents of broad definitions of including "everything but the kitchen sink." In fact, it may well be true that including too many behaviors under the rubric of "violence" may result in a breakdown of social exchanges between people as they label each other's actions as abusive or violent (Duffy and Momirov, 1997). Further, it is more difficult to study fifty behaviors at once than one or two. Nonetheless, many women and men have discovered to their regret that there is little truth to the suggestion that "sticks and stone may break my bones but words will never hurt me." In fact, women who have experienced male violence often say that it is the psychological, verbal, and spiritual abuse that hurts the most and longest (Renzetti, 2008). As noted above, some women say that most physical wounds heal, but the damage to their self-respect and ability to relate to others caused by emotional, verbal, and spiritual violence affects every aspect of their lives (DeKeseredy and Schwartz, 2009).

This point is buttressed by this statement made by a woman interviewed by DeKeseredy and MacLeod (1997):

> I was raped by my uncle when I was 12 and my husband has beat me for years. For my whole life, when I have gone to a doctor, to my priest, or to a friend to have my wounds patched up, or for a shoulder to cry on, they dwell on my bruises, my cuts, my broken bones. My body has some scars . . . that's for sure. . . . I don't look like anything like I did 15 years ago, but it's not my body that I really wish could get fixed. The abuse in my life has taken away my trust in people and in life. It's taken away the laughter in my life. I still laugh, but not without bitterness behind the laughter. It's taken away my faith in God, my faith in goodness winning out in the end, and maybe worst of all, it's taken away my trust in myself. I don't trust myself to be able to take care of my kids, to take care of myself, to do anything to make a difference in my own life or anyone else's. That's the hurt I would like to fix. I can live with my physical scars. It's these emotional scars that drive me near suicide sometimes. (p. 5)

Psychologically abusive acts are common events and thus should be considered part of any definition of violence against women. Moreover, as we have seen from the examples in this chapter, physical abuse, sexual abuse, psychological abuse, and other types of assaults on women are not mutually exclusive. For example, 80 percent of forty-three rural Ohio women we interviewed were victimized by two or more variants of woman abuse (DeKeseredy and Schwartz, 2009). Certainly, male-to-female assaults are multidimensional in nature. Even the U.S. federal government recognizes this reality. For example, the Centers for Disease Control's National Intimate Partner and Sexual Violence Survey measured physical and sexual violence, stalking, psychological aggression, and control of reproductive or sexual health (Black et al., 2011). Unfortunately, while such a conceptualization of violence is a strong feature of this study, the use there of gender-neutral terms such as "intimate partner violence" is highly problematic, for reasons presented in the next section.

Gender-Neutral or Bidirectional versus Gender-Specific Definitions

Chapter 2 shows that thousands of women around the world experience "extraordinary abuses in ordinary places" (Salter, 2013). The names commonly given to these assaults are "domestic violence" and "intimate partner violence." Some government agencies and community groups favor these gender-neutral labels because they claim that they are more inclusive and address the fact that there is also violence in same-sex relationships (Denham and Gillespie, 1999; Sinclair, 2003). However, the most strident advocates of such degendered definitions are antifeminist organizations (e.g., fathers' rights groups), politicians, journalists, and researchers who assert that women are as violent as men. They do not just advocate more attention to male victims.[5] Rather, they demand the renunciation of feminism and the research, laws, and programs they deem feminist (Dutton, 2006, 2010; Girard, 2009).

Despite lacking strong empirical support, claims that violence is gender-neutral are increasingly becoming "common sense" in North America (Dragiewicz and DeKeseredy, 2012b; Minaker and Snider, 2006). Further, these assertions are having a major impact on policy, practice, and police officers' beliefs and attitudes. Consider this e-mail sent by a Durham Regional Police Service officer to Walter DeKeseredy on January 24, 2012[6]:

Hello Dr. DeKeseredy,
I regularly present to police officers about Domestic Violence. In the last few courses that I have presented to police officers, I have come up against officers saying that the police perspective of Domestic Violence is very biased against men; that men are assaulted as often by women but they never report it; women lie and some other comments that are consistent with the usual arguments that it is a gender-neutral crime. I am responding with statistics of male offenders versus female offenders, male privilege and explaining power and control issues. Yet, I feel I'm not rebutting these arguments in the best way.

Another example is the experience of the friend of Walter DeKeseredy's student mentioned previously in this chapter:

One night they got into an argument, it escalated until she became desperate, hid in the bathroom and called the police. Four officers [came], two male and two female. Her boyfriend calmly sat on the couch and talked to one officer while she spoke to another in another room. She was shaken, he had never hurt her like that before. Her boyfriend left, the officers told her that he could return the next day and they could work on things. She found out the next day when she, confused, went to obtain a copy of the police report and spoke to the officers. The report stated that she had attacked him, was suffering from postpartum depression and wasn't in control of her actions (his words), which is why they had decided not to arrest HER [emphasis in original]. He apparently had scratches on him to prove his point.

By this time, her bruises had set in, half of her face was black and blue, she had other bruises (later found out he had fractured her ribs and damaged her kneecap). She spoke to the officers, explained that she never had postpartum, that he attacked her, that she was just trying to get away when she scratched him and that she was afraid now that by believing him, they are telling him it is okay. They stood by their report, said she was the aggressor, and that her story wasn't as well put together as his, thus, she must have being lying.

What leads people to believe that women are as violent as men? Certainly, there anti-feminists who don't care what any type of data say and are determined to roll back the political, economic, and social gains women have achieved in their ongoing struggles for equality (Dragiewicz, 2011). Then, there are others who are not necessarily right-wing, but who accept, at face value gender symmetrical data such as those generated by government surveys that use some version of the Conflict Tactics Scale (CTS) (e.g., Statistics Canada, 2011). First developed by Murray Straus (1979) and later modified by him and his colleagues (Straus, Hamby, Boney-McCoy, and Sugarman, 1996), the CTS typically generates statistics showing that men and women are equally violent in intimate heterosexual relationships. This quantitative tool is designed to solicit information from men and women about the various tactics they used to resolve conflicts in their relationships. Most versions of the CTS consist of at least eighteen items that measure at least three different ways of handling interpersonal conflict in relationships: reasoning, verbal aggression (referred to by some researchers as psychological abuse), and violence.

Although widely used, the CTS is a highly controversial measure and must be administered with caution.[7] For example, as discussed earlier, the context of the very survey makes a difference in the answers that one receives. Here the total emphasis is laid out in the name: the Conflict Tactics Scale. Questions are asked about tactics that people use when engaged in conflict. What if you live in a house of terror where seemingly for no reason your spouse will suddenly attack you? Or if your spouse controls your movements, spending, friends, schooling, or even eating patterns? Are these situations of conflict to the person being interviewed? What if your husband announces that he is going to kill you tonight, and spends the day cleaning his guns and sharpening his knives, discussing aloud which tactic he will use to kill you? Believing him, you hit him on the head with a frying pan, take the truck keys, and drive to safety? Simple, you are a violent woman, according to the CTS. Your husband never touched you.

The common CTS finding that women hit men as often as men hit women (*sexual symmetry*) is deceptive for several reasons. One of the most important is that the CTS provides only crude counts of behaviors and ignores the contexts, meanings, and motives of violence. Much female and male violence is used for different reasons, with female violence used mainly in self-defense or fighting back and male violence used primarily as a means of patriarchal control (De-Keseredy, 2011a). Therefore, Desmond Ellis reminds us that, "[i]gnoring context, meaning and motive is misinforming . . . [a]nd not separating different types of violence is misleading" (cited in Foss, 2002, p. 2). In other words, unless we know exactly why people use violence, it is wrong to draw conclusions about the causes of such behavior based solely on crude counts of hits, kicks, slaps, and the like.

In addition to using CTS data to support the claim of bidirectionality of violence,[8] proponents of sexual symmetry artificially narrow the definition of violence between intimates to obscure injurious behaviors that display marked sex asymmetry, such as sexual assault, strangulation, assault during the process of separation or divorce, stalking, and homicide. While some might insist that such behaviors constitute an unacceptable or hysterical broadening of the definition of violence, in fact they are rather commonly part of abused women's experiences (DeKeseredy and Dragiewicz, 2007; Dragiewicz, 2011).

That *some* women strike *some* men, sometimes with the intent to injure, should not be the subject of debate. Every competent survey ever done has found battered men, some battered by other men and some battered by women, including intimate partners. However, the concept of "exceptions that prove the rule" makes sense here. The point of the exercise should be to identify the typical or the most common case, without losing sight of the fact that all true victims are indeed victims. Still, relying on simple counts of actions divorced from their meaning and ignoring a broad range of hurtful behaviors does not mitigate or change the meaning of the conclusion that women are the overwhelmingly predominant victims of intimate adult violence. This is why we and many other feminist scholars use gender-specific terms such as "woman abuse," "woman battering," and "violence against women." And, of course, there are decades of rich qualitative and quantitative research that strongly support the use of such terms. Note, too, that despite the ongoing efforts of antifeminist scholars and activists to narrow definitions of violence and to make gender-neutral terms widely accepted, the terms "woman abuse" and "violence against women" are still used by some North American government agencies (e.g., Ontario Women's Directorate and the U.S. Office on Violence Against Women) and practitioners, and have been since the mid-1980s (DeKeseredy, 2012b). As well, much to the dismay of fathers' rights groups in Canada, the Ontario government publicly endorsed a commissioned feminist report that refutes the notion that intimate violence is sexually symmetrical (see DeKeseredy and Dragiewicz, 2009). This is not to say, though, that gender-neutral language will not dominate the discourse on violence in private places in the near future. In fact, gender-neutral terms are rapidly replacing gender-specific ones in federal government publications and in some academic circles (Dragiewicz and DeKeseredy, 2012b).

Typologies of Violence in Intimate Relationships

Some scholars try to bridge the gap between gendered and gender-neutral definitions by offering typologies (Eckhardt, Holtzworth-Munroe, Norlander, Sibley, and Cahill, 2008; Johnson, 2008; Johnson and Ferraro, 2000). Perhaps the best known of these is Michael P. Johnson's typology of intimate terrorism, violent resistance, and situational couple violence. All of these are serious forms of violence, rather than minor events that neither side experiences as violent or coercive. The CTS is not the only means of operationalizing typologies such as Johnson's (2008), but studies based mainly on the CTS or other decontextualized measures provide no information that can be used to characterize incidents as representative of one type of violence or another (DeKeseredy and Schwartz, 2011; Dragiewicz and DeKeseredy, 2012b). Certainly the seriousness of an act can be measured in such a decontextualized way. For example, being hit or stabbed by a partner is usually more serious an event than being pushed or slapped, although this is not automatically the case: being stabbed with a letter opener that doesn't break your skin might be less harmful than being pushed down a flight of stairs. However, when one moves to imputing the motives of an act, it gets more difficult. Is the push or stab part of a terroristic attempt at control, or a situational out-of-character event? It is usually impossible to make accurate claims about the motives of violence based on numbers of acts, as DeKeseredy pointed out in his critique of Johnson's typology at the National Institute of Justice's Gender Symmetry of Violence Workshop (National Institute of Justice, 2000). Indeed, motivations for violence and control vary and even Johnson acknowledged, "qualitative research and rich interview data would be necessary to thoroughly understand the meaning and social context" (cited in National Institute of Justice, 2000).

Another problem with Johnson's typology is that he claims to identify a very small number of cases that to him exemplify "mutual violent control." In such cases, he contends,

> both members of the couple are violent and controlling, each behaving in a manner that would identify him or her as an intimate terrorist if it weren't for the fact that their partner also seems to be engaged in the same sort of violent attempt to control the relationship. (p. 12)

What makes this assertion highly problematic is that, as Evan Stark (2006) observes, while there is evidence that *some* women often use force to control their male partners, "they typically lack the social facility to impose the comprehensive levels of deprivation, exploitation, and dominance found in coercive control. I have never encountered a case of coercive control with a female perpetrator and male victim" (p. 1024).

There is some empirical support for typologies such as those developed by Johnson and by Amy Holtzworth-Munroe and her colleagues (e.g., Holtzworth-Munroe, Meehan, Herron, Rehman, and Stuart, 2000; Leone, Johnson, and Cohan, 2007). Still, critics like Ellen Pence and Shamita Das Dasgupta (2006) and DeKeseredy and Dragiewicz (2009) caution that such typologies are likely to be misused. They note that it is all too easy for abusers and their allies to paint individual incidents as "situational" or aberrant violence even when they are not, and that this can have life-and-death consequences. Although shelter staff and scholars recognize that not all violence is the same, and not all violence that takes place in the home is necessarily battering (Dasgupta, 2002; Osthoff, 2002), there is no tool that can discern whether an individual act is part of a broader pattern of coercive control. Accordingly, antiviolence advocates continue to call for assessments that place violence and abuse in the context of the relationship, family, community, culture, and history (Bonisteel and Green, 2005).

Summary

Throughout North America but also in other parts of the world social problems like violence and abuse are subject to the "politics of need interpretation" (Fraser, 1989, p. 292), wherein social issues are hotly contested in public discourse. Nancy Fraser argues that in late-capitalist welfare-state societies, discursive struggles over social resources and power are often framed in terms of competing needs. Power struggles are played out in debates over which social issues or behaviors should be framed as legitimate political concerns and which should be enclaved as nonpolitical matters (p. 294). Specifically, this chapter shows that there are highly visible struggles associated with the very definition of violence.

In what is still one of the most widely read and cited social scientific articles in the world, Howard Becker (1967) asks sociologists, "Whose side are we on?" Here, we are on the side of women and are heavily influenced by feminist "ways of knowing" (Ryan, 2001). Hence, the definition of violence used in this book is broad and gender specific. We have explained how some assert that such an approach is simply a leftist political agenda (Dutton, 2010; Winstock, 2011). As feminists, we have no problem being labeled *political*. After all, "all writing is political" (Sartre, 1964), including the work of antifeminist scholars. Moreover, we, like many of our colleagues, contend that no scientific method, theory, or policy proposal is value free. Still, our definition is not simply a political enterprise. Rather, it is heavily influenced by years of empirical work and numerous data sets revealing that women are the primary targets of intimate violence and that the abuse they endure is multidimensional in nature. Furthermore, following British radical feminist Liz Kelly (1988), we regard violence as existing on a continuum that ranges from nonphysical acts such as obscene phone calls to physical acts such as beating someone up. Although the idea of a continuum is often used to portray moving from the least to the most serious, like Kelly we view all of these behaviors as serious, with none automatically considered more serious than another. Although a punch is generally viewed as worse than a slap, a slap can break teeth. A shove can result in a fall backwards, a blow to the head, and major head trauma or death (DeKeseredy, 2011a; Smith, 1987). In the next chapter, we examine the extent and distribution of cruel behaviors situated on the continuum of violence.

2 | The Extent and Distribution of Violence against Women

The past four decades have seen an explosion of information about the serious problem of violence against women. It is now commonly understood that women and girls across the globe experience a wide range of violence, from female infanticide to sexual trafficking of young girls to rape as a weapon of war. Violence is far too common in the lives of women from the very young to the elderly.
—*Shana L. Maier and Raquel Kennedy Bergen, "Critical Issues in Intimate Partner Violence"*

Since the early 1980s, over one hundred fifty scientific articles on the extent of male violence against female marital and/or cohabiting partners have been published, with most of them written by U.S. social scientists (Machado, Dias, and Coelho, 2010). This is not surprising, because the United States is the world's center for crime survey research. For the same reason, it is also not surprising that U.S. researchers have produced most of the statistics on sexual assault and other forms of woman abuse in a variety of private and public places. Thus, the bulk of the incidence and prevalence data presented in this chapter are not global in scope. Incidence here refers to the percentage of women who were assaulted and the percentage of men who were abusive in the past twelve months. Prevalence here is the percentage of women who were victimized by men and the percentage of men who assaulted women during a much longer time period, such as ever in their lifetime (Basile and Black, 2011; DeKeseredy and Schwartz, 1998a).

This is not to say that scholars from other countries do not gather statistics on violence against women. Canadian researchers, for example, are very active in the field. Indeed, Statistics Canada's (1993) Violence Against Women Survey (VAWS) was the world's first national survey specifically designed to investigate multiple types of male-to-female violence (Jacquier, Johnson, and Fisher, 2011). Consequently, this study yielded much higher prevalence rates of violence and abuse than earlier surveys designed to measure either crime or family conflict (Dobash and Dobash, 1995).[1] The impact of the path-breaking methodological developments made in the VAWS is still felt today and it was replicated in countries such as Australia, Finland, and Iceland (Walby and Myhill, 2001), as well as in regional studies like the Chicago Women's Health Risk Study (Block et al., 2000).

The Canadian national survey of woman abuse in university/college dating (CNS) was also the first country-wide study of its kind (DeKeseredy and Kelly, 1993a; DeKeseredy and Schwartz, 1998a), expanding on the scope of an earlier U.S. national survey of sexual assault on campus (Koss, Gidycz, and Wisniewski, 1987). Additionally, Canadian scholars like Douglas Brownridge (2009) have been at the forefront of the examination of violence against women during and after separation and divorce.

The abuse of women by intimate male partners is not restricted to North America, and researchers from different nations developed collaborative projects showing that it is a global public health problem. For instance, the World Health Organization conducted a multicountry study of the health effects of gendered violence. Over twenty-four thousand women who resided in urban and rural parts of ten countries were interviewed. The research team found that the percentage of women who were ever physically or sexually assaulted (or both) by an intimate partner ranged from 15 percent to 71 percent, with most research sites reporting between 29 percent and 62 percent (Garcia-Moreno, Jansen, Ellsberg, Heise, and Watts, 2005).

Another major international study carried out with the help of Canadian criminologist Holly Johnson—the International Violence Against Women Survey (IVAWS)—conducted interviews with twenty-three thousand women in eleven countries. The percentage of women who revealed at least one incident of physical or sexual violence by any man since the age of sixteen ranged from 20 percent in Hong Kong to between 50 percent and 60 percent in Australia, Costa Rica, the Czech Republic, Denmark, and Mozambique. In most countries examined, rates of victimization were about 35 percent (Johnson, Ollus, and Nevala, 2008). In looking at international rates one might also consider that in Australia, Canada, Israel, South Africa, and the United States, 40 to 70 percent of female homicide victims were murdered by their current or former partners (DeKeseredy, 2011a; Krug et al., 2002). Another unsettling truth is that fourteen girls and women are killed each day in Mexico (DeKeseredy, 2011b; Mujica and Ayala, 2008). Of course, male violence against women around the world takes many other shapes and forms, such as honor killings, dowry-related violence,

2.1 Honor Killings or Femicide?
A Modern Domestic Horror Show

A case that achieved tremendous media attention throughout North America, sparking frenzied discussions about the nature of Islam, turned out to be one of the more dramatic examples in recent history of femicide and domestic horror. Mohammad Shafia, his wife, Tooba Yahya, and eldest son, Hamed, were convicted in January 2012 after a three-month trial, and each was sentenced to life in prison with the option of parole only possible after twenty-five years. They were convicted of killing the couple's three teenage daughters and Shafia's first wife, to whom he was still married.

The case was presented in the media and a good part of the public discussion as an example of "honor killings," which led to intense debates about whether Islam sanctioned such murders and intense protests from the Muslim and Afghan immigrant community that such acts were not only unsanctioned, but were anti-Islamic. The dead included Rona Amir Mohammad, the wife who was cast aside for the crime of being unable to conceive children, and three daughters: Zainab, 19, Sahar, 17, and Geeti, 13. Much was made of Shafia's anger that his eldest daughter had a Pakistani boyfriend, which he felt made her no better than a whore and which allegedly explained why three members of the family decided to murder all four people, including teenage girls acculturated to the norms of Montreal rather than those of remote Afghan villages. As Hashimi (2013) notes, "Unfortunately, since the Shafias were Muslims, the case reinforced the blatantly incorrect notion that murders in response to the perceived tarnishing of family honour are sanctioned by Islamic teachings."

The news angle that was less discussed was that the case represented a horrific but all-too-common act of violence against women in which females who are considered inconvenient are disposed of by males who feel a need to express power and control. Women and children in intimate relationships are murdered every day in North America, almost exclusively by non-Muslims. Stripped of obscuring questions about honor, the case simply involved the murder of a

continued

wife who was trapped in a bigamous relationship, telephoning people in several countries to complain that she was about to be killed by an abusive family. The presiding judge in the case concluded: "The apparent reason behind these cold-blooded, shameful murders was that the four completely innocent victims offended [the defendant's] completely twisted concept of honor . . . that has absolutely no place in any civilized society" (Dalton, 2012, p. 1). The problem was that this wasn't a case of an uncivilized medieval peasant following his values, but of a controlling bigamist abuser living out his modern misogynist values.

genital cutting, and acid-burning (Fontes and McCloskey, 2011; Sev'er, 2008; Silvestri and Crowther-Dowey, 2008; Watts and Zimmerman, 2002). Annually, approximately five thousand women and girls lose their lives to honor killings around the world (Proudfoot, 2009). Box 2.1 describes a recent case that occurred in Kingston, Ontario, Canada, and that garnered much media attention in many countries. Even the popular news channel CNN covered this murder.

A much longer list of atrocities committed against women around the world could easily be presented in the sections that follow. However, since male peer support theories were developed to explain male violence against current and former North American female partners, mainly U.S. and Canadian data on such abuse will be reviewed. It is to intimate femicide that we turn first.

"If I Can't Have You, No One Can!"
Intimate Femicide

The first part of the above heading "echoes through the data on homicide in the context of sexual intimacy" (Polk, 2003, p. 134). It is also a common theme in the intimate femicide literature. We define intimate femicide as "the killing of females by male partners with whom they have, have had, or want to have, a sexual and/or emotional relationship" (Ellis and DeKeseredy, 1997, p. 592). Regrettably, government statistics on intimate femicide are "bone dry" and are bereft of the sociological imagination briefly mentioned in the introduction to this book (Jones, 1980). Drawing upon Mills's (1959) critique of abstracted empiricism (e.g., research divorced from theory), what Websdale (1999) stated about U.S. domestic homicide data still holds true:

> Abstracted empiricism dominates American criminology and has limited the overall understanding of homicide in general, and of domestic homicide in particular. Amidst a plethora of causal models, regression analyses, controls for the supposedly "discrete" variable or that, criminologists lose sight of domestic homicide as a process. Rather, homicides are frozen onto the pages of a supplemental homicide report and then grafted onto some model or subjected to the latest statistical obscurity. Like packaged frozen vegetables that have long since lost touch with a field or the earth, homicide statistics and the data sets they become a part of are convenient but usually bereft of flavor. In short, the use of abstracted empiricism to understand homicide produces accounts and explanations that are about as far removed from social life and historical change as the dead bodies that generated those statistics in the first place (p. 2).

Most current U.S. data on intimate homicide are derived from the FBI's Supplementary Homicide Reports (SHR) and these data are collected yearly, and published by the U.S. Bureau of Justice Statistics. At the time of writing this chapter, the most recent official report on homicide patterns and trends presents data from 1980 through 2008, as well as overall rates for 2009 and 2010 (detailed data on these years were not available) (Cooper and Smith, 2011). Below are some salient findings presented in this report:

- There were roughly twenty-three thousand homicides in 1980 and nearly fifteen thousand in 2010.
- Roughly one out of five homicide victims (16.3 percent) was killed by an intimate partner.
- Females were substantially more likely than males to have been killed by an intimate partner. Two out of five female murder victims were killed by an intimate.
- The rate of females killed by an intimate decreased from 43 percent in 1980 to 38 percent in 1995. After 1995, that percentage increased, reaching 45 percent in 2008.
- In every age group ranging from twelve to sixty or older, female victims were more likely than male victims to have been killed by an intimate.
- The rate of females killed by an intimate increased by 5 percent from 1980 to 2008.

why they are as
we disposable ....

More recently, the FBI's (2010) Uniform Crime Reports show that 12,996 people were murdered that year, with 603 wives killed by their husbands, compared to 110 husbands killed by their wives. The same data set shows that 492 girlfriends were killed by their boyfriends, while 131 boyfriends were killed by girlfriends. In sum, then, women are more likely to be killed by an intimate partner than by all other types of perpetrators combined (Basile and Black, 2011). However, the key problem with official homicide data such as the above is that they do not provide information on intimate relationship status variations in femicide. For example, the relationship category "wife" includes married women, females in common-law relationships, and ex-spouses. This is hardly a trivial problem, given that three decades of academic research shows that some relationships are more dangerous than others, with separated women being at the highest risk of intimate femicide (Brownridge, 2009; DeKeseredy and Schwartz, 2009). In fact, in the United States, close to 50 percent of men on death row for domestic murder killed their wives or lovers in retaliation for leaving (DeKeseredy, 2011a; Stark, 2007). These findings support Diana E. H. Russell's (2001) claim that femicide is "some men's 'final solution' for women" (p. 176).

Probably the greatest "risk factor" for intimate homicide is being African American, with these women two to three times more likely to be killed by men than are White women. Native American and Hispanic women also have higher rates than White women, but lower than African Americans (Basile and Black, 2011; Campbell, 2008). Unsurprisingly, the "number one" risk factor for intimate femicide is a history for the male of violence against a female partner (Auchter, 2010; Campbell, 2007; Johnson and Dawson, 2011). A risk factor suggests that it is not automatic or guaranteed that a batterer will become a murderer, but looking at the murderers, one thing that they are most likely to have in common is that they previously had battered intimate partners. There are other important correlates, or risk factors, including:

- Past use of a weapon to scare or harm the victim
- Possession of a weapon
- Past threats of suicide or homicide
- Stalking behavior
- Jealousy
- Alcohol and/or drug abuse by the perpetrator (Adams, 2007; Campbell et al., 2003)

In sum, every day in the United States, roughly four women are killed by a current or former male partner (DeKeseredy and Schwartz, 2009; Stout,

2001). In Canada, the so called "kinder, gentler nation" with so much smaller a population than the United States, still sixty women a year are victims of intimate femicide and every six days a woman dies from domestic violence (DeKeseredy, 2011a; Kettani, 2009). These data constitute what Toronto lawyer and activist Pam Cross (2007) refers to as "a horrific and preventable death toll that should cause outrage in the citizens of this country" (p. A8). Unfortunately, reducing the rate of femicide is not a political priority on either side of the border.

Nonlethal Physical Violence

A review of studies of the incidence and prevalence of nonlethal physical violence in intimate relationships supports claims made in chapter 1. Michelle L. Meloy and Susan L. Miller (2011) summarize the situation: "The existing research and writing reflects a lack of consensus on how violence should be conceptualized, what behaviors should be asked about, and how findings should be interpreted and reported for policy makers" (p. 62). There are many attempts to answer the question "how much violence against women takes place behind closed doors?" but there is no consensus about the extent of this problem. Still, all survey researchers in the field are likely to agree with this point: There is no reason to believe that overreporting is a problem in this area and many reasons to believe that underreporting is a problem (Schwartz, 2000). Despite all of the social scientific and methodological advances made over the past thirty years, "obtaining accurate estimates of the extent of woman abuse in the population at large remains the biggest methodological challenge in survey research on this topic (Smith, 1987, p. 18).

There are many reasons why both abused women and male offenders might not disclose incidents. Some people are completely embarrassed to find themselves in such a situation, and don't want to let others know about it. Another common reason is a fear of reprisal. Many women report that they were told that if they ever told anyone or called the police, that they would be much more severely hurt or killed. Methodologists often worry about forward and backward telescoping. Here a person who has been beaten often might be unable to accurately place each of those in a specific time period, such as when asked how often something happened in the past six months. Anyone who has ever felt that a series of events all ran together in their mind would understand this problem. There is also simple memory error: people who work hard to put unpleasantness out of their mind could in fact just plain forget. Finally, of course, there is purposeful deception (DeKeseredy and Schwartz, 1998a; Meloy and Miller, 2011; Schwartz, 2000).

As suggested in chapter 1, others have argued that an important cause of underreporting comes from framing a study as a crime survey (see chapter 1). There are many other possible reasons for nonreporting, including a reluctance or inability to subject oneself to the unpleasantry of recalling traumatic behaviors or events. Surprising to some people, but not to workers in the field is a belief among some victims and offenders that violent or psychological assaults are too trivial or inconsequential to mention (Smith, 1994; Straus, Gelles, and Steinmetz, 1981). Some women might not yet have given up on their marriage and might be holding out hope that the violence can be stopped and it can be saved. However, they may feel that if they report the violence that might be a step that will signal the end of the relationship. As well, many batterers are involved in a complex process of attempting to remain in control of relationships (Bancroft, 2002; DeKeseredy and Schwartz, 2009). They may not be ashamed of their violence because of the pain it caused, but they might be ashamed of the violence because it represents a last-ditch action needed to compensate for their inability to maintain control through the use of masculine authority (DeKeseredy and Schwartz, 1998a; Rae, 1995).

New technologies always have pluses and minuses. For example, advances in technology has made it easier than ever before for researchers who collect data on violence to interview a random sample of people who own landline telephones. Yet, that is also the problem. More and more people, and especially younger ones, only have cell phones and cannot be interviewed on land lines. Others without access to landlines might be low-income people, homeless people (including women driven from their homes because of violence), women who are in mental health institutions or prisons (both of whom have high rates of violence victimization). There are other problems that contribute to underreporting (e.g., language barriers) and all of them are difficult to overcome and not likely to be eliminated in the future. However, there have been some significant attempts to minimize the sources of underreporting, but it is beyond the scope of this chapter to describe them here.[2]

Some surveys elicit higher estimates than others, and government surveys typically generate lower rates of violence against women than those conducted by university-based researchers. For example, Statistics Canada's (1993) national Violence Against Women Survey (VAWS) found that, in the context of dating, 2 percent of female respondents reported being physically abused in the past year and 18 percent of them experienced this harm since the age of sixteen. It should be also noted that these figures include both sexual and physical assaults. In sharp contrast, the Canadian national survey of woman abuse in university/college dating (CNS), also a national-level representative sample study, uncovered these rates of physical and sexual violence:

- Of the male respondents, 13.7 percent indicated that they had physically assaulted their dating partners in the year before the survey, whereas 22.3 percent of the female participants stated that they had been victimized in such a way during the same time period.
- About 35 percent of the women reported having been physically assaulted, and 17.8 percent of the men stated that they had used physical abuse since leaving high school.
- Approximately 28 percent of the female participants stated that they were sexually abused in the past year, whereas 11 percent of the males reported having victimized a female dating partner in this way during the same time period.
- Of the women, 45.1 percent stated that they had been sexually assaulted since leaving high school, and 19.5 percent of the men reported at least one incident of abuse in the same time period (DeKeseredy and Schwartz, 1998a).

The main reason for the different rates is that the VAWS defined physical and sexual violence in narrow legalistic terms, while the CNS used broad definitions of such assaults, which help researchers uncover higher and more accurate estimates of these problems. Some things don't change, and more recent U.S. and Canadian government surveys continue to underestimate the extent of violence against women for the same reason. Consider the critique of the U.S. National Violence Against Women Survey (VAWS) featured in chapter 1. Again, it found that 1.8 percent of the women in the sample stated that they were victimized by one or more of these "intimate intrusions" in the past year (Stanko, 1985): rape, physical assault, rape and/or sexual assault, and stalking (Tjaden and Thoennes, 2000). On the other hand, most university-based studies of just physical violence in marital/cohabiting relationships show that at least 11 percent of North American women in these contexts are physically abused by a male partner on an annual basis (DeKeseredy, 2011a).

Government public health surveys also elicit very low annual rates of physical violence against women. For instance, the Centers for Disease Control's National Intimate Partner and Sexual Violence Survey (NISVS)[3] only uncovered a twelve-month rate of 4 percent, and this figure includes violence committed by a same-sex partner (Black et al., 2011). Yet the lifetime rate is much higher (33 percent), which is consistent with prevalence rates generated by all kinds of surveys of violence against women. Unfortunately, due to a combination of government cutbacks and right-wing political pressure to ignore or minimize the extent of violence against women, it is unlikely that we will see new large-scale university-based surveys that elicit higher rates in the near future.

The Distribution of Nonlethal Physical Violence[4]

Anne Menard (2001), Director of the National Resource Center on Domestic Violence (NRCDV), is one of many feminist scholars and activists who points out that in North America, violence against women "occurs in all demographic and social groups, cutting across age, race, ethnicity, sexual orientation, and economic circumstances" (p. 708). To the extent that one is arguing that violence takes place in every part of society, this is true. But this is not to argue that it takes place equally in every part of society. All women are not at equal risk of being victimized by male intimates; some are at much higher risk than others. For example, one might consider the women who live in public housing. In the Quality of Neighborhood Life Survey, which was administered to residents of six public housing projects in the west end of a metropolitan center in Ontario, Canada, DeKeseredy, Alvi, Schwartz and Tomaszewski (2003) found that 19.3 percent of the female sample were physically assaulted by intimate partners in the year before the survey. This figure is much higher than the 4 percent rate uncovered by the NISVS.

Renzetti and Maier's (2002) Camden, New Jersey, study provides further support for the assertion that women residing in public housing are at higher risk of violent victimization than their more affluent counterparts. The women in their sample reported a lifetime violent victimization rate of 64 percent by husbands, boyfriends, relatives, or acquaintances such as neighbors. As Holzman, Hyatt, and Dempster (2001) remind us, "demographic, economic, and geographic factors associated with high incidence of violent victimization of women appear to find a nexus in public housing" (p. 665). Indeed, regardless of whether they live in public housing, a large empirical literature shows that low-income women report higher rates of intimate violence than more privileged females (Renzetti, 2011).

There are also age, race and ethnicity differences in rates of violent offending. Males between the ages of sixteen and twenty-four assault women more than older men (DeKeseredy, 2007a). Another difference is that rates of such abuse reported by African Americans, American Indians and Alaska Natives, and mixed races are higher than those for other racial/ethnic groups (Basile and Black, 2011; Wood, Myrstol, Rosay, Rivera, and TePas, 2011). However, this has nothing to do with biological makeup, skin color, or culture. Rather, a greater percentage of minorities are poor, unemployed, and are members of the working class, which provides much greater explanatory power for the higher rates of violence (DeKeseredy, Dragiewicz, and Rennison, 2012).

However, there has been extensive criticism of many of the measures of race and ethnicity used in large-scale U.S. surveys, such as the VAWS. For instance, the above "pan-ethnic categories" are treated as homogenous groups but in reality include "diverse subpopulations that have very distinct ethnic, religious, historical, philosophical, and social values that may have important roles in the dynamics" of violence against women (Perilla, Lippy, Rosales, and Serrata, 2011). Certainly, not all Black people are the same and there are different rates of violence among African Americans, African Caribbeans, and Africans. A similar critique can be made when talking about violence within other ethnic groups, such as those officially designated as "American Indian/Native Alaskan" (Aldarondo and Castro-Fernandez, 2011). To the best of our knowledge, the National Alcohol and Family Violence Survey is the only major U.S. survey specifically designed to overcome or minimize these limitations and hopefully other large-scale studies will follow suit (Aldarondo, Kaufman-Kantor, and Jasinski, 2002; Kaufman-Kantor, Jasinski, and Aldarondo, 1994).

There is growing body of research showing that immigrant and refugee women are "vulnerable populations" (Basile and Black, 2011; Brownridge, 2009; Fong, 2010; Sokoloff, 2005; Villalon, 2010). As is often said, though, more research needs to be done because these women's experiences are not adequately addressed in large national samples and these women are often misclassified as "White." Related to this problem is that some common types of abuse directed at immigrant/refugee women, such as using immigration status as a method of coercive control, are not operationalized in mainstream surveys and not included in widely used measures such as the Conflict Tactics Scale (CTS) (Dutton, Orloff, and Hass, 2000; Perilla, Lippy, Rosales, and Serrata, 2011). Also, it is essential to avoid stereotyping or constructing perpetrators of violence against ethnic/minority and immigrant/refugee women as "others." As Fontes and Mc-Closkey (2011) remind us, "there are few forms of violence that belong exclusively to any particular culture" (p. 152).

Cohabiting women are at much higher risk of being beaten than are married women (Brownridge and Halli, 2001; DeKeseredy, 2011a). So are separated and divorced women. Some explanations for these intimate relationship status variations are provided in chapter 4, but note that they are heavily influenced by what we will describe as male peer support, as well as other factors, such as poverty, unemployment, and the social context of alcohol consumption. These and other variables are also strongly associated with violence against women in rural areas, and there is growing evidence suggesting that rural women are at higher risk of being physically abused than suburban and urban women in the United States (Basile and Black, 2011; DeKeseredy and Schwartz, 2009; Maier and Bergen, 2012; Rennison, DeKeseredy, and Dragiewicz, in press). Additionally, a review of cross-cultural research shows that violence against women is more common in rural areas around the world than it is in industrialized contexts (Garcia-Moreno, Jansen, Ellsberg, Heise, and Watts, 2006; Machado, Dias, and Coelho, 2010).

More research demonstrating variations in physical violence across different categories of women could easily be presented here. However, the main point is that not all women are equally likely to experience physical violence in intimate relationships. The same can be said about sexual violence, which is also prevalent in the United States, Canada, and other parts of the world.

"Not a Love Story": Sexual Violence[5]

As described in chapter 1, sexual violence takes different shapes and forms and is not restricted to forced penetration. Younger women are at the highest risk of victimization by sexual violence. Both large- and small-scale North American surveys consistently show that approximately 25 percent of female undergraduate students experience some variation of this crime on an annual basis (DeKeseredy and Flack, 2007). However, many people continue to dismiss or trivialize this widespread problem. For example, in March, 2006, Walter DeKeseredy and William F. Flack Jr. met with a lawyer for a small private university in the United States to discuss sexual assault on his campus and its immediate surroundings. The lawyer stated that a recent study of unwanted sex among students at his school was flawed and, at best, revealed a high rate of "regretted sex." When DeKeseredy told him that unless his institution of higher learning developed an effective prevention plan, there was a strong chance that victims' parents would sue, this lawyer replied that he was more worried about lawsuits filed by "alleged perpetrators." Such a concern presumes that false allegations of sexual assault are more significant problems than true ones. However, less than 2 percent of campus rapes reported to the police are false allegations (De-

Keseredy, 2011a), which is a particularly small number when compared to the extraordinary underreporting of this crime on college campuses, and the consistent finding that 25 percent of college women suffer from some variant of sexual assault while in school.

On top of gathering rich data on the extent of sexual assault on the college campus, social scientists have identified many risk factors associated with it, such as patriarchal male peer support (Schwartz and DeKeseredy, 1997), alcohol and drug consumption (Fisher, Daigle, and Cullen , 2010; Schwartz, DeKeseredy, Tait, and Alvi, 2001), "hooking up" (Bogle, 2008; Flack et al., 2007), and experiencing sexual assault prior to coming to college (DeKeseredy and Schwartz, 1998a). Still, theoretical developments have not kept pace with the empirical literature. Schwartz and Pitts's (1995) feminist routine activities theory and male peer support models presented in chapters 3 and 4 are exceptions to the criticisms that work in this field has been hampered by what some leading experts in the field refer to as "consistent lack of theoretical grounding" (Fisher, Sloan, Cullen, and Lu, 1998).

Until the recent NISVS, the only nationally representative U.S. estimates of a wide range of sexual assaults were collected from college samples (Fisher, Cullen, and Turner, 2000; Koss, Gidycz, and Wisniewski, 1987). Table 2.1 presents the NISVS lifetime and twelve-month rates of sexual violence reported by women in the sample. An important finding is that about one in five women reported being raped in her lifetime, which translates to nearly 22 million female residents of the United States. Furthermore, close to one in two women (44.6 percent) experienced sexual violence other than rape at some time in their lives (Black et al., 2011).

The Distribution of Sexual Violence

Statistics presented in Table 2.1, as well as other data, tell us that sexual violence is a widespread problem in the United States. However, as is the case with nonlethal physical violence and femicide, some subgroups of women face special risks and some subgroups of men are more likely to be perpetrators. For example, it is estimated that 20 to 40 percent of women in the military have experienced some type of sexual assault (Campbell and Townsend, 2011; Suris and Lind, 2008).

A key risk factor for the victimization of women is alcohol and drug consumption because such activity usually occurs close to young men who are at high risk of assaulting them (Johnson and Dawson, 2011). Using Canadian

Table 2.1 Lifetime and Twelve-Month NISVS Rates of Sexual Violence

Type of Assault	Lifetime		12-Month	
	Weighted %	Estimated Number of Victims*	Weighted %	Estimated Number of Victims*
Rape	18.3	21,840,000	1.1	1,270,000
Completed forced penetration	12.3	14,617,000	0.5	620,000
Attempted forced penetration	5.2	6,199,000	0.4	519,000
Completed alcohol/drug facilitated penetration	8.0	9,524,000	0.7	781,000
Other Sexual Violence	44.6	53,174,000	5.6	6,646,000
Made to penetrate	X	X	X	X
Sexual coercion	13.0	15,492,000	2.0	2,410,000
Unwanted sexual contact	27.2	32,447,000	2.2	2,600,000
Non-contact unwanted sexual experiences	33.7	40,193,000	3.0	3,532,000

*Rounded to the nearest thousand
X Estimate is not reported; relative standard error > 30 percent or cell size < 20.
Source: Black et al. (2011, p. 18)

national survey data (CNS), Schwartz, DeKeseredy, Tait, and Alvi (2001) found that undergraduate men who went out drinking two or more times a week and who had friends who gave them peer support for both emotional and physical partner abuse were nine times as likely to report committing sexual assault as men reporting none of these three characteristics. Furthermore, alcohol is a common feature of many men's social groups, such as fraternities, and is commonly used as a tool to make women unable to resist sexual aggression. Inside men's groups, alcohol is commonly used in contexts that support patriarchal conversations about women's sexuality and how to control it (DeKeseredy, Alvi, and Schwartz, 2006; Hey, 1986; Schwartz and DeKeseredy, 1997).

Contrary to popular belief, women are much more likely to be sexually assaulted by an intimate partner or acquaintance than by a stranger (Fisher, Daigle, and Cullen, 2010; Wykes and Welsh, 2009). For example, the NISVS found that nearly one in ten women has been raped by an intimate partner in her lifetime (Black et al., 2011). Dating is a particular risky context for women, and so is separation or divorce (DeKeseredy and Schwartz, 1998a, 2009).

Turning now to race/ethnicity, the variations reported in the previous section are similar. For instance, rates of reported sexual assault by African Americans, American Indian/Alaska Natives, and mixed races are higher compared to other racial/ethnic groups (Black et al., 2011; Tjaden and Thoennes, 2000). In Canada, Native or Aboriginal women are particularly vulnerable, with some studies estimating that eight in ten women have endured sexual assault (Johnson and Dawson, 2011; McIvor and Nahanee, 1998). In the United States, Hamby (2004) also found very high rates, with 12 percent to 49 percent of Native American women experiencing sexual violence in their lifetime and most knew the perpetrators. Of course, many Native women live in rural areas and there is growing evidence females who live in these communities are more likely to be raped or sexually assaulted than their urban counterparts (Maier and Bergen, 2012; Rennison, DeKeseredy, and Dragiewicz, in press).

The men most likely to sexually assault current or former intimate partners are those who:

- are physically and verbally abusive (Knight and Sims-Knight, 2011)
- hold strong patriarchal beliefs (DeKeseredy, 2011a)
- frequently consume pornographic material (DeKeseredy and Olsson, 2011)
- have patriarchal male peer support (DeKeseredy and Schwartz, 2009; Maier and Bergen, 2012; Schwartz and DeKeseredy, 1997)
- abuse alcohol and drugs (Basile and Black, 2011)

Concern for Victimized Women

Obviously, a broad spectrum of women are affected by a serious and injurious event like sexual assault over the course of their lives. Given how harmful it is, it is often surprising to find how little concern is generated about them by politicians, journalists, and the general public. Sexual assault survivors are still routinely blamed and stigmatized today (Johnson and Dawson, 2011). One recent example is described by Ben Armbruster (2012) in box 2.2. This disturbing event took place in early February 2012 at a time when North American crime discussion is still dominated by cries of "what about victims' rights," along with calls for more prisons, more executions (and reinstating the death penalty in Canada). Nevertheless, it remains widely popular to belittle female victims

2.2 Fox Pundit Says Women in the Military Should "Expect" to Be Raped

The Pentagon announced new rules last week easing the ban on women serving in combat. While conservatives like Rick Santorum are a little uneasy with the news, the announcement only formalizes military practices that were already taking place.

But Fox News contributor Liz Trotta's commentary on the matter took the issue to a whole other level. She's not really concerned about the "controversy" surrounding the Pentagon's announcement. For Trotta, the issue is having "women once more, the feminists, going, wanting to be warriors and victims at the same time." She cited a recent Pentagon report that violent sex crimes in the military have increased over the past six years and said women should "expect" it, decrying more levels of bureaucracy to support women who have been "raped too much."

Trotta said "But while all of this is going on, just a few weeks ago, Defense Secretary Leon Panetta commented on a new Pentagon report on sexual abuse in the military. I think they have actually discovered there is a difference between men and women. And the sexual abuse report says there has been, since 2006, a 64 percent increase in violent sexual assaults. Now, what did they expect? These people are in close contact, the whole airing of this issue has never been done by Congress, it's strictly a question of pressure from the feminists."

"And the feminists have also directed them, really, to spend a lot of money. They have sexual counselors all over the place, victims' advocates, sexual response coordinators. . . . So, you have this whole bureaucracy upon bureaucracy being built up with all kinds of levels of people to support women in the military who are now being raped too much."

To his credit, Fox host Eric Shawn tried to talk Trotta down a bit. "You certainly want the people fighting the war to be protected from anything that could be illegal," he said. But Trotta wouldn't have it. "Nice try Eric," she said, "This whole question of women in the military has not been aired properly, and it's the great sleeping giant."

Source: Ambruster (2012). Used by permission of ThinkProgress.org.

when they are attacked by people they know, and box 2.2 provides a major example of this.

For sexual assault survivors, statements such as Liz Trotta's constitute a "second rape" (Madigan and Gamble, 1989), and there is no way of knowing just how many women are deterred from disclosing their experiences for fear of enduring responses like hers. What we do know, however, from the data presented in this chapter and elsewhere is that an alarming number of women do not get the help they need (Campbell and Townsend, 2011).

Stalking

Stalking is defined here as "the willful, repeated, and malicious following, harassing, or threatening of another person" (Melton, 2007a, p. 4). It involves a variety of fear-inducing behaviors, such as unwanted phone calls and e-mails, showing up at a woman's home when such a "visit" is unwanted, and sneaking into a person's home or car to let her know that the offender was there (Black et al., 2011). We often hear of the stalking experiences of movie stars and other celebrities, but most stalking quietly occurs in our own neighborhoods and typically involves men targeting current or former intimate female partners (Black et al., 2011; Logan, Cole, Shannon and Walker, 2006; Klein and Hart, 2012). Stalking is also strongly correlated with physical and psychological abuse, and it escalates when women leave their male partners (Mechanic, Uhlmansiek, Weaver, and Resick, 2000; Mechanic, Weaver, and Resick, 2000; Melton, 2007b).

There are very few recent national estimates of stalking in the United States (Basile, Swahn, Chen, and Saltzman, 2006; Baum, Catalano, Rand, and Rose, 2009). The most up-to-data national data are derived from the NISVS. This study found the following:

- One in six women (16.2 percent) was victimized by stalking over the course of her lifetime.
- Four percent of female respondents were stalked in the year before the survey.
- One in five Black non-Hispanic women was stalked in her lifetime and the prevalence of stalking for White, non-Hispanic and Hispanic women was similar (one in six and one in seven, respectively).
- One in three multiracial non-Hispanic and one in four American Indian/Alaska Native women were stalked during their lifetime.

- Over three-quarters of female stalking victims (78.8 percent) received unwanted calls, including voice or text messages, or hang ups.
- Fifty-eight percent of female victims reported being approached and 39 percent were watched, followed, or tracked with an electronic device.
- Sixty-two percent of the women were stalked by a current or former intimate partner and 24 percent were victimized by an acquaintance, with nearly 13 percent stalked by a stranger.
- Eighty-three percent of female stalking victims were only stalked by men.
- More than 50 percent of female victims were stalked before the age of 25 (Black et al., 2011).

The motivations for stalking vary, but among those identified in the literature are obsession, jealousy, revenge, a need to control the victim, and the desire to reestablish a relationship (Melton, 2007b; National Institute of Justice, 1996; Roberts and Dziegielewski, 1996). It may be painfully obvious, but worth stating nonetheless: regardless of what causes men to stalk, their illegal behavior generates much fear and concern. As one woman told Logan, Cole, Shannon, and Walker (2006):

> I'm afraid that he will feel like a man with nothing to lose and he will kill me. That's what I am afraid of. I think he would rather see me dead than to see me happy or to see me with someone else. (p. 22)

In light of the femicide data presented earlier, women who exit relationships and are stalked have every right to be fearful. Many men do not leave their ex-partners alone, and their visits can be lethal. Another important point to keep in mind is that abusive men are at high risk of being more abusive when their relationship ends (Melton, 2007b).

Psychological Abuse

Chapter 1 made explicit that psychological abuse by intimates is a major problem. Nevertheless, compared to physical and sexual violence, it receives relatively little empirical and theoretical attention except as a feature of violent relationships. In some cases, this is fully appropriate. However, there remains the disconcerting problem that in a great many cases psychologically abusive relationships go undocumented and unattended to because they are not also physically or sexually abusive (Nash Chang, 1996; Stark, 2007). Ignoring psychological abuse becomes a serious problem when it turns out that we are ignoring a major form of woman abuse. To be clear, easy as it is to trivialize such abuse as "he failed to compliment me on my new shoes," the problem, rather, is serious aggression up to the point of maintaining a fearful and terroristic household. As noted earlier, this can lead to much longer-term consequences than actual physical abuse.

The good news, though, is that psychological abuse is emerging as a topic of concern and scientific interest. One sign of this newer and growing scientific interest is that Haworth Press now publishes *The Journal of Emotional Abuse*. The NISVS focus on the incidence and prevalence of "psychological aggression" in intimate relationships is even more important evidence. This study measured "expressive aggression (such as name calling, insulting or humiliating an intimate partner) and coercive control, which includes behaviors that are intended to monitor and control or threaten an intimate partner" (Black et al., 2011, p. 37).

NISVS data show:

- About 50 percent of women in the United States were victimized by at least one type of psychological aggression in their lifetime, with four in ten reporting some variant of "expressive aggression" (e.g., humiliation or insult) or coercive control.
- Fourteen percent of women experienced some form of psychological aggression in the past year.
- The most commonly reported behaviors were expressive forms of aggression such as being called stupid or ugly (64.3 percent), witnessing a partner act angry in a manner that appeared dangerous (57.9 percent), and being insulted, humiliated, or made fun of (58 percent). Another commonly reported behavior was demanding to know a woman's whereabouts (61.7 percent) (Black et al., 2011).

It is unclear from these data which groups of women in the United States are the most vulnerable and which groups of men are most likely to be perpetrators, as variations across different socioeconomic categories had not been released as of this writing. But there is literature revealing what Nash Chang (1996) discovered some years ago: "The husband maintains a dominating position, functioning more like a parent or controlling boss. He acts against his wife who becomes his object" (p. 85). A similar pattern exists in many dating relationships and cohabitating or common-law relationships (Stosny, 2008). For example, it was a common feature in Schwartz's Violence against Women class for many years to discuss this problem. Despite many warnings against self-disclosure unless the student felt fully comfortable about it, it was common for one or two students in every class to disclose that as a first-year student living in a dormitory her boyfriend, who attended a different university, forbade her to leave her dorm room except to eat or attend class. He would call her at all hours of the day and night to check up on her whereabouts.

There are many different types of psychologically abusive men. Another example identified by Lundy Bancroft (2002) is the "Water Torturer":

> The Water Torturer's style proves that anger doesn't cause abuse. He can assault his partner psychologically without even raising his voice. He tends to stay calm in arguments, using his own evenness as a weapon to push her over the edge. He often has a superior or contemptuous grin on his face, smug and self-assured. He uses a repertoire of aggressive conversational tactics at low volume, including sarcasm, derision—such as openly laughing at her—mimicking her voice, and cruel, cutting remarks. . . . [H]e tends to take things she has said and twist them beyond recognition to make her appear absurd, perhaps especially in front of other people. He gets to his partner through a slow but steady stream of low-level emotional assaults. . . . He is relentless in his quiet derision and meanness. (p. 84)

Much more research on psychological abuse is needed. Also, we do not have, as yet, a widely accepted definition of psychological abuse, which, in turn, affects our knowledge of the extent, distribution, and key sources of this harm (Basile and Black, 2011). Then again, the same can be said about the other types of abuse covered in this chapter.

Summary

This chapter describes the alarming scope of violence against women. Although the statistics presented here are "hotly debated" (Campbell and Townsend, 2011), they underestimate the incidence and prevalence of nonlethal forms of woman abuse. The harms examined in this chapter often overlap and they are not the only assaults that many women experience. For example, numerous women are economically abused by their intimate partners (Klein and Hart, 2012), but we don't have reliable national estimates of such victimization, or even a reliable definition of when such a situation is serious enough to count as abuse. For example, a relative of one of the authors of this book graduated college and got married, going to work while her new husband went to graduate school. He had her turn over her paycheck to him, and she had to ask him for anything she wanted, such as fifty cents to put into a newspaper machine.

She would hotly deny that she was abused by this. How do we count whether or not she was? The field has begun to generate some valuable small-scale studies, and Adams, Sullivan, Bybee, and Greeson (2008) helped fill a major research gap by developing the Scale of Economic Abuse, one of the first attempts to measure this. Klein and Hart (2012) discuss other instruments that attempt to measure this.

Intimate violence is certainly not restricted to the groups of women covered in this chapter. Pregnant women, elderly women, women in same-sex relationships, homeless women, and women with disabilities are also vulnerable populations (Basile and Black, 2011; Brownridge, 2009; Jasinski, Wesely, Wright, and Mustaine, 2010), but it is beyond the scope of this book to review the empirical and theoretical literature on every type of woman abuse and every group of women that is hurt by intimate violence. This is not to say, however, that the pain and suffering of women excluded from the purview of this book is less important than women abuse in the contexts examined in subsequent chapters.

Despite budget cuts, the anti-feminist backlash, and a host of other obstacles and challenges, men and women involved in the violence against women movement have achieved much over the past four decades. Abused women now have more resources to choose from, but the data scattered throughout this chapter show that they are not markedly safer. Without doubt, separated and divorced women are still at an increased risk of being killed if they lived with abusive and/or controlling men (DeKeseredy, 2011a). Moreover, young women are still sexually assaulted in "numbers that would numb the mind of Einstein" (Lewis cited in Vallee, 2007, p. 22), recalling Katz's (2006) claim that "It takes a village to rape a woman" (p. 149). Sadly, thousands of women will continue to be killed, beaten, sexually assaulted, stalked, and so forth until the major causes of woman abuse are recognized, understood, and addressed by policy makers and the general public (Johnson and Dawson, 2011; Wolfe and Jaffe, 2001). In Chapter 7 we suggest some effective means of helping to achieve this goal and for making the feminist struggle to end violence against women a "usual rather than unusual part of public policy" (Hearn, 1998, 113).

3 | The History of Male Peer Support Theory

Many boys and men in our society have been taught to view violence as a requisite of masculinity. Even though feminism has made significant strides in changing attitudes toward women, males are still encouraged by both peers and adult figures in their lives to be manipulative, domineering, and controlling toward girls and are often rewarded for displaying such "typical" masculine behavior. . . . Many students and even adults in a school community—the schools' gender police—expect boys to make comments about girls' bodies, talk about them derisively with one another, and keep the upper hand in any sexual interactions. Perceived infractions against these kinds of codes can incur the wrath of a boy's peers (and even adult role models) and the boy may chastise himself as well.   —Jessie Klein, *The Bully Society*

What accounts for the high rates of violence against women presented in chapter 2? Social scientific answers to this question range from simple single-factor explanations to complex multivariate offerings.[1] Regardless of their degree of sophistication, they are not, as many people argue, "irrelevant antonyms of fact" or "just fanciful ideas that have little to do with what truly motivates real people" (Akers and Sellers, 2009, p. 1). On the contrary, in the words of Kurt Lewin (1951), the founder of modern social psychology, "There is nothing so practical as good theory" (p. 169). Surely, to both prevent and control violence against women, more than accurate data is required. We need to explain this problem. Thus, in this chapter we trace the history of the original male peer support theories, which, along with perspectives reviewed in chapter 4, influenced the development of progressive policies and practices recommended in chapter 7.

The Historical, Social, and Intellectual Roots of Male Peer Support Theory

Male peer support theories grew out of seeds planted in several places at York University, situated in Toronto, Canada, and at the 1987 American Society of Criminology meetings in Montreal where the authors of this book first met. As stated in the introduction, these theories are heavily shaped by social support theory and other social scientific perspectives that address the relationship between all-male peer group dynamics and woman abuse. However, it cannot be emphasized enough that the male peer support models developed by us would not have emerged without the guidance, advice, and inspiration of colleagues affiliated with the LaMarsh Center for Research on Violence and Conflict Resolution that was based in York University.[2] It no longer exists, but the Center's impact is still felt around the world today.

The Contribution of the LaMarsh Center

The LaMarsh Center was established in 1980 under the leadership of sociologist Desmond Ellis. Walter DeKeseredy completed three degrees in sociology under Ellis's supervision, and he became heavily involved in LaMarsh Center intellectual activities in 1985 as a doctoral student. Among the Center's Executive Board at that time were psychologists David Weisenthal, Richard Goranson, James Check, and sociologists Michael D. Smith and Alice Propper. All of these colleagues were engaged in vibrant and timely intellectual projects, including empirical and theoretical work on woman abuse. However, it was Ellis and Smith who had the greatest impact on DeKeseredy's scholarly trajectory.

In 1985, the study of woman abuse in dating had a "short history" (Riggs and O'Leary, 1989). There were a few studies of sexual assault in dating conducted in the late 1950s and late 1960s,[3] but physical violence in this intimate context received limited, if any, empirical and theoretical attention until James Makepeace (1981) published the first study of "courtship violence" among U.S. college students. This survey opened the door to a number of others in the general community in the 1980s that challenged the "marriage license is a hitting license thesis" (Straus, Gelles, and Steinmetz, 1981). This thesis includes two main contentions. First, marriage is a special institution that places women at high risk for abuse. Second, married women are more likely to be beaten than unmarried women (Gelles, 1982).[4] However, in the mid-1980s, there were no comparable Canadian data that contradicted this claim made by Murray Straus and his colleagues. So, this research gap helped launch DeKeseredy's PhD thesis in sociology.

In 1985, Michael D. Smith was in the process of developing a representative sample survey of woman abuse in Toronto and Desmond Ellis was doing pioneering research on post-separation woman abuse. DeKeseredy asked them to be on his PhD supervisory committee and they agreed, but Ellis was adamant about avoiding abstracted empiricism at all cost. He told DeKeseredy (and correctly so) that obtaining exploratory survey data on male-to-female physical violence in Canadian university/college dating was not good enough. He also said that an original thesis entails rigorous theoretical work and that DeKeseredy needed to find a relevant theory and operationalize its key concepts. At that time, though, responding to Ellis's concerns seemed a daunting task because the extant literature on male physical violence in post–secondary school dating was basically atheoretical (DeKeseredy, 1988c).

From November 1985 to the early part of 1986, DeKeseredy toiled in York University's enormous Scott Library looking for theoretical guidance, and his frustration was growing stronger with each passing day. Then, in the fall of 1986, while in York University's *Cock and Bull Pub* drinking his morning coffee and preparing for an undergraduate tutorial that he was to shortly lead, one of the most important events in his life transpired. At a nearby table was a group of six undergraduates, and DeKeseredy overheard them offering "solutions" to one group member's dating problems. The recipient of advice was deeply disturbed because he took a woman out for dinner and she refused to have sex with him at the end of the evening. Some of his peers suggested that he stop seeing her, while others stated that he should have physically forced her to have sex with him.

At that moment, DeKeseredy remembered Eugene J. Kanin's (1967a) reference group theory. He was the first North American sociologist to tackle this important question: How do homosocial (all-male) groups make sexual abuse in courtship legitimate to their members? Furthermore, how do they perpetuate this problem over time? DeKeseredy then, with an improved outlook on the future, went to his tutorial and shortly after told Smith about his experience. Smith had a keen interest in the violent subculture hypothesis derived from Wolfgang and Ferracuti's (1967) work and he tested it using interview data gathered from over 700 hockey players (see Smith, 1979, 1983). Smith was also familiar with the literature on what was then referred to as "wife beating," and he asked DeKeseredy to read Lee Bowker's (1983) book *Beating Wife-Beating*, which included, for its time, one of the more developed male peer support theories of wife abuse. This was one of the best suggestions DeKeseredy ever received, and he and Schwartz have consequently cited Bowker's book numerous times. In chapter 1 we noted Bowker's claim that the male patriarchal subculture of violence is "spread through all parts of society" (p. 136). He was right.

After reading Bowker's work and revisiting Kanin's (1967a) theory, De-Keseredy decided to broaden his analysis of woman abuse in dating to include sexual and psychological abuse and to examine how male groupings contribute to the multidimensional nature of "the dark side of the ivory tower" (Sloan and Fisher, 2011). However, he still couldn't put all the theoretical pieces together until Desmond Ellis introduced him to social support theory in the fall of 1986.

Social Support Theory[5]

Social support theory is generally used by social psychologists to explain the role of social support in health maintenance and disease prevention. Their arguments are derived from a large empirical literature that shows that people with friends and family members who offer them psychological and material resources are healthier than persons with few or no supportive contacts (Caplan, 1974; Cassell, 1976; Cohen, and Wills, 1985; Sarason and Sarason, 1985). Ellis (1988) and Hoff (1990) were the first researchers interested in violence against women to recognize social support theory's explanatory value and to reconceptualize it to suit their empirical and theoretical interests. A few years later, Francis T. Cullen (1994) modified social support theory to show the broader criminological community how certain sociocultural factors insulate people from committing crimes. Cullen, though, never applied social support theory to his collaborative work on the sexual victimization of college women.

Social support theory is mainly psychological, but Ellis (1988) argues that it has sociological roots in the writings of pioneering sociologists Emile Durkheim (1951) and George Herbert Mead (1934). Durkheim maintained that high or low levels of social integration are related to suicide. For example, strong group integration may result in altruistic suicide and weak social integration may result in egoistic suicide. For symbolic interactionist Mead, the development of an individual's mind and self is based on social exchanges with various people. An important part of much of sociology is that people are not born with innate personalities that emerge full-blown as the body develops (Agnew, 2011), but rather that mind and self develop uniquely in each person, based on the way in which they interact with other people. Hence, one of the stronger legacies of sociology, based on the writings of both Durkheim and Mead, is that social integration and the quality of interactions within social networks have significant individual and social consequences.

Contemporary social support theorists examine the relationship between social support, health, and physical and psychological well-being. Two perspectives in particular explain the relationship between social support and people's ability to cope with stressful life events: (1) the main- or direct-effect model and (2) the buffering model. Proponents of the former contend that an increase in social support produces an increase in well-being regardless of whether people are under stress or the level of support received (Thoits, 1983; Wills, 1985). Integration into large social networks provides a "positive effect, a sense of predictability in one's life situation" (Cohen and Wills, 1985, p. 311). Social networks can also help people avoid negative experiences, which can increase the chance of physical or psychological problems. Advocates of the buffering model also contend that social support leads to well-being, but only for persons under stress (Cohen and Hoberman, 1983; Wilcox, 1981). Social support "buffers" or protects people from the negative effects of stressful life events.

Social Support Theory and Woman Abuse

Ellis (1988) turned social support theory upside down and with his help DeKeseredy (1988a) shortly followed suit. In other words, they argued that social support can threaten women's health under certain conditions. According to Ellis's application of social support theory, lawyers, police officers, mediators, and other professionals who deal with woman abuse differ in the emphasis they place on safety compared to other factors, such as their own professional standing, income, the law, and the couple's relationship. These alternative concerns direct attention away from the physical protection of separating or separated women and can result in further abuse by their estranged husbands.

For example, Ellis provides an "atrocity tale" (Goffman, 1961) that is directly relevant to this discussion. A battered woman went to a male lawyer to ask him to help remove her violent husband from their home or to get him to provide her with financial support so that she could move out temporarily. She also reported that her husband beat her the previous night and that she was worried about her safety. The lawyer responded to her request for help by stating that he required some money as a deposit and advised her to return to her husband. Furthermore, he told her to come back to his office when the injuries she received from her spouse were more severe. This woman's experience is an example of inappropriate assistance that may have serious health consequences for women.

More empirical support for Ellis's approach is offered by Ellis and Wight's (1987) study of lawyering as mode of social support. They found that the type of assistance women receive from lawyers will influence whether or not they are abused after divorce or separation. Their survey data reveal, for example, that wives who were abused before separation and who consulted conciliatory lawyers were more likely to report being abused after separation than abused wives who consulted adversarial lawyers.

Thus, the argument is that the social support provided by some of those ostensibly responsible for helping abused women increases the probability of many women's victimization or further victimization. DeKeseredy (1988a) added to this by arguing that the same can be said about the resources offered by some male peer groups. Presented in figure 3.1, DeKeseredy's original male peer support model contends that many men experience various types of stress in dating relationships, ranging from sexual problems to threats to the kinds of authority that a patriarchal culture has led them to expect to be their rights by virtue of being male. Simply put, dating can be stressful. Heavily influenced by Bowker (1983), DeKeseredy argued that when a male finds that the male domination that society has taught him is his natural right is threatened or is perceived to be challenged, psychological stress is most likely to be experienced. Some men try to deal with these problems themselves, or turn to an older generation for advice, or might talk to women or girls for advice. However, many men turn to male friends for advice, guidance, and various other kinds of social support when they are in some psychological distress, and particularly the kind of stress that comes from dating and relationships with females. Of course, it is common for men to obtain excellent advice from their friends, to find that others share the same fears, and to find that they are able to relax or calm themselves down.

The problem is that one thing we have seen in most ethnographic studies of male culture is an emphasis on masculinity demonstrations. Studies of gangs, delinquency, workplace cultures, street corner societies, or school groups almost invariably show that boys and men tell exaggerated stories of their success sexually with females, their success in dominating females, and their ability to control other people to get what they want. The advice that they are likely to give to a young man in conflict over what he sees as a challenge to his patriarchal rights in many groups will encourage and legitimate the physical, psychological, and sexual abuse of women. They might tell the young man to slap or hit a female who talks back to them. They might insist that if she refuses sex that he should force the issue, to maintain his rights. In other words, the social

DATING RELATIONSHIP → STRESS → MALE PEER SUPPORT → WOMAN ABUSE

Figure 3.1 DeKeseredy's original male peer support model

support that friends offer to one of their members in psychological stress can be to abuse her physically or sexually.

Such male peer support can also motivate men to mistreat women regardless of stress. As just suggested, most of the male peer support studies done before and after DeKeseredy constructed the model in figure 3.1 do not discuss stress as a prerequisite for men interacting with male peers or receiving support for abusive behaviors. Groups such as fraternities, sports teams, regular bar patrons, colleagues at work, club members, or other male groups take on the task of teaching members that engaging in woman abuse is acceptable or preferred behavior under certain conditions.

DeKeseredy maintained that one of the things that male peer groups will do is teach or support or suggest to members that they should not put up with women's challenges to their authority and that they should strike back. Outside the realm of dating to exemplify this point is British anthropologist Ann Whitehead's (1976) ethnographic data showing that husbands' pub peers influenced them to beat their wives to maintain dominance and control by furnishing informational and esteem support. Informational support is "help defining, understanding, and coping with problematic events. It has also been called advice, appraisal support, and cognitive guidance" (Cohen and Wills, 1985, p. 313). Cohen and Wills defined esteem support as "information that a person is esteemed and accepted" (p. 313).

In the context of teasing each other about their marriages, Whitehead found, male pub patrons proclaimed that a married man is supposed to do what he wants after marriage. He is required to row with his wife, hit her, or "lay down the law." Further, quarrels in which he "has the upper hand" bring him esteem. However, if his wife argues with him, locks him out of the house, or refuses to cook for him, he loses esteem. Whitehead also observed a man receive verbal encouragement from male pub patrons while he pinned a woman down and gave her a "love-bite" on her neck against her will. Whitehead argues that this behavior is an example of "joking abuse" used by men to control the behavior of women.

Like Bowker (1983), DeKeseredy asserted that male peer support also enables men to resist attempting to end their abusive behavior. There is a literature showing that after beating female intimates, some men display contriteness and offer pleas for forgiveness (e.g., Bancroft, 2002; DeKeseredy, 1988b; Walker, 1977–78, 1979, 1983). However, peers alleviate such post-abuse-related stress by assuring the man that what he did was correct and right. They can encourage the post-abuse men to continue asserting their authority through harmful means.

In sum, the theoretical work of Ellis and DeKeseredy, and statistics gleaned from tests of their theories, challenge traditional social support theory, which emphasizes only the beneficial features of social support (Heller and Swindle, 1983). Data gathered by us over the past twenty-five years confirm Vaux's (1985) argument that "social support may facilitate the resolution of problems or the management of distress, but there are no guarantees that such a resolution is free of cost" (p. 102). Even so, DeKeseredy's original model has some pitfalls and they were addressed five years after he published it with the assistance of Martin Schwartz.

A Chance Meeting at the 1987 American Society of Criminology Conference[6]

The 1987 American Society of Criminology (ASC) conference in Montreal was an exciting event for several reasons. Both of us self-identified as critical criminologists, which was a newer discourse that succeeded conflict theory, and emphasized not only social and economic inequality in society, and its effect on crime, but also gender and race differences in victimization and offending. New directions in critical criminology were emerging in those days, with such subfields as postmodernism, feminism, left realism, and the beginnings of restorative justice models (Schwartz, 1989). A large and vibrant cohort of young scholars were making important historical advances at this international gathering by offering new ways of thinking critically about crime, law, and social control.[7] Two in particular—feminism and left realism—were garnering much attention. They were major influences on us then, and they continue to influence our empirical, theoretical, and policy work on male peer support.[8] Critical criminologists like us view hierarchical social stratification and inequality along class, racial/ethnic, and gender lines as the major sources of crime. Another common feature that critical criminologists share is the rejection of policies and practices such as "zero tolerance" policing (e.g., criminalizing begging on the streets), "three strikes, you're out" sentencing, private prisons, coercive counseling therapy, and other punitive approaches that view crime as a manifestation of individual deviancy. Rather, critical criminologists regard major structural and cultural changes within society as essential to reducing crime and facilitating social justice (DeKeseredy and Dragiewicz, 2012a; J. Young, 1988). However, because major structural transitions are not coming soon in this current neoliberal political economic era, critical criminologists also advance progressive short-term reforms that "chip away" at patriarchal capitalism (Messerschmidt, 1986), some of which are described in chapter 7.

Martin Schwartz was, and still is, an active critical criminologist and he played a key role in the creation of the ASC's Division on Critical Criminology (DCC).[9] Schwartz was also appointed as the DCC's first Vice Chair in 1990. DeKeseredy accidentally met him at the 1987 ASC conference book exhibit. At one of the displays, Schwartz overheard DeKeseredy criticizing a colleague's textbook for "only paying lip service" to critical criminological theories such as those developed by feminist scholars. Schwartz turned to DeKeseredy and said, "Why don't you write the author?" Then he looked at DeKeseredy's name tag and enthusiastically said, "I need to talk to you!" DeKeseredy had applied for a job in Ohio University's sociology and anthropology department, and Schwartz read his application file, which included a paper on DeKeseredy's original male peer support model. They went for coffee and Schwartz told DeKeseredy that his chances of getting the job were slim because Ohio University, which only had male criminologists at that point, was interested in diversity in that central part of the department, especially considering the large number of female students in the program. DeKeseredy fully supported that position but still wanted to exchange ideas with Schwartz because he was, at that time, one of the few men in criminology deeply committed to feminist principles of scholarship and praxis. We went on to establish a strong friendship and working relationship.

Since publishing our first coauthored piece (Schwartz and DeKeseredy, 1988), we revised the original DeKeseredy male peer support model in ways described in the next section of this chapter. Moreover, we were the first North American scholars to publish feminist critiques of left realism, a new direction in critical criminology that, especially in the United Kingdom, sent "shock waves through radical criminology, opening up personal disputes and ideological cleavages that endure to this day" (Hayward, 2010, p. 264). Our other projects included studying woman abuse in Canadian public housing (DeKeseredy, Alvi, Schwartz, and Tomaszewski, 2003), jointly responding to the neoconservative backlash against feminist studies of woman abuse (DeKeseredy and Schwartz, 2003), examining separation and divorce sexual assault in rural communities (De-Keseredy and Schwartz, 2009), and collaborating on a Canadian national representative survey of woman abuse in university/college dating (DeKeseredy and Schwartz, 1998a; Schwartz and DeKeseredy, 1997).

We were, and still are, deeply moved by the activist and educational work done by members of the feminist men's movement, such as Rus Funk (1993, 2006), Jackson Katz (2006), and Tony Porter (2006a, 2006b). These and other feminist men (together with feminist women) inform the policy proposals we advance in chapter 7 and elsewhere (e.g., DeKeseredy, Schwartz, and Alvi, 2000). As stated previously, these policies are also guided by our theoretical models, especially the modified male peer support model that has roots in our Montreal meeting.

The Modified Male Peer Support Model[10]

The original impetus to change the male peer support model came from our own criticism that the earlier DeKeseredy (1988a) model seemed too focused on individual factors. The early rendition tried to explain woman abuse while using only variables related to stress and male peer support. Given the empirical support that DeKeseredy (1988b) found for his theory (see chapter 5), there is no question that he was right in claiming that these variables are related. However, what was missing from figure 3.1 was the recognition that there are quite a number of other related factors that can influence whether a man abuses a woman. Reality, we felt, was much more complex than simply putting a man living in social stress in with friends who supported patriarchal practices and discourses. Certainly, since both of us are sociologists, we were attracted to models that bring into focus a broad variety of social forces that at various times and places have an effect on human behavior. Certainly, we made no attempt or claim to explain every single factor that could be related to male peer support and the abuse of women. However, we did feel that there were four particularly important factors that needed to be added to the model: the ideologies of familial and courtship patriarchy; alcohol consumption, membership in social groups (e.g., fraternities and sports teams), and the absence of deterrence. Since an extended explanation of these factors is offered in earlier publications (DeKeseredy and Schwartz, 1993; Schwartz and DeKeseredy, 1997), they will be more briefly discussed here.

Again, the DeKeseredy model is focused on individual behavior, but we felt that actions such as beatings, psychological abuse, sexual assaults, and the like do not operate in a vacuum. A substantial number of male actions, values, and beliefs, we felt, are micro-social expressions of broader patriarchal forces. Of course, we fully understood that the definition of patriarchy is much debated within sociology and feminism; it is still widely used because, as noted by Gwen Hunnicutt (2009), "it keeps the gaze directed toward social contexts rather than toward individual men who are motivated to dominate" (p. 554). Still, there is a need to develop a working or usable definition of patriarchy that is more than just this device to keep us pointed in the right direction. Here, we draw from Dobash and Dobash (1979), who note that patriarchy is made up of two elements. Structurally, the patriarchy is a hierarchical organization of social institutions and social relationships that allows men to maintain positions of power, privilege, and leadership in society. As an ideology, the patriarchy rationalizes itself. That means that it provides a means of creating acceptance of subordination not only by those who benefit from such actions, but even by those who are placed in such subordinate positions by society.

Most definitions of patriarchy are fairly simple, like the one that we use, but in reality there are different types of male power systems. *Social patriarchy* is often used to refer to male domination at the societal level, but there is a subsystem, often called *familial patriarchy*, that refers to male control in domestic or intimate settings (Barrett, 1985; Eisenstein, 1980; Ursel, 1986). However, even if patriarchy is divided into these two variants, neither can be understood without reference to each other (Smith, 1990). As Hunnicutt (2009) puts it, "Micro- and macro-patriarchal systems exist symbiotically. Interpersonal dynamics are nested within the macro-level gender order" (pp. 557–58).

Our original concern was to attempt to explain violence between friends or dating partners on college campuses. A problem was that even if one accepts the legitimacy of the dichotomy between social patriarchy and familial patriarchy, there is some room for debate on whether it is actually familial patriarchy we are concerned with on college campuses. Dating has certainly changed today, and we have recently seen a significant shift from dating to hanging out and "hooking up"[11] on college campuses. Certainly the terms "dating" and "dates" are used much less frequently than they were in 1993 (Bogel, 2008) when we crafted our modified model as seen in figure 3.2. At that time, some scholars argued that students who engaged in dating relationships were mirroring patriarchal marriages in which the male partner has superior power and privilege (Dilorio, 1989; Lamanna and Reidman, 1985; Laner and Thompson, 1982; Mercer, 1988). Lloyd (1991), however, argued that courtship is not merely a mirror, but a patriarchal system in and of itself, where the rules and customs of male

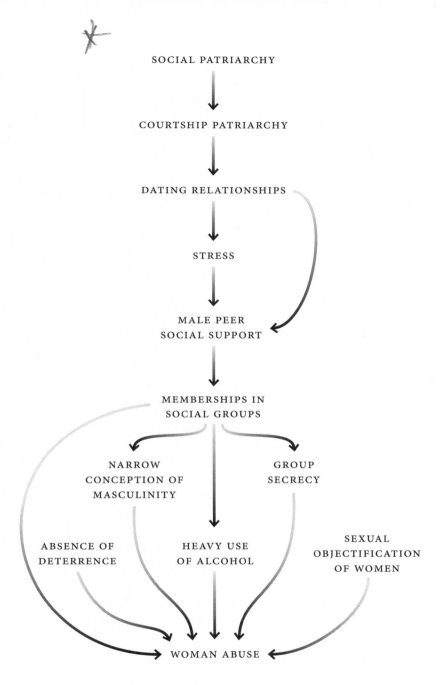

Figure 3.2 Modified male peer support model

dominance play out differently. For example, the ideal of romanticism may be more important in courtship than in marriage. In either case, researchers argue that the more couples agree on the right of control by men, and the greater the dependence of women on men, the greater the potential for violence and exploitation. Further, most of the research on pro-abuse male peer groups has found a social support discourse that reflects the ideology of courtship or familial rather than social patriarchy.

Part of Smith's (1990) definition of familial patriarchy informs the one offered here: a discourse that supports the abuse of intimate partners who violate the ideals of courtship patriarchy. Relevant themes of this ideology are an insistence upon women's obedience, respect, loyalty, dependency, sexual access, and sexual fidelity. That some women do not conform to these "norms" is stressful for many men. Such women are also considered appropriate targets for abuse by some of the male friends of these men (Brennan, 2012a), and as described in box 3.1, there is growing evidence that a large portion of North American males still approve of assaults on women if they challenge their authority. Peers tell their friends to sexually, physically, and psychologically mistreat dating partners who violate the above norms and who refuse to provide them with sexual gratification (DeKeseredy, 1988a). Several studies have described social networks that approve of sexual assaults on certain dating partners as "teasers," "economic exploiters," "bar pickups," and "loose women" who do not engage in sexual intercourse (DeKeseredy and Schwartz, 1998a; Kanin, 1985). These male homosocial cohorts often provide sexually aggressive members with a "vocabulary of adjustment" so that their violent actions do not alter their conceptions of themselves as normal, respectable men (Kanin, 1967b). The same can be said about many agents of social control, such as the Toronto police officer who inspired the "Slut Walk" discussed in box 3.2.

Thus, a system of patriarchy where society assumes the dominance of men and teaches this lesson well, was added to the model. And, for reasons described in boxes 3.1 and 3.2, as well as throughout other parts of this book, this powerful determinant is still very much alive today. In the words of Maier and Bergen (2012), the foundation of male peer support for violence against women "rests on the normalization and acceptance of gender inequality and the recognition that 'real' men are superior to women and naturally have authority over them" (p. 332).

Another variable added to figure 3.2—*alcohol consumption*—also continues to be strongly related to various types of woman abuse in intimate relationships. Although the United States and Canada are not among the world's leaders in

3.1 Is Hitting Women Still Considered OK?

A recent survey of over a thousand men in the Canadian Province of Alberta showed that while many men seem to be increasingly aware of domestic violence issues, serious problems remain. For example, roughly half of the men surveyed agreed that women who wear provocative clothing are putting themselves at risk for rape.

While much can be read into such attitudes, less ambiguous were responses to the survey question asking participants whether they agreed with the statement that it is never acceptable to physically assault a woman, even if she did something to incite anger. About one in ten disagreed, meaning that they felt it was acceptable to strike a woman if she made a man angry. A slightly larger proportion (13 percent) felt that violence is less serious if it is the result of people becoming so angry that they lose control. And it was not only violence against women that was approved, as 21 percent of respondents said it was acceptable behavior to slap a child in the face (Stephanson, 2013), a finding that Alberta Premier Alison Redford said "made me sick to my stomach" (Brennan, 2012b).

The survey poll was conducted by Leger Marketing, a national polling firm, under contract to the Alberta Council of Women's Shelters. It covered a variety of issues, including attitudes toward sexual assault, where it found that most men in the survey believed that women often say no to sexual activity when they really mean yes, and 40 percent disagreed with a statement that "women rarely make false claims of being raped" (ACWS, 2012). "This is the first study of its kind that has been done in Alberta and I believe in the rest of the country," said Ian Large, vice-president for the Alberta branch of Leger Marketing. The ACWS said it would use the results to inform programming, so that messages could be targeted appropriately (Brennan, 2012b).

alcohol consumption per capita, drinking rates have continued to climb and now stand at a twenty-five-year high (Gallup, 2010). However, the relationship is somewhat complex, because there is no direct causal relationship between alcohol consumption and woman abuse. Removing alcohol completely doesn't end abuse; most abusive men continue to harm current and former female in-

3.2 Slutwalks Expand around Globe

Toronto Police Constable Michael Sanguinetti unwittingly set off a worldwide social movement when he told a York University student meeting on safety that, although he had been warned against saying so, "women should avoid dressing like sluts in order not to be victimized."

Sanguinetti's may have been an off-hand remark, but the outrage it engendered, and the belief that such victim-blaming attitudes are endemic within the criminal justice system, led some students at the university to begin a process of attempting to reclaim the word "slut," redirecting it away from the notion that women who are sexually active are automatically less entitled to safety and freedom from assault.

The students began to organize a Toronto Slutwalk, with the hopes that about fifty people would march on police headquarters to demand an end to slut-shaming and sexual profiling (Flack 2011). Within a month, it became obvious that thousands of women and many men planned to take part in the April march. The provocative nature of the demonstration's name and the obvious, pent-up anger and frustration that it released, that the emphasis in sexual assault too often is on the victim's behavior rather than on the offender's behavior, made for an instant worldwide phenomenon. A flood of articles and media mentions led to quickly expanding lists of sponsors, allies, and marchers. People in other cities became interested, not only in Canada, but throughout the United States. From Nevada to Florida, from Texas to Boston to the District of Columbia, local slutwalks were successfully staged and popularly supported. The movement then spread to the United Kingdom, New Zealand, Argentina, the Netherlands, Sweden, and Australia (Crawford 2011).

timates after they reach sobriety (DeKeseredy, 2011a; Gelles and Cavanaugh, 2005). Still, while not causal, alcohol is related to woman abuse in many ways.

The heavy and frequent use of alcohol is a common feature of many men's social groups (Bogle, 2008), such as fraternities. Particularly for the young, alcohol is consumed socially, with groups of peers actively working with each other to help binge drinkers to explain away, rationalize, and excuse embarrassing, unsightly, and even violent behavior (Vander Ven, 2011) such as aggressive and violent behavior toward women. For many years alcohol has been commonly used as a tool to render women unable to resist sexual aggression (Flack et al., 2007; Messman-Moore, Coates, Gaffey, and Johnson, 2008). Back in the 1920s the writer Dorothy Parker was considered the exemplar of New York wit when she penned the ditty "Candy is dandy, but liquor is quicker," but many generations of women have found alcohol used as a weapon against them to accomplish sexual acts that they would not submit to when sober. Although there may not be a direct link between drinking and sexual aggression (in other words, drinking does not automatically cause such aggression), there certainly is an indirect link. Through our many years of study we have discovered over and again that men who admit (anonymously) to being sexual aggressors are also among the heavier drinkers in the sample (Schwartz and Nogrady, 1996; Schwartz et al., 2001). Years ago, we cited Ward, Chapman, Cohen, White, and Williams (1991) on the relationship, and it still describes very well the state of the scientific literature in the field:

> While this may not be sufficient evidence of a causal connection between alcohol use and sexual aggression, it shows, at a minimum, that alcohol is an important part of the student lifestyle and that unwanted sexual experiences are a product of that lifestyle. (p. 68)

Further, as noted earlier, alcohol is also used in contexts that support patriarchal conversations about women's sexuality and how to control it. Recall what we outlined earlier about what Ann Whitehead heard and observed in a British pub. We argued, and continue to do so today, that many of these same messages are heard by college men who are in fraternities, live in all-male dormitories, have regular friends in the neighborhood bar, play sports, or have other homosocial networks. In fact, cross-cultural data reveal that pro-abuse peer relations often sleep together in residences apart from women (Levinson, 1989). Aggressive male sports teams are also fertile breeding grounds for the abuse of women, especially sexual aggression (Benedict, 1998; Burstyn, 2000; Forbes, Adams-Curtis, Pakalka, and White, 2006). They are regularly exposed to messages from teammates suggesting that a real man is not under the control of a woman; a real man has sex on demand and does not accept attacks on his masculine authority. The scandal at Penn State University is mostly known for the actions of former coach Jerry Sandusky, but an important part of the

3.3 Hockey Players and Sexual Entitlement

The story may have seemed familiar. Police arrested two members of a university's elite sports team on charges of sexual assault. The county prosecutor, of course, dismissed the charges against one player and accepted a guilty plea to a drastically reduced charge for the other. In this case, however, the president of Boston University, Robert A. Brown, took the uncommon approach of convening a broad-based and powerful task force to examine the hockey team, an important sport at BU, and the university's attitudes toward and procedures for dealing with rape and sexual assault. Obviously, many believed that the events that led to the arrests were not isolated but were part of a regular pattern.

In fact, the task force found that the team operated in a culture of sexual entitlement, which the task force defined, in a delicately worded passage, as "frequent sexual encounters with women absent an emotional involvement." The task force also said that not only hockey players but students generally were in need of sexual assault prevention training to protect the community (Jahnke, 2012).

Less circumspect findings located in the subcommittee reports that were not made public, but which were obtained by *The Boston Globe*, outlined extensive group sex, drinking and sex parties in the locker room, and the conclusion that at least some of the team members had "the perception that they need not seek consent for sexual contact" (Carmichael 2012).

local conversation was the discussion of a sports culture that protected student athletes from the regular student judiciary process and gave some of them support for the notion that if they were good enough at football, they were excused from any actions of misbehavior off the field. Such a culture is not at all rare among both large and small universities, with police, local prosecutors, and school officials all taking part in conspiracies to cover up "misbehavior," which all too often involved either sexually or physically abusing women (see, e.g., Benedict, 1998). However, this pro-abuse culture is now, as described in box 3.3, slowly being recognized by a growing number of university administrators.

An Absence of Deterrence

The *absence of deterrence*, an important element in the modified male peer support model, remains a major problem on college campuses. Most often studies center on the presence of deterrence. Thus, one might ask if blue lights, locked front doors, curfews, and police patrols would reduce the amount of violence against women, particularly on a college campus. Here, however, we are centering on the *absence* of deterrence, asking the question of whether a lack of punishment or the absence of negative consequences is partially responsible for the amount of the violence against women today. How is it possible that as many as one-quarter or more of all college women report being victimized by sexual aggression during their time on campus? It can't all be because men hear messages approving of such behavior, since there are also many messages on every college campus disapproving of sexual aggression.

Most people in North America, after years of our law enforcement systems, believe in deterrence, and the effect of formal social control such as police and corrections systems. If asked why they did *not* commit a burglary in recent weeks, virtually everyone will report that they didn't want to go to prison. However, that really is only true for a smaller group of people. Most North Americans don't commit burglary because they think that it is wrong. They learned values from their parents, or believe in what their religion teaches them, or often find that even if they are not churchgoers that they retain many of the values and beliefs inculcated into them as children. Others are deterred by informal social control. If being caught in a burglary will bring you social shame, cause you to lose your job, embarrass you before your family, lose you friends, get you in trouble with your sorority, or anything similar, then you are being deterred by informal social control. Still others make a cold calculation. For example, sometimes college students who are already in debt for twenty or more years because of college tuition loans calculate that getting a criminal record can destroy all of their expensive plans for a good life, especially if they are expelled from school, dropped from ROTC, unable to get a good job later, or rejected by many potential marital partners.

The relevance here is that many men find no deterrence at all for sexual aggression. Their friends either overlook or actively support their behavior. No one they know or even hear about has ever been arrested for sexual aggression against a date or a friend. It has been many years, if ever, since their school expelled a student for rape. If they do get arrested, their team's coaches work with police and prosecutors to get the charges dropped, and pressure the school's judicial system to let the student go without major punishment. Of course, the biggest problem on college campuses is that few such crimes are reported to the police. In our own work over the years, we have surveyed or interviewed many hundreds of sexually assaulted college women, very few of whom ever reported the crime to officials. Many were pressured not to report by other students such as members of their sorority, others were convinced that they would be publicly embarrassed if they reported, and a tremendous number believed what they had been told, that they were to blame for the attack because they had been drinking, they were in a man's dorm room, they had been taking drugs, or engaging in some other behavior that society uses to tell women that they are responsible for men's bad behavior. Unsurprisingly, Schwartz and Leggett (1999) found that 25 percent of women in their sample who had been raped because they were too intoxicated by alcohol or drugs to fight back effectively assigned themselves 100 percent of the blame for what happened. However, they also found about one-quarter of the women who were raped by force or threat of force took 100 percent of the blame for the rape (and many more accepted partial blame).

One of the reasons why women accept this blame is that they hear messages blaming them from friends, relatives, peers and university administrators. In any forced sex situation it continues to be difficult to convince at least some people throughout the community that it is wrong to rape women. In any university there are students, parents, teachers, and administrators who all stand ready to claim that the woman was drunk and therefore shares responsibility. Then there are those, such as the university lawyer discussed in chapter 2, who minimize the extent of sexual assault on their campuses and who refer to this crime as "regretted sex." Another common way to avoid facing the problem comes from many high-level college administrators, who claim that most threats to students come from outside campus communities (Millar, 2009).

Interestingly, there is something about the intersection of sex and female victims that breeds these kinds of responses. Few would suggest that a woman who passes out from drinking too much in a bar bears the responsibility for having her purse stolen. Not many would argue against prosecuting the thief after he was caught driving her car and using her credit cards. Yet if the man instead removed her clothes and raped her, there would be a never-ending line of apologists for him claiming that she was to blame for being drunk. For example, in the college town of Athens, Ohio, a neighbor of one of the authors here came home from an evening in the bars and telephoned for a pizza delivery. By the time it arrived, an hour later, she had fallen into a deep sleep.

The delivery man opened the door to yell inside that he had arrived. When he saw the unconscious woman, he later said, he felt that he had come across a "freebie," partially disrobed her and proceeded to engage in sexual intercourse. When he was arrested under a 75-year-old statute that forbids intercourse with a woman who was not conscious enough to give meaningful consent, the town was split. For weeks the local newspapers printed an array of letters with about half defending the man by attacking the woman for being drunk in her own house behind a closed door.

To this day, despite numerous studies of campus sexual assault, as well as scores of education and awareness programs, when the topic is sexual assault, people often find the "facts" confusing, and talk about the "muddy waters" of such situations. "Isn't it true that a woman is asking for sexual intercourse if she agrees to allow a man to buy her dinner or if she dresses provocatively?" Many people would agree with this statement. Professors serving on judicial boards have reported to us that they voted to acquit a man accused of rape for such reasons as the woman posted on her Facebook account a week later a picture of herself having a good time. Both of us have given many community presentations, and have been asked questions such as: "Don't you think the problem is due to how girls dress today?" One of the more noted examples of this occurred in Madison, Wisconsin, where Dane County Judge Archie Simonson justified placing on home detention only a fifteen-year-old boy convicted of taking part in a gang rape of a high school girl in the stairwell of the school. With the way that girls dressed today, the judge said, it would be a normal reaction for a red-blooded male to commit rape (Woliver, 1993). His attempt to blame the girl for her own rape, however, backfired when the story was widely publicized and Judge Simonson became the first judge ever recalled in Wisconsin. If he had just kept his mouth shut, he could have just placed the rapists on probation, as is still done across the country every day. In a noted recent Texas case, for example, where twenty men and boys were arrested for the gang rape of an eleven-year-old girl, the adult courts were sentencing men to as much as ninety-nine years, while the juvenile court was putting other rapists on probation (Stebner and Associated Press, 2012).

Thus, even when the facts seem completely clear (e.g., the Wisconsin boy was convicted of rape), there are many people who find such "facts" ambiguous and muddy. The result is that particularly on high school and college school grounds, many males seem to have an immunity from punishment; there will be no negative consequences on many campuses even in fairly serious cases of gang rape (DeKeseredy and Flack, 2007). As the lead detective at a major state university campus explained in an interview to Martin Schwartz, "All of the claims of rape on this campus come from girls who are trying to get out of taking exams." What message do you think that rapist men receive on that campus as a result of their actions?

In the past few years, there has been extensive discussion and condemnation of the Pennsylvania State University administration over covering up the crimes of a former coach. Despicable as their acts were, it is hard to believe that this cover-up could not have happened on many campuses throughout North America. Hiding the number of rapes on campus is a game played across the country. As one example, during all of the years that Schwartz taught at Ohio University and was developing a reputation for a series of articles based on survey research into rape victimization, these publications were never mentioned in university publications or press releases, although even very minor conference papers were usually mentioned. The news bureau editor explained (on his last day at work before going to a new job) to Schwartz that it was university policy to refuse to mention any of his works for fear that parents would find out that there were sexual assaults on that campus and remove their daughters.

All of these influences come together to provide a climate that protects men and convinces many women to accept blame much of the time when they are victimized. Schwartz and Leggett (1999) conclude that in a society that accepts male sexual aggression on women as normative:

> If too many men act like they can force sexual intercourse on a woman any time they wish on college campuses and get away with it, it is because it is too often true. In fact, they *can* often act with impunity. . . . When approximately five percent of victimized women are reporting even forcible rape, there is very little reason for a rapist to fear any consequences of his action. (pp. 266–67)

Other Factors in the Model

Box 3.3 deals with portions of a problematic culture that sometimes surrounds sports teams. There are other negative features of the climate often associated with combative male sports, and certainly many other places in society also, that are related to violence against women. One in particular is a *narrow conception of masculinity*, or what Bruce Kidd (1990) refers to as the "gross sexism and homophobia of that inner sanctum of patriarchy, the locker room" (p. 42). Of course, such conceptions are found in fraternities, men's clubs, bars and pubs, and many other groupings of men besides sports teams, where masculinity is socially constructed out of other ideologies: race, class, gender, and of course, sports identities. Certainly, many people have found such a culture in inner-city male gangs, and connected that behavior to violence against females (Ulloa, Dyson, and Wynes, 2012; Miller, 2008). Within many fraternities, the approved masculinity that is taught is indeed narrow. Men are supposed to be clean cut, athletic, have money, have a high tolerance for alcohol, and be successful with a variety of women (Schwartz and DeKeseredy, 1997). They learn to distance themselves as far as possible from anything that sounds effeminate, including studying in majors or even taking coursework in fields such as social work, education, nursing, or art. They learn that real men have sex on demand from a variety of women. Of course, none of them do, but in what social psychologists often call "pluralistic ignorance" (Chia and Lee, 2008), members can become convinced from listening to stories and hearing bragging throughout the group that they are the only ones who are not successful at being exceptionally sexually active. In fact, most of the group may secretly feel the same way, as they are all acting in ignorance. The men who feel the most deprived and alienated in this manner tend to see women as the gatekeepers to their self-image, and they are prime candidates to be the ones who force women into sex. This might also explain why many feel that first- and second-year students are the most dangerous to women; they haven't been around long enough to learn the truth: that they are not sexually inactive relative to the group's reality but only to the bragging.

Another value and factor in the modified male peer support model, is one that is also endemic to fraternities and many locker rooms: *group secrecy* (Schwartz and DeKeseredy, 1997; Sanday, 1990), which keeps men from revealing the deviant behavior of their peers or teammates to outsiders. Groups like organized crime or street criminals or even the police are noted in popular culture for maintaining a protective silence in the face of an investigation into wrongdoing by authorities, but student affairs personnel on college campuses often have similar stories to tell about fraternities, dorm groups or sports teams. In at least one case, Penn State University, the NCAA found that there was a "culture of reverence" for football that went far beyond silence into actively covering up felony crimes (Wolff, 2012).

Such a wall of silence can indeed protect the team or organization from criminal investigations, but it also does an excellent job of telling the violent men in the group that their actions are not wrong, or at least are fully tolerated and supported. Silence is one of the more effective ways that all-male groups legitimate and perpetuate sexual assaults.

At the same time, the men in these groups learn to *sexually objectify women*. There are a number of ways to accomplish this, but most depend on the use of language that eventually informs and helps to form viewpoints. Edwin Schur (1984) explains that in such organizations men learn to see and visualize women through a lens in which the only important quality is their femaleness, rather than their accomplishments, position, intelligence, or status. Of course, this is done throughout a society where most female rock and country stars have to appear half naked, female athletes are rated by their looks as much as or more than by their talent, and even ratemyprofessors.com encourages students to rate their faculty teachers on their sexual attractiveness. However, in these homosocial male groups under consideration here the effort is taken to the extreme.

As we will discuss in chapter 6, another way that many of the men in fraternities and other social groups develop attitudes and maintain their sexual objectification of women is the viewing of pornographic media while "drinking with the boys" (DeKeseredy and Olsson, 2011). Theorists in the field argue that pornography can lead to desensitization about the seriousness of sexual assault (Dines, 2010; Jensen, 2007).

Moving Forward

In 2011 and 2012, the sports world's greatest scandal ever (Wolff, 2012) involved the covering up of sexual assault crimes (in this case child sexual assault) in the name of protecting Penn State University and to some degree its football team and management. Many people have misunderstood the NCAA punishment, which was not a punishment of Penn State because one of its coaches turned out to be a child molester. It was for the actions of the Penn State coaches and top administration members, who decided that it was more important to hide the crimes of a felon child assaulter than it was to report these crimes. The accusation against Penn State is that, knowing that Coach Sandusky was using the university after his retirement to commit these acts, the coaches and administration not only took no steps to report him to the proper authorities (as required by law) but, further, did not even remove his keys or forbid him to bring little boys into the locker and shower rooms. These are the accusations that formed the basis behind the punishment that was meted out. Salter (2013) refers to Penn State's actions as organized child sexual abuse.

However, how unusual was the action of Penn State's administration? How rare is it that an administration takes the position that protecting the school's reputation is more important than punishing rapists? How rare is it that a school would take active steps to hide the number of rapes on campus from authorities and the student body, although it is federally required that all rapes be reported to the Department of Education? Unfortunately, it is not unusual at all. Some people have been outraged that in the Penn State case no attempt was made by the school authorities to discover the identities of the children being molested and raped, and no attempt was made to provide social services to them as victims. However, those who attack Penn State might first wish to check out the level of services provided by their own favorite schools to the many victims of sexual assault who are raped annually in campus facilities, and the efforts that the school makes to find out who they are if they don't self-report immediately. What would be particularly shocking would be to find a college or university that *did* make such efforts.

We are excited about the number of new empirical and theoretical developments in the study of sexual assault. However, for women who are victimized by sexual assault on or near their institutions of higher learning, new developments have little to offer unless they inform effective policies, which, again, are in shorter supply at most campuses across this continent. Clearly it is time to move beyond what the California Coalition of Sexual Assault (CALCASA) labels "traditional responses to the problem," and to convince administrators to become more concerned with providing services to sexual assault victims than with protecting the school's reputation.

Although our modified male peer support model is better than the original, it also has some limitations. Perhaps the most important one is that although some of the individual elements have been repeatedly tested empirically, there has not yet been a test of the entire model. In fact, given its complexity, it may have more value as a heuristic or teaching model than as a predictive model. In other words, its greatest value may lie in summarizing the complex literature, rather than in isolating and predicting which specific men on college campuses are most likely to abuse women.

Our expanded model also does not account for the way in which social networks that favor and promote the abuse of women develop. Rather, it starts with the proposition that these groups already exist and discusses their role in women abuse. For example, one empirical question that remains is whether pro-abuse social groups shape and mold men to learn these new behaviors or whether they simply attract pro-abuse-oriented young men who need nothing more than a hockey jersey or a new sweatshirt with Greek letters sewn on. A central element of Peggy Reeves Sanday's (1990) theory is that fraternity rituals mold this behavior. She argues that the young man comes to college and then goes through fraternity initiation ceremonies that involve the "transformation of consciousness": "By yielding himself to the group in this way, the pledge gains a new self" (p. 135). Robin Warshaw (1988), on the other hand, as well as some large-scale survey data (e.g., DeKeseredy and Schwartz, 1998a), suggest that men with sexist ideologies seek out patriarchal all-male social groups so that they will receive support for their attitudes and behavior. Similarly, we do not know whether men who beat their wives or cohabiting partners and who have strong social support networks are truly influenced by these networks to adopt new attitudes toward their female partners or whether men who already hold such attitudes are attracted to other like men in order to gain support for their already existing views (DeKeseredy and Schwartz, 1998b).

Summary

We now know that different distinct types of male peer support influence North American males to victimize their partners. However, prior to 1988, few attempts were made to theorize how membership in all-male friendship networks, and the functions they provide, motivate men to physically, sexually, and psychologically harm female intimates. This chapter chronicles a sociological and personal journey, one that has resulted in twenty-five years of theoretical and empirical work on one of the most powerful determinants of woman abuse in a variety of intimate settings. Not only have the theories reviewed here informed much research on woman abuse, but they have also guided theories of other social problems. For example, using our modified male peer support model, Cortney Franklin (2005) explains how the police subculture operates to oppress women in policing. Further, she constructed a visual model very similar to ours.

More work on male peer support needs to be done and probably will be done. Certainly, the limitations of the theory presented in figure 3.2 have not been addressed and variations in male peer support across different ethnic/cultural groups have yet to be examined. Hopefully, a new generation of scholars will focus on these issues and apply male peer support theory to relevant substantive topics such as sexual violence and war, sexual harassment in the military, and bullying.[12] We contend that despite their pitfalls, the two models reviewed here could be the backbones of new male peer support models on a variety of topics that fall under the category of masculinities and crime, as they are for the perspectives reviewed in chapter 4.

4 | Contemporary Male Peer Support Theories

> Sexual assaults and sexually coercive behaviors in youths' neighborhoods were often an extension of the broader sexualized treatment young women experienced. This is largely why young women were so leery of groups of men. As with sexual harassment, young women's risks for sexual assault and coercion were varied. Among peers, alcohol and drugs were often used to lower a young woman's level of awareness or incapacitate her. Rapes involving physical force more frequently involved adult men, though they happened with peers as well.
> —*Jody Miller, Getting Played*

There is a famous scene in the movie *The Godfather, Part III*, where Al Pacino, in the role of Michael Corleone, leader of an organized crime network, says, "Just when I thought I was out . . . they pull me back in!" Similarly, in 1999, just when we thought we were going to pursue new empirical and theoretical directions and move out of the realm of studying college students, our colleague Alberto Godenzi pulled us back in.[1] He made us "an offer we couldn't refuse,"[2] so to speak, by inviting us to coauthor a theoretical piece that integrates Travis Hirschi's (1969) social bond theory with some of our own work on male peer support. The purpose of this chapter is to describe and evaluate this offering, as well as subsequent male peer support models that prioritize economic, rural, and intimate relationship status issues. There are many theories of woman abuse, but integrated perspectives are still rare. What all the theories reviewed in this chapter have in common is that they bring together several bodies of knowledge, including feminism, masculinities, and of course, male peer support.

A Gendered Social Bond/Male Peer Support Theory of University Woman Abuse[3]

Among the many theories of woman abuse, few attempt to engage the major theoretical contributions of criminologists who are themselves not directly writing on such abuse (Cardarelli, 1997). The gendered social bond/male peer support model presented here responded to Miller and Wellford's (1997) call for theory integration in explaining male-to-female victimization and follows a growing trend among criminologists to develop integrated theories (e.g., Agnew, 2011; Barak, 2009). Further, like the theoretical contributions made by Ellis (1989), Young (1999), and Branch, Sellers, and Cochran (2001), our model shows that consensus or middle-range theories that have been sharply attacked for ignoring gender may still have useful theoretical constructs if they are combined with critical insights.

Our starting point was that no woman abuse theory had attempted to examine one of the most popular theories in criminology and delinquency, and unsurprisingly so, since Travis Hirschi's (1969) social bond perspective is an inherently conservative account. It does not seem likely to enhance a feminist sociological understanding of woman abuse. As is typical of criminological theories of the past, social bond theory was developed in a social and historical context that ignored any notion of gendered power (Belknap, 2006). Hirschi explicitly ignored female experiences, excluding their self-report data from his statistical analysis, although he does report that this exclusion is "difficult to justify." In his book *Causes of Delinquency*, Hirschi states in a footnote that "in the analysis which follows, the 'non-Negro' becomes 'white,' and the girls disappear" (1969, p. 35). Following this, virtually all studies of social bond theory have used all-male samples.

The gendered social bond/male peer support theory we developed also deals with a problem with Hirschi's original formulation by placing more emphasis on group processes. As Sampson (2000) has pointed out, criminological theorizing has been held back by a static logic that focuses attention on only a few explanatory categories and the failure to integrate individual-level theories with explanations of social processes that involve the communal aspects of life. Relying on limited and static theories robs us of explanatory power and improved public policy, which are reason enough to proceed even if Hirschi himself had no interest in providing a theory that included motivation and a gendered analysis.

The need to understand gendered power and the emphasis on group processes are both essential parts of the criminological enterprise. In criminology's past, some study of groups and male peer support was a central feature of criminological thought, at least in the form of gangs, and certainly in a gender-blind manner for the most part. While there were some problems in using gangs as a surrogate for all peer-influence groups for delinquents, the invention of self-report surveys, and the example set by Hirschi moved the entire field out of group processes and into an analysis of individual behavior by the 1970s (Kreager, Rulison, and Moody, 2011).

Today, within mainstream criminology the study of peer influence on delinquent behavior continues to become at least more mathematically sophisticated. McGloin (2009) argues that "the deviant peer group consistently emerges as one of the most robust correlates of offending behavior across a host of methodological specifications" (p. 35), and is echoed more recently by Young, Barnes, Meldrum, and Weerman (2011), who argued that "peer delinquency is a national correlate of delinquent and criminal behavior" (p. 599). As an example of recent mainstream research on the subject, Haynie and Osgood (2005) found adolescent youth have a higher frequency of committing delinquent acts if they have highly delinquent friends and spend a great deal of time in unstructured socializing with these friends. Others have similarly found that delinquent peers affect the commission of delinquent acts (Weerman, 2011), even among those youth who deny that there is such an influence (McGloin and Stickle, 2011). Perhaps a bit more convincing are those who attempt to argue that the relationship is more than just exposure to the group. Rather, some measure of susceptibility or conditioning to peer influence greatly amplifies the group's effect on the individual (Miller, 2010). A few studies have made some attempt to study woman abuse as a consequence of gang socialization, although Ulloa, Dyson, and Wynes (2012) argue in a review of this literature that it is in its infancy and scattered. Still, they report that every sign is that there is such a relationship.

Overall, however, Miller and Brunson (2000) argue that the study of group processes is vital to understand the community's role in "shaping young men's normative beliefs about gender and the treatment of young women" (p. 421). This critique also applies to other theories, such as Cohen and Felson's (1979) routine activities theory—a traditional perspective to which Schwartz and Pitts (1995) added a gendered analysis to explain sexual assault on U.S. college campuses (see also Schwartz, DeKeseredy, Tait, and Alvi, 2001).

Miller and Burack (1993) argue that a gender-blind theory of crime hides as much as it makes clear, but Schwartz et al.'s (2001) work shows that a previously gender-blind crime theory can be improved and made useful when integrated with one or more strands of feminist thought. In our work on Hirschi's theory, we attempted to extend that insight to show that a richer understanding of the common crime of woman abuse results when Hirschi's social bond perspective is brought together with male peer support theories. Integrated theory has a variety of meanings (Barak, 2009), but our emphasis is on taking feminist and male peer support theories, which are strong in providing arguments on why offenders are motivated to harm women, and tying these arguments to the suggestions that Hirschi made about the criminal bond. Feminist theories are strongest where Hirschi is weakest, and the combination of the two has value in explaining male-to-female violence.

We turn much of Hirschi's argument upside down by arguing that bonds to conventional institutions can increase woman abuse in a variety of circumstances because gender inequality is an unacknowledged norm. The value of this approach is in developing a heuristic model. Our theory is less an attempt to improve Hirschi's social bond theory than to take out certain useful parts with explanatory value that can be combined with critical and feminist theoretical perspectives.

The next section discusses the valuable aspects of Hirschi's work and briefly reviews our theory, but there are some very different basic presumptions between our work and his. We do not start from a Hobbesian proposition that people are naturally inclined to commit crime, as Hirschi does, but rather that abusive behavior is learned from groups who teach that woman abuse is legitimate behavior.

Rethinking Hirschi's Conception of Conformity and Deviance

Informed by Hobbes (1651/1963), Hirschi presupposes that people are naturally deviant or criminal, and that there is no need to explain something that is natural. Rather, that which is unnatural—conformity—is what must be theorized. He contends that criminal or delinquent acts result when the bond to conventional society is weak or broken. People who have a strong social bond to conventional peers and social institutions (e.g., schools, nuclear family, religion, etc.) are more likely to obey the law because these bonds all promote mutual respect and pro-social behavior.

Hirschi's formulation has been criticized on the grounds that a young man's social bond might be to antisocial peers and institutions. What has not been discussed, however, is the problem that conventional institutions and peers might be the ones that are directly or indirectly supporting attitudes of gender inequality, which in turn support gendered violence. What if some behaviors criminologists define as deviant are actually acts of conformity to conventional norms—like gender inequality—that are naturalized by the prevailing ideology?

As one example of conformity that can lead to deviance, one might consider corporations. As Messerschmidt (1993) notes, it is not uncommon for an old-boy network to encourage and justify corporate crimes, such as price fixing and violations of occupational health and safety standards. Junior members, almost always men, are recruited who share the network's norms, attitudes, values, and behavioral standards. Attachment, commitment, involvement, and belief in these "legitimate" institutions set the stage for recidivist corporate criminality that harms workers, consumers, and the environment (Friedrichs, 2010).

Like corporations, colleges are conventional institutions that can, under certain conditions, legitimate race, ethnic, class, and gender inequality. Some university organizations may take an active role in legitimating these inequalities, which help to develop a social bond that fosters and justifies woman abuse in an atmosphere that is conforming rather than deviant. It is not an accident that so many university campuses have very low rates of other serious or violent crime, but at the same time have alarming rates of woman abuse, with more than 25 percent of college women reporting rape or attempted rape victimization in most surveys (DeKeseredy, 2011a; DeKeseredy and Flack, 2007). These figures do not even include beatings, harassment, and other gender violence. Further, differing studies have found, depending on the question, that between 25 percent and 60 percent of male college students reported some likelihood that they would rape a woman if they could get away with it (Briere and Malamuth, 1983; Russell, 1998). Thus, in this setting, rather than a rare event committed by a few deviant men, "the experience of violent intrusion—or the threat of such intrusion—is a common thread in the fabric of women's everyday lives" (Renzetti, 1995, p. 3).

Our social bond/male peer support perspective, like Hirschi's, is a theory of conformity. We argue that in subcultures of extensive victimization, it is men who do not engage in woman abuse who are the deviants and whose bond to the dominant patriarchal social order is weak or broken. Somewhat like Agnew's (2011) attempt to build a unified criminology, as we approached the new millennium, one of our key goals was, as Rock (1992, p. xi) suggests, to end "the criminological cold war and the facile ideological oppositions of the 1970s and 1980s." Our main objective, though, was to provide an integrated theory of conformity that attempts to help explain why men who belong to patriarchal peer groups engage in woman abuse and other sexist practices. This theory suggests that abuse is a byproduct of the men's attempt to maintain a social bond with a conventional or traditional social order marked by gender inequality (Mooney, 1996; Young, 1999).

This finding is important because the claim that campus woman abuse is relatively uncommon (e.g., Roiphe, 1993) has found a responsive chord both inside and outside the academic community (Dragiewicz and DeKeseredy, 2012a). This position is politically comfortable for some university officials, students, and faculty, as it avoids having to reexamine the nature of male-female relationships. Our theory represents an alternative position on sexual assault and physical abuse, suggesting that they are normal events on the college campus, which is not the same as saying they are morally valid. Rather, they occur frequently, and they are culturally normal in that they are generally supported by much of North American culture and society (Maier and Bergen, 2012).

Of course, Hirschi's view of a social control theory is that it tries to explain why a man who believes in a norm is willing to violate it. If, as we suggest, this man learns an alternative set of beliefs that legitimate the behavior, and nullify societal beliefs against this behavior, then, as Hirschi (1969) puts it, "there is, within the context of the theory, nothing to explain" (p. 23). We contend that woman abuse is socially learned in societies, small groups, or institutions that view woman abuse as a normal and legitimate way of interacting with women. The purpose of our work, however, was not to show that Hirschi's formulation was correct, but that the addition of a gendered sensitivity and the insights of male peer support theory could make Hirschi's offering useful in explaining the existence of woman abuse on college campuses.

The Economic Exclusion/Male Peer Support Model[4]

Until 2002, virtually all work on male peer support dealt with the influence of college men on other college men. However, it certainly exists in many other places. Just as one example, Jody Miller (2008) notes at the start of this chapter that pro-abuse male peer support is found in poor inner-city neighborhoods. We always suspected such male peer support existed off the college campus, but it was not until 1996 that we started moving toward examining brutal male peer group dynamics that extend beyond academic settings and their immediate surroundings. The starting point was Walter DeKeseredy's discovery of William Julius Wilson's (1996) seminal book *When Work Disappears: The World of the New Urban Poor.* While perusing the chapter titled "The Fading Inner-City Family," DeKeseredy found this passage, which prompted us to start thinking about developing yet another male peer support theory:

> Males especially feel pressure to be sexually active. They said that the members of their peer networks brag out their sexual encounters and that they feel obligated to reveal their own sexual exploits. Little consideration is given to the implications or consequences of sexual matters for the longer-term relationship. (p. 99)

In the winter of 1997, DeKeseredy was involved in a seminar at Carleton University in Ottawa, Canada, on new directions in criminology, which involved a critical reading of *When Work Disappears.* Here a skeptical PhD student questioned its relevance to the Canadian context. She asserted that Canada does not have pockets of urban poverty and related social problems (e.g., high rates of crime) similar to those in Chicago and other major metropolitan sections of the United States. Was she right or was she wrong? In an exhaustive search for evidence, a handful of studies were located that showed that Canada then had a higher rate of urban poverty than the United States.[5] We also followed up this literature review by conducting the first Canadian study of the relationship between poverty, joblessness, and crime in Canadian public housing. The woman abuse data generated by this collaborative project helped spawn our economic exclusion/male peer support model later developed at Ohio University (DeKeseredy and Schwartz, 2002).

In the first volume of the international journal *Violence against Women,* editor Claire Renzetti (1995) stated that, "The problem of violence against women manifests itself in a terrifying array of forms throughout the world" (p. 6). Quantitative and qualitative data uncovered by two colleagues and us show that Canadian public housing complexes are no exception, and was published in *Under Siege: Poverty and Crime in a Public Housing Community* (DeKeseredy, Alvi, Schwartz, and Tomaszewski, 2003). On top of "living in conditions that . . . are unimaginable" (Renzetti and Maier, 2002, p. 50), struggling to feed themselves and/or their family, and coping with a host of other poverty-related problems (e.g., depression), many women in our sample endured a substantial amount of intimate violence, as well as gender, racial, and homophobic harassment in public places. For example, about one-fifth (19.3 percent) of the women who completed our survey stated that they had experienced one or more types of intimate violence in the past year (DeKeseredy, Alvi, Schwartz, and Perry, 1999). This incidence rate is higher than those elicited by the majority of North American representative samples surveys that used a similar form of the version of Straus, Hamby, Boney-McCoy, and Sugarman's (1996) Conflict Tactics Scales (CTS-2) that we employed, although it is similar to the 16.7 percent one-year rate found in Renzetti and Maier's (2002) study of thirty-six female residents of public or Section 8 housing in Camden, New Jersey.

Why do female public housing residents experience more violence than women in the general population? Prior to the development of the theory presented in figure 4.1, there were no social scientific attempts to answer this question. Perhaps this neglect was rooted in feminist challenges of the myth that only poor women are targets of abuse (Schwartz, 1988a), or perhaps from fear that research on class "will be misused by bigots" (Ptacek, 1999, p. 33). Others, at that time, did not believe that female public housing residents are victimized. For example, a social worker at a public meeting explained: "There isn't as much domestic violence in public housing because the women living in public housing projects actually live alone with their children and men aren't allowed to be there" (cited in Raphael, 2001a, p. 699). There are other explanations for the marginalization of both poverty issues and public housing residents in the literature on woman abuse; but they are described in detail elsewhere (see Ptacek, 1999). Fortunately, today there is a critical mass of feminist scholars doing pioneering work on the relationship between class, race, and woman abuse.[6] Certainly, this observation made close to thirty years ago is no longer relevant today:

> [F]eminists have dealt inadequately with the question of whether some women are *more* vulnerable than others. Eager to repudiate class and race-biased analyses of abuse, we have promoted universal risk arguments, criticizing methodologies that define some women as more vulnerable than others. But this refutation of classism and racism obscures our ability to wrestle with this question of vulnerability and therefore eligibility criteria. (Fine, 1985, p. 397, emphasis in original)

We do not claim that the physical conditions in which these women live constitute the primary cause. Instead, we offer a sociological theory that is heavily informed by Sernau's (2001) web of exclusion model, Wilson's (1996) inner-city poverty research, our expanded male peer support model (see figure 3.2), and Jock Young's (1999) work on social exclusion. Although, the study of public housing woman abuse was in its infancy in the late 1990s and at the start of the new millennium, we could not agree more with Raphael (2001b) who claimed in her commentary on the state of knowledge that the empirical work done at that time "makes it clear that economic variables need to be better incorporated into the current theoretical mix than they have been heretofore" (p. 454).

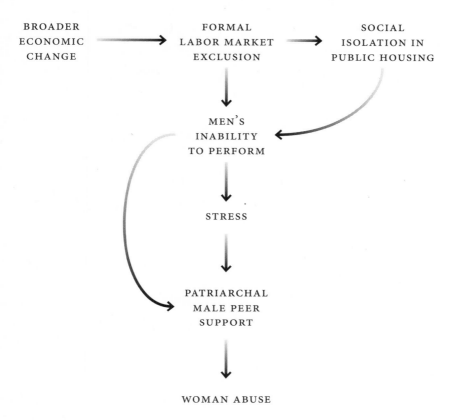

BROADER ECONOMIC CHANGE → FORMAL LABOR MARKET EXCLUSION → SOCIAL ISOLATION IN PUBLIC HOUSING

MEN'S INABILITY TO PERFORM

STRESS

PATRIARCHAL MALE PEER SUPPORT

WOMAN ABUSE

Figure 4.1 Economic exclusion/male peer support model

Figure 4.1 contends that recent major economic transformations (e.g., the shift from a manufacturing to a service-based economy) displace working-class men and women (and they continue to do so today) who often end up in urban public housing or other "clusters of poverty" (Sernau, 2001). Unable to support their families financially and live up to the culturally defined masculine role as breadwinner, socially and economically excluded men experience high levels of life-events stress because their "normal paths for personal power and prestige have been cut off" (Raphael, 2001a, p. 703). For example, because they cannot afford to look after both their partners and their children, some women evict male intimates or "invert patriarchy" in other ways by making decisions for the household and having the lease and car in their names (Edin, 2000). Such actions are perceived by patriarchal men as "dramatic assaults" on their "sense of masculine dignity" (Bourgois, 1995, p. 215).

Some men deal with stress caused by their partners' inversions of patriarchy by leaving them, while others use abuse as a means of sabotaging women's attempts to gain economic independence (Bourgois, 1995; Raphael, 2001b). Other men, however, turn to their male peers for advice and guidance on how to alleviate stress caused by female challenges to patriarchal authority. Large numbers of socially and economically excluded male peers in and around public housing view wife beating as legitimate means of repairing "damaged patriarchal masculinity" (Messerschmidt, 1993; Raphael, 2001a), and they often serve as role models because many of them beat their own intimate partners (DeKeseredy et al., 2003).

Figure 4.1, like most of our male peer support theories, is not a predictive model. Like figure 3.2, it is a heuristic perspective and does not attempt to isolate specific offenders. Even so, unlike most woman abuse theories developed prior to this one, ours attempts to explain how broader economic changes (e.g., deindustrialization) that have occurred in recent decades contribute to one of North America's most pressing social problems. Further, this model calls for moving the experiences of those whom William Julius Wilson (1987) refers to as the "truly disadvantaged" to the center of empirical and theoretical work on the ways in which all-male social networks perpetuate and legitimate woman abuse.

While the economic exclusion/male peer support model helped fill several gaps in the literature on woman abuse, like any social scientific perspective, it can be improved. For example, consistent with the other male peer support theories reviewed in this book, it does not specifically address whether members of patriarchal male peer support groups are intentionally recruited into these alliances or whether they gravitate to such groups as a way of selectively attempting to sustain or receive support for their earlier-acquired values and behavior. Further, it does not specify that men may interact with and be influenced by peers who live away from public housing. Another point to consider is that like every other male peer support model, racial/ethnic variations in male peer support dynamics remain to be examined. Nevertheless, again, there is evidence of pro-abuse male peer support in some U.S. inner-city communities of color and in some Puerto Rican neighborhoods (e.g., Bourgois, 1995; Miller, 2008; Wilson, 1996).

A Feminist/Male Peer Support Model of Separation/Divorce Sexual Assault[7]

To say that rural crime has ranked among the least studied social problems in criminology is an understatement. However, there is now an emergence of critical criminological research and theoretical work on drug use, woman abuse, racism, and other social problems that plague rural areas in Canada, the United Kingdom, the United States, Australia, and elsewhere.[8] Collectively, rural studies reviewed by DeKeseredy (2011b) and Donnermeyer (2012) show that rural communities are not less criminogenic than urban areas, a discovery that challenges conventional wisdom. In fact, rural rates may be higher than urban rates in particular types of rural places and for specific kinds of crime (Donnermeyer, Jobes, and Barclay, 2006). Note that Rennison, DeKeseredy and Dragiewicz (2012) found that rural separated/divorced women were markedly more likely to be sexually assaulted than urban women.

Gagne's (1992, 1996) feminist work on rural woman abuse played an important role in sparking contemporary critical interpretations of rural crime and social control. Shortly after came Websdale's (1998) *Rural Woman Battering and the Justice System: An Ethnography.* Nonetheless, the flames did not emerge until the latter part of the last decade, with the publication of a spate of scholarly books, journal articles, and chapters,[9] many of which continued along the feminist path broken by Gagne and Websdale. Our feminist/male peer support model of separation/divorce sexual assault presented in figure 4.2 was among that group of critical theoretical and empirical offerings that departed from "criminological and sociological urbanism" (Hogg and Carrington, 2006, p. 1). Not only were we interested in developing a richer theoretical understanding of gendered violence in the U.S. heartland, but we also wanted to help fill a gap in the literature on heterosexual intimate relationship status variations in sexual assault.

Since the 1970s, social scientists have greatly enhanced an empirical and theoretical understanding of various types of woman abuse in ongoing heterosexual relationships. However, although we know that breaking up with a violent man is one of the most dangerous events in a woman's life (see chapter 2), relatively little attention has been paid to the victimization of women who want to leave, are in the process of leaving, or who have left their marital/cohabiting partners. Furthermore, the limited work that has been done on this topic focused on lethal and nonlethal physical violence.[10] Woman abuse, of course, is multidimensional in nature and a growing number of studies show that women are also at high risk of being sexually assaulted during and after separation/divorce.[11] Still, until we conducted our study of such victimization in rural southeast Ohio (see DeKeseredy and Schwartz, 2009), the bulk of the research on this problem, regardless of whether it is qualitative or quantitative, was done in urban areas, such as Boston and San Francisco. Further, the extant literature was bereft of theory. Constructed with the help of our former Ohio University MA student McKenzie Rogness, figure 4.2 constitutes a collaborative attempt to address this problem.

Central to this theory is the role of patriarchal dominance and control, which is also a major theme in the marital sexual assault literature (Bergen, 2006; Gillum and Tarrezz Nash, 2011; Mahoney and Williams, 1998; McGregor, 2012). For example, McKenzie Rogness's (2002) integrated theory contends that macro-level factors like societal patriarchy (see chapter 3) work together with male micro-level forces such as patriarchal male peer support to influence men to rape their marital/cohabiting partners. Guided by her integrated theory and Jana Jasinski's (2001) call for "acknowledging the existence of multiple risk factors" when doing theoretical work on woman abuse in general, societal patriarchy, "male proprietariness" (Wilson and Daly, 1992), and patriarchal male peer support are the major components of this model. Here, we briefly discuss these and other variables in it.

Figure 4.2 situates separation/divorce sexual assault within the larger context of societal patriarchy. North America is well known for being a continent characterized by gross gender inequity. For example, in thirty-three U.S. states, under law, a man can be awarded conditional exemptions if he raped his wife (Caringella, 2009). Many more examples of patriarchal practices and discourses could easily be provided. Nevertheless, a constant such as societal patriarchy cannot explain a variable like changes in the frequency and severity of male sexual assaults on women who want to or who have left them (Ellis and DeKeseredy, 1997). In other words, if we live in a patriarchal society that promotes male proprietariness, why, then, do some men sexually assault during or after the exiting process, whereas most others do not? Certainly, data generated by a number of researchers using patriarchal ideology scales of one kind or another indicate that there are variations in male proprietariness (DeKeseredy et al., 2004; DeKeseredy and Schwartz, 1998a; Smith, 1990), which is "the tendency [of men] to think of women as sexual and reproductive 'property' they can own and exchange" (Wilson and Daly, 1992, p. 85). Proprietariness refers to "not just the emotional force of [the male's] own feelings of entitlement but to a more pervasive attitude [of ownership and control] toward social relationships [with intimate female partners]" (p. 85).

Most women in abusive relationships or in nonviolent relationships characterized by other means of patriarchal dominance and control are not weak people who are unable to take steps on their own behalf. In fact, most women resist or eventually will resist their male partners' proprietariness in a variety

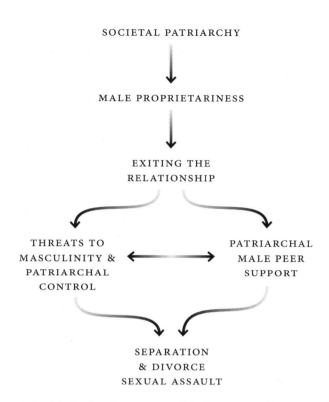

SOCIETAL PATRIARCHY

MALE PROPRIETARINESS

EXITING THE
RELATIONSHIP

THREATS TO
MASCULINITY &
PATRIARCHAL
CONTROL

PATRIARCHAL
MALE PEER
SUPPORT

SEPARATION
& DIVORCE
SEXUAL ASSAULT

Figure 4.2 A feminist/male peer support model of separation/divorce sexual assault

of ways, such as arguing, protesting, fighting back, or leaving the relationship
if they have been abused (DeKeseredy and Schwartz, 2009; Sev'er, 2002). For
example, one southeast Ohio woman told us: "With me being a strong-headed
woman, I did not like that and I refused to cook for him, I refused to do his
laundry. I told him to do it his damn self because I don't want to be his slave. He
didn't like that. . . . That would usually have me end up with a fist in my face or
my head bashed against a wall."

The precise number is unknown of how many women defy men's control
by exiting or trying to exit a relationship. This might involve emotional separation, obtaining a separate residence, and/or starting or completing a legal
separation/divorce. Emotional separation, a major predictor of a permanent
end to a relationship, is defined as a woman's denial or restriction of sexual relations and other intimate exchanges (Ellis and DeKeseredy, 1997). Emotionally
exiting a relationship can be just as dangerous as physically or legally exiting
one because it, too, increases the likelihood of male violence and sexual abuse

(Block and DeKeseredy, 2007; Kirkwood, 1993; DeKeseredy and Schwartz, 2009). For instance, of the one hundred sexually abused women who participated in McFarlane and Malecha's (2005) study sponsored by the U.S. National Institute of Justice, 22 percent reported an emotional separation before the first time they were sexually assaulted.

Regardless of how a woman does it, her attempt to exit or her successful departure from a sexist relationship challenges male proprietariness, and may result in violence, including homicide (Dobash, Dobash, Cavanagh, and Medina-Ariza, 2007; Websdale, 2010). As Lundy Bancroft (2002) puts it, "The abuser's dehumanizing view of his partner as a personal possession can grow even uglier as a relationship draws to a close" (p. 219). Still, exiting alone, like all single factors, cannot on its own account for sexual assault. For example, many abusive patriarchal men who abuse women during or after separation/divorce have male friends with similar beliefs and values, and these peers reinforce the notion that women's exiting is a threat to a man's masculinity (DeKeseredy et al., 2006). Furthermore, many members of patriarchal peer groups view beatings, rapes, and other forms of male-to-female victimization as legitimate and effective means of responding to "damaged" patriarchal masculinity and re-affirming a man's right to control his female partner (Messerschmidt, 1993; Ray, 2011). Not only do these men verbally and publicly state that sexual assault and other forms of abuse are legitimate means of maintaining patriarchal authority and domination, they also serve as role models because many of them physically, sexually, and psychologically harm their own intimate partners. Consider that 47 percent of the 43 rural survivors of separation/divorce assault we talked to said that they knew their partners' friends also physically or sexually abused women. In fact, Betty, one of our respondents, told us that all of her ex-partner's friends hit women or sexually assault them, and several interviewees told us that they directly observed their partner's friends abusing female intimates.[12]

In short, patriarchal male peer support contributes to the perception of damaged masculinity and motivates sexually abusive men to "lash out against the women . . . they can no longer control" (Bourgois, 1995, p. 214). Moreover, if a patriarchal man's peers see him as a failure with women because his partner wants to leave or has left him, he is likely to be ridiculed because he "can't control his woman" (DeKeseredy et al., 2004). Hence, like many college men who rape women, he is likely to sexually assault her to regain status among his peers. Similar to other men who rape female strangers, acquaintances or dates, the sexual assaults committed by men during or after the process of separation/divorce may have much more to do with their need to sustain their status among their peers than either a need to satisfy their sexual desires or a longing to regain a loving relationship (Godenzi et al., 2001).

Figure 4.2 guided our study of separation/divorce sexual assault in rural Ohio and it garnered some empirical support, resulting in the publication of *Dangerous Exits: Escaping Abusive Relationships in Rural America* (DeKeseredy and Schwartz, 2009). Still, there are obviously other factors that contribute to the danger in women's exits from intimate relationships, such as male consumption of pornography (DeKeseredy in press; DeKeseredy and Olsson, 2011). As well, figure 4.2 served as a starting point for future theoretical work and the next section features a subsequent perspective that addresses some major rural issues that we overlooked at the time of its development.

A Rural Masculinity Crisis/Male Peer Support Model of Separation[13]

Rural social and economic transformations, challenges to masculine identity, and male peer support are major components of figure 4.3. Following Sernau (2006), this model asserts that in rural U.S. communities, "male privilege is persistent but precarious" (p. 69). For example, prior to the end of the last century, many rural men obtained an income from owning family farms or working in extractive industries such as coal mining (Jensen, 2006; Lobao, and Meyer, 2001; Sherman, 2005). Further, buttressed by a patriarchal ideology, most of these men's marriages were typically characterized by a rigid gendered division of labor in which men were the primary "bread winners" and women had "an intense and highly privatized relationship with domestic production," such as childrearing and doing housework (Websdale, 1998, p. 49; Ni Laoire and Fielding, 2006). This is not to say, though, that such gender relations are nonexistent today. They are still evident in a sizeable number of rural communities (Lobao, 2006). Reflect on the experiences of this rural Ohio woman we interviewed:

> His favorite thing was, "If you are not going to be at work, you're going to be here cooking and cleaning, doing laundry. And if I ever catch you sitting on your ass, I am going to beat the fuck out of you, you know."

Even so, rural men's power has become fragile due to major challenges to their masculine identity spawned by changes that have occurred over the last forty or more years (DeKeseredy et al., 2007; Johnson, 2006; Sherman, 2005). For example, there is a major decline in the number of family-owned farms because many people cannot make a reasonable living from them (Jacobs, 2005;

| RURAL SOCIAL AND ECONOMIC TRANSFORMATIONS | → | CHALLENGES TO MASCULINE IDENTITY | → | MALE PEER SUPPORT | → | SEPARATION AND DIVORCE SEXUAL ASSAULT |

Figure 4.3 A rural masculinity crisis/male peer support model
of separation/divorce sexual assault

Towes, 2010). Furthermore, the closing of sawmills, coalmines, and other key sources of income have devastated many rural U.S. communities that relied on a small number of industries for employment (Jensen, 2006; U.S. Department of Agriculture, 2011). Also, many women seek employment or get jobs when their husbands become unemployed or when their farms become unsustainable or less profitable—another factor that has the potential for weakening the overall power of men (DeKeseredy and Schwartz, 2009; Lobao and Myer, 2001). As Gallup-Black (2005) correctly observed when considering the vast literature on the linkage between disadvantage and homicide in urban locations, "But the relationship between violence and economic hardship . . . defined by job loss, unemployment, poverty, and population loss—can be just as pronounced in rural or small population areas" (p. 165). For example, the rural rate of homicide in Canada is higher than those for urban and small urban areas (Donnermeyer, DeKeseredy and Dragiewicz, 2011).

This transition in the area of employment often generates marital instability because many economically displaced males who cannot meet their perceived responsibilities as the man of the household feel deprived of intimate and social support resources that give them self-worth (DeKeseredy and Schwartz, 2009). A sizeable portion of unemployed rural men who strongly adhere to the ideology of familial patriarchy compensate for their lack of economic power by exerting more control over their wives (DeKeseredy et al., 2007; Sherman, 2005), a problem that can influence these women to consider leaving or to exit their marriages. Numerous other major social and economic transitions have spawned "the crisis in the rural gender order" (Hogg and Carrington, 2006, p. 181), such as women's rights to own property and inherit wealth, an increase in the number of rural women's associations, and the "delegitimation" of some forms of rural masculinity (e.g., via tougher drinking and driving laws).

Some unemployed rural men have "managed to remake masculinity" through means that do not involve intense patriarchal domination and control of their wives or common-law partners. For instance, Sherman's (2005) study of families harmed by the closure of sawmills in a rural California community reveals that some unemployed men became active, progressive fathers and delighted in spending much time with their children while their wives worked.

Too many other unemployed rural men, however, deal with the aforementioned "masculinity challenges" by spending much time drinking with men in similar situations (DeKeseredy et al., 2006), which is one of the key reasons why their wives leave or try to leave them (Sherman, 2005). Frequently, the contexts of drinking, such as bars and pubs, are locations where definitions of masculinity are played out (Campbell, 2006), what Campbell (2000) referred to as the "glass phallus." Further, as we uncovered in three rural Ohio counties (see DeKeseredy and Schwartz, 2009), many rural men have peers who view various types of woman abuse as legitimate and effective means of repairing damaged masculinity. Similar to many unemployed urban counterparts, these men serve as abusive role models (DeKeseredy and Schwartz, 2002).

When women terminate relationships because of their partners' substance abuse, violent behavior, or other problems generated in part by unemployment, rural men often perceive this move as another threat to their masculinity. Additionally, many of them are influenced by their male peers to engage in separation/divorce sexual assault to regain control and to avoid losing status (DeKeseredy et al., 2007). Status is a factor that is also closely related to fear of ridicule, which is a mechanism of informal social control in many societies (Beirstadt, 1957; Warr, 2002). For example, if abusive men's peers see them as failures with women due to separation/divorce, they will face group ridicule, lose status, and thus assault the women they can no longer dominate (Bourgois, 1995). This process is similar to the dynamics behind the presentation of self by males in rural pubs, as described by Campbell (2000). It is not so much demonstrating masculinity as it is being seen by peers as less than masculine. Hence, control and abuse prevents loss of status.

Figure 4.3 is heavily informed by variants of critical criminological thought and does not reduce, like mainstream perspectives [e.g., Hirschi's (1969) social bond theory], gender to an afterthought or to a control variable in a regression equation. Moreover, like figure 4.2, it is a rare attempt to explain the plight of a group of women who have historically suffered in silence. Indeed, if battered lesbians, women of color and female members of other ethnic/racial groups have been delegated to the margins by orthodox criminology and "white" liberal and radical feminists (Potter, 2008; Sokoloff and Dupont, 2005; Villalon, 2010), the same can be said about socially and economically excluded rural women who endure beatings, sexual assaults, and the like.

In addition to being critical and bringing marginalized abused women's experiences to the center of criminological analysis, figure 4.3 responds to some of the problems in the state of male peer support theory and to research that needs to be done in the future. Chief among these limitations is the question of where there are regional variations in male peer support for sexual assault and other types of woman abuse (DeKeseredy and Schwartz, 1998b). As stated before, there has been very little empirical and theoretical work on men outside the mostly white, middle-class confines of large university campuses—for example on working-class men of the same age in rural communities—to see if their experiences are the same. As well, to the best of our knowledge, except for figure 4.2 crafted by DeKeseredy et al. (2004), there has been no other previous attempt to apply male peer support theory to any type of abuse during separation/divorce. Thus, figure 4.3 moves male peer support research and theorizing beyond the limited realm of academic settings and focuses on a very high-risk relationship status category. Moreover, it addresses the fact that rural women's individual experiences are parts of a larger set of economic and social structural factors (Donnermeyer, Jobes, and Barclay, 2006). The same can be said about the social and economic exclusion model of separation/divorce woman abuse in public housing presented in figure 4.4.

The Social and Economic Exclusion Model of Separation/Divorce Woman Abuse in Public Housing[14]

In the middle of the last decade, no North American study tried to identify the groups of women living in public housing or "cities-within-cities" that are the most risk of being assaulted by male partners (Venkatesh, 2000). Together with Shahid Alvi (see DeKeseredy et al., 2008), we hypothesized that separated/divorced female public housing residents are more likely to be hurt by intimate violence than their married counterparts. Guided by the theoretical model described in figure 4.4 and using data from the Quality of Neighborhood Life Survey (DeKeseredy et al., 2003), we tested this hypothesis, and the data are discussed in chapter 5. Figure 4.4 builds on our economic exclusion/male peer support model of public housing woman abuse (see figure 4.1), DeKeseredy et al.'s (2003) theory of post-separation woman abuse in public housing, and Sernau's (2001) web of exclusion model. Figure 4.4, like figure 4.1, asserts that the rapid deindustrialization that has occurred in North America since the 1970s produced an alarmingly high rate of unemployed men who end up living in socially isolated public housing communities. This isolation within such centers of concentrated urban disadvantage can further contribute to unemployment because many employers believe that public housing residents are more likely than others to steal, miss work, and abuse substances, especially if they are people of color (Wilson, 1996; Wilson and Taub, 2006). Obviously, not every employer has this perception and many businesses will hire public housing residents (albeit at low wages). Still, with the suburbanization of employment, even many low-paying jobs are now only found far from inner-city housing projects. Thus, it is difficult to get or sustain a job if people cannot afford cars or expensive public transportation.

It is not surprising that a large number of jobless men turn to alcohol and drugs to cope with the day-to-day problems associated with being economically and socially excluded (Stevens, 2011). Staying "clean and sober" is almost impossible in many poor places, especially if sizeable portions of your peers do not have the courage, motivation, or desire to abstain from using drugs and alcohol. Elliott Currie (1993) developed the *saturation model* to explain this problem. He asserts that after decades and generations of limited economic opportunity, some urban areas become marked by pervasive hopelessness. Drug use becomes more and more widespread, until it virtually saturates the entire community. People don't really make a conscious effort to become drug users but just seem to drift into doing what everyone else is doing. Again, in a community saturated with drugs, quitting can become nearly impossible. One of Erich Goode's (1989) informants writes: "Whenever I saw my friends, they were shooting up, too. . . . The problem with kicking heroin . . . is that all of your friends aren't kicking at the same time" (p. 252).

Excessive drug and alcohol consumption generates considerable relationship stress and is strongly associated with male-to-female violence (DeKeseredy, 2011a). Not surprisingly, many women do not want to live with men who abuse substances and who are violent. Hence, they exit or try to terminate their relationships: As one Chicago woman told Kathryn Edin (2000):

> I married [my first husband] a month after I had [our son]. And I married him because I couldn't afford [to live alone]. Boy, was that stupid. And I left him [two years after that] when our daughter was five months old. I got scared. I was afraid because my kids were starting to get in the middle. [My son] still to this day, when he thinks someone is hurting me, he'll start screaming and crying and beating on him. He had seen his father [beat me up]. I didn't want him to see that. I remarried six months later because I couldn't make it [financially]. And I got into another abusive marriage. And we got separated before the year was even up. He would burn me [with cigarettes]. He was an alcoholic. He was a physical abuser, mental [too]. I think he would have killed me [if I had stayed].

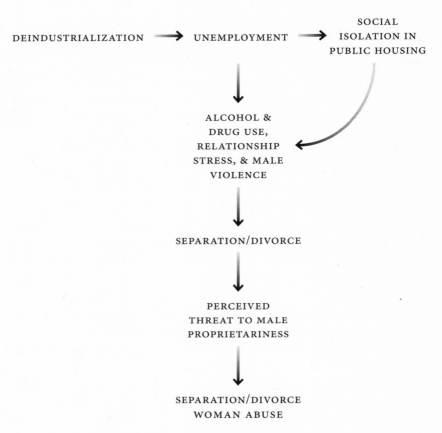

DEINDUSTRIALIZATION → UNEMPLOYMENT → SOCIAL ISOLATION IN PUBLIC HOUSING

ALCOHOL & DRUG USE, RELATIONSHIP STRESS, & MALE VIOLENCE

SEPARATION/DIVORCE

PERCEIVED THREAT TO MALE PROPRIETARINESS

SEPARATION/DIVORCE WOMAN ABUSE

Figure 4.4 A social and economic exclusion model
of separation/divorce woman abuse in public housing

Not all women who separate or divorce their partners end up leaving their homes, particularly if it is their name that is on the lease. Some "invert patriarchy" by evicting the male partner that they see as irresponsible, or who may be too difficult to house and feed (Bourgois, 1995; DeKeseredy, Alvi, and Schwartz, 2006; Edin, 2000). Regardless of how the relationship ends, many male public housing residents, like other "truly disadvantaged" men (Wilson, 1987) strongly adhere to the ideology of familial patriarchy. Thus, they are more prone to interpreting women ending relationships as a challenge to male proprietariness which, if it is not already clear, can result in violent retaliation.

Some of the QNLS data described in *Under Siege* (DeKeseredy et al., 2003) and in the next chapter partially support figure 4.4 and Bourgois's (1995) argument that by abusing women, many socially and economically excluded inner-city men are "desperately attempting to reassert their grandfathers' lost autocratic control over the household" (p. 500). Women who resist or challenge their partner's patriarchal expectations are at a substantially elevated risk of being assaulted (DeKeseredy and Schwartz, 2009; Smith, 1990; Yllo, 1983). Certainly in homicide we know that women who leave or attempt to leave controlling partners are under increased risk of being killed, especially if she leaves for another partner (Campbell et al., 2003; DeKeseredy et al., 2008).

A New Left-Realist Gendered Subcultural Theory[15]

In chapter 3, we briefly described our association with left realism. This variant of critical criminology emerged in the mid-1980s in the United Kingdom and in the United States. The roots of left realism are found in the writings of Jock Young (1975, 1979), Tony Platt (1978), and Ian Taylor (1981), but this school of thought was not expressed formally until the publication of John Lea and Jock Young's (1984) *What Is to be Done about Law and Order?* Shortly after this seminal work came Elliott Currie's (1985) *Confronting Crime: An American Challenge*, which arguably marked the official birth of North American left realism and is still, today, one of the most widely read and cited progressive texts of its kind.

Left realism has been "rediscovered" and one its British founders, Roger Matthews (2009), offers a "refashioned" version that "prioritizes the role of theory" (p. 344). The concepts of class, the state, and structure are emphasized in his recent attempt to create a "coherent critical realist approach" to explaining crime and punishment (p. 341). More evidence that this school of criminology is just as exciting as it was in its early years is that the journal *Crime, Law and Social Change* published a special issue on left realism in 2010, edited by us (see vol. 54).

Over the years, we have jumped back and forth from studying woman abuse and theorizing it to writing articles and book chapters on left realism, many of which were critiques heavily informed by feminist schools of thought. Still, it was not until 2010 that we developed our own left-realist perspective. Similar to what noted mainstream juvenile delinquency theorist Albert Cohen (1955) argued, left realists contend that people lacking legitimate means of solving the problem of relative deprivation (poverty experienced as unfair) may come into contact with other frustrated disenfranchised people and form subcultures, which in turn, encourage criminal behaviors (Lea and Young, 1984).[16] Absent from this theory is an attempt to address how, today, subcultural development in North America and elsewhere is heavily shaped simultaneously by the recent destructive consequences of right-wing Milton Friedman or Chicago School economic policies and marginalized men's attempts to live up to the principles of hegemonic masculinity. Our new left-realist offering emphasizes these two key determinants and offers a more gendered understanding of the linkage between broader social forces and subcultural development.

We, among many other social scientists and activists, assert that the harmful effects of "laissez-faire" economic policies informed by Friedman (1962) and others on the right have caused a relatively "new assault" on workers and have helped make North America "categorically unequal" (Massey, 2007), including corporations moving to developing countries to use cheap labor and take advantage of weak environmental and workplace safety laws (DeKeseredy, 2011b; Sernau, 2006; Waquant, 2008). The main point is that they have excluded a substantial number of North Americans from the labor market, which challenges men's masculine identity (Brotherton, 2008). A major source of many male youth's discontent is their unemployment and "material shortage" relative to the employment and "material abundance" of male members of other social class groupings (Ellis and DeKeseredy, 1996; Tanner, 2012). Scores of these socially and economically excluded youths, regardless of whether they live in urban or rural communities, experience "status frustration" that puts them at great risk of teaming up with others to create a subculture that promotes, expresses, and validates masculinity through violent means (Cohen, 1955; DeKeseredy and Schwartz, 2005; Messerschmidt, 1993).

We further assert that in communities damaged by, for example, deindustrialization, the loss of family-owned farms, or the closing of sawmills and coalmines there is a greater proportion of all-male peer groups that promote violence against women. Men at the bottom of the socioeconomic ladder flocking together with members of all-male sexist subcultures that perpetuate and legitimate woman abuse is not surprising, since they are more likely than their more affluent counterparts to adhere to the ideology of familial patriarchy (DeKeseredy, 2011b; Smith, 1990). Arguably, such subcultures are likely to flourish in the near future because areas with high levels of poverty and unemployment are fertile breeding grounds for male-to-male and male-to-female violence (Currie, 2012). This is not to say, however, that middle-class men and boys do not engage in violence. They certainly do, and this book reviews a large literature on the strong association between patriarchal male peer support and various types of woman abuse in university/college dating, which involves, for the most part, middle- and upper-class young adults.

Despite Matthews's (2009) attempt to offer a new left-realist criminology, for this school to truly move forward, it must not minimize the importance of gender, which most left realists did in the past. Our theoretical perspective, summarized here, addresses this concern, as well as answers mainstream and progressive calls for criminological integration (Agnew, 2011; Barak, 2009). But, as is the case with earlier realist theoretical work, our attempt to refashion realism will likely receive more criticism from the left than from the right. This is because the right holds Cohen's (1955) subcultural theory in much higher regard than do most critical criminologists. For example, although he is sharply opposed to what C. Wright Mills (1959) refers to as abstracted empiricism (e.g., research divorced from theory) and positivism,[17] Majid Yar and Sue Penna (2004) labeled British pioneering critical criminologist Jock Young a positivist for his continued application of strain and subculture to an understanding of crime and control.[18] Among critical criminologists, this label is typically seen as a stigma because it situates one as an ally of mainstream criminology.

The roots of Cohen's (1955) work are based in Emile Durkheim's (1951/1897) sociological ideas. Although some critical criminologists have found Durkheim's approach too biological and inherently conservative (Taylor, Walton, and Young, 1973), a few progressive scholars show that much of his work can be of great value to "help specify a realistic set of socialist goals" (Pearce, 1989, p. 10). Further, consistent with the original left-realist subcultural theory (Lea and Young, 1984), we assert that like our gendered social bond/male peer support theory of university woman abuse, our refurnished left-realist version demonstrates that concepts derived from gender-blind orthodox theories are still useful when combined with critical criminological insights.

Summary

Mark Warr (2002) correctly points out that "[c]riminal conduct is predominantly social behavior. Most offenders are imbedded in a network of friends who also break the law, and the single strongest predictor of criminal behavior known to criminologists is the number of delinquent friends an individual has" (p. 3). Nonetheless, unless we missed something, nowhere to be found in his book and in most other mainstream criminological works is there any mention of peer influence as a cause of woman abuse. This is a major omission, one that we have continually responded to since we started our intellectual relationship. As other criminological perspectives on the role of peers have evolved since the development of Edwin Sutherland's (1939) differential association theory, this chapter shows that our theoretical contributions have also changed and become more complex. Nevertheless, one feature that continues to remain the same is our commitment to linking macro-level forces with micro-social factors and we started down this path in 1993 (see chapter 3). As well, our theoretical work moved out of institutions of higher learning and into poor inner-city communities and rural areas. The next step is to address what Warr (2002) labels the "virtual peer group." As yet, we have not constructed a theory of how Internet peer groups contribute to woman abuse, but we have done some empirical work on the new media and male peer support, which is presented in chapter 6.

We assume by now that readers with a strong affiliation for positivism are probably asking, "What do the data say?" This is not surprising, due in large part to reasons offered by Jock Young (2011): "[A]bstracted empiricism has expanded on a level which would have surely astonished Mills himself. How in much of the social sciences reality has been lost in a sea of statistical symbols and dubious analysis" (p. viii). In chapter 5, we answer this question; but, all our qualitative and quantitative research done so far is guided by one or more of the theories presented in this chapter and in chapter 3. True, as feminists and left realists, our work is grounded in critical criminology, but chapter 6 helps challenge the popular myth that critical criminological theories are simply "rhetorical" (Wheeler, 1976), "ideologically charged ideas" (Liska, 1987), and are "untestable" (Akers and Sellers, 2004).

5 | What Do the Data Say?

Be a good craftsman: Avoid any rigid set of procedures. Above all, seek to develop and to use the sociological imagination. Avoid the fetishism of method and technique. Urge the rehabilitation of the unpretentious intellectual craftsman, and try to become such a craftsman yourself. Let every man be his own methodologist: let every man be his own theorist; let theory and method again become part of the practice of a craft. Stand for the primacy of the individual scholar; stand opposed to the ascendancy of research teams of technicians. Be one mind that is on its own confronting the problems of man and society.
—C. Wright Mills, *The Sociological Imagination*

North American criminology is characterized by a diverse and wide-ranging variety of theoretical perspectives. Yet, one would not know this if she or he only read *Criminology* and *Criminology and Public Policy*, which are the two official journals of the American Society of Criminology, or *Justice Quarterly*, the primary official journal of the Academy of Criminal Justice Sciences. Positivism and empiricism dominate mainstream American criminology and these journals are classic examples of this orthodox way of thinking. If one is only interested in complex mathematical models of criminal and criminal justice system behavior, then American criminology is the place to go. And, of course, this methodology is greatly influential in the rest of the world. As Jock Young (1988) stated twenty-five years ago: "American criminology is a powerhouse of ideas, research techniques and interventions which understandably dominate Western thinking about crime" (p. 293).

More recently Young (2011) has reminded us that "abstracted empiricism has expanded on a level which would have surely astonished Mills himself" (p. viii). Something else that would have amazed Mills is the simultaneous expansion of feminism. Michael Burawoy (2008) points out some of the gender-blind nature of Mills's work in his open letter to him:

Finally, we turn to the modern history of feminism. This is an area of social thought quite beyond your ken. Students were appalled by your condescending characterization of women in *White Collar*,[1] especially the sections on the "salesgirls" and "the white-collar girl." I was surprised you so completely missed the boat on gender since your hero Thorstein Veblen[2] was such an ardent feminist and spoke about the exploitation of women in a consumer culture with such vitriol. (p. 368)

Some readers may be asking, "If Mills was not a feminist, why, then, in the introduction do you state that your gendered theories are heavily grounded in his concept of the sociological imagination?" There are four main answers to this question. First, in the words of Burawoy, "It is, indeed, a powerful idea" (p. 368). Second, we are critical criminologists, which like "Mills' radicalism," puts us on "the periphery of American Sociology" and criminology for that matter (Ritzer, 2008, p. 213). Third, Mills compels us to look beyond the personal troubles of one or two women assaulted by a male partner and rather to look at the broader problem of woman abuse in our society. Finally, like the writings of Hirschi (1969) and Cohen (1955), Mills's contributions can be useful when integrated with strands of feminist thought.

Another reason for drawing from Mills is that he was a strong advocate of linking theory with research and this has always been a primary concern for us. In fact, almost all of the research on male peer support, ranging from the early work of Eugene J. Kanin (1967a, 1967b) to our most recent study (DeKeseredy and Schwartz, 2009), is driven by some theoretical perspective that, in the spirit of Mills, converts the *personal troubles* of woman abuse into *public issues.* This chapter reviews an extensive array of qualitative and quantitative studies guided by male peer support theories, and we suggest new directions in theory and research.

College/University Studies

Kanin's Research[3]

Eugene Kanin pioneered empirical and theoretical work on male peer support in institutions of higher learning, and his offerings continue to influence us. He argues that some men come to college with either a history of sexual aggression or a desire to engage in this behavior. These are often men who were highly trained as far back as elementary school to treat women as sexual objects and to use women simply as things to achieve their own desires: "scoring," or engaging in sexual activity. After interviewing 341 male undergraduate unmarried students (1967b), he asserted that sexually aggressive college men do not need training on this subject when they arrive in college. Rather, they selectively seek out male friends who support and sustain sexually exploitative behavior they learned in high school or earlier.

In other words, Kanin suggests that sexually aggressive young men don't just happen to come under the influence of aggressive male peers who teach the new students a brand new set of college values based on the exploitation of women. They simply need to locate other similarly minded men to make friends and to tell each other they are acting properly. Men already interested in exploiting women tend to seek out social groups, such as finding out which fraternities on campus have a reputation for this behavior.

This support of other men does not have to be verbal, according to Kanin (1967b), but it is important that the group explicitly and openly encourages the new member to exploit or to force women physically into sexual acts. More likely, these "erotically oriented" peer groups "stress the value of the erotic goal so that the male will be prone to become physically aggressive at the point when it is apparent that the usual seductive approaches are not going to be productive" (p. 497).

Thus, it is Kanin's (1985) argument that that there exists on most campuses men who are socialized by their friends or groups into a "hypererotic" subculture that produces extremely high or exaggerated levels of sexual aspiration. In other words, these men are taught to *expect* to engage in a very high level of consensual sexual intercourse, or what is to them sexual conquest. The problem, of course, is that for most men such goals are impossible to achieve. When they fall short of what they see as their friends' high expectations, and perhaps short of what they believe their friends are all actually achieving, some of these men experience relative deprivation. This sexual frustration, caused by a "reference-group-anchored sex drive," is what Kanin (1967b) feels can result in predatory sexual conduct. These men are highly frustrated, not because they are deprived of sex in some objective sense, but because they feel inadequate or unable to engage in what they have defined as the proper amount of sex.

The last point is important enough to repeat. How much sex does a man need to feel fulfilled? Certainly, as anyone who has looked at voluntary celibacy knows, the answer is none. In fact, many men choose to have little or no sex at all, without ill effect. Other men decide that if they are not having sexual intercourse once a week, then they are deprived. Then there are others who require three or four acts of sex a week to feel emotionally satisfied (Hill, 2008). Kanin's argument is that it is the latter group from which date or acquaintance rapists often emerge. Many years ago some people felt that rapists were men who were unable to engage in voluntary sexual activities because of a sexual imbalance, or because there weren't enough women to go around. Kanin is making the opposite argument. These are men who feel sexually frustrated even while they are actually engaging in more sex than is typical for male undergraduates. Their expectations and goals are so high that they are dissatisfied and feel disappointed and even angry at being deprived by women (sex objects) of even more sex. The date rapists Kanin studied were primarily interested in scoring as often as possible and reported that their friends would approve of forced sex against at least some women. Kanin believes these friends actually exist—that there is on many college campuses a male "hypererotic" subculture that approves in some instances of forced sex.

What about college men who are not in such a subculture? Without pressure from their peers for sexual conquests, Kanin (1967a) argues, these men are more likely to be satisfied with their sexual accomplishments, or at least less likely to experience dissatisfaction with them, which means that they are less likely to sexually abuse women.

One problem with this formulation is that it is hard for many people to believe that the men with high sexual expectations who force women into sexual intercourse obviously against their will can somehow justify their behavior as a legitimate "conquest." Particularly when they are using physical force, they must be aware that this behavior will often be defined as deviant or criminal not only by other students, but also by the police, courts, and campus administrators. According to Kanin, this is one more area where male peer support groups provide a service to their members. These all-male alliances provide the *vocabulary of adjustment* discussed in chapter 3.

A major strength of Kanin's work is that hypotheses based on his theory can be tested using both quantitative and qualitative data. In fact, empirical support for some of his assertions is provided by several studies. For example, we analyzed data generated by the Canadian National Survey of woman abuse in university/college dating (CNS) and found that men begin patterns of sexual abuse in elementary and high school and bring them to college (DeKeseredy and Schwartz, 1998a). More recent surveys conducted in Canada and the United States found that 11 percent to 19 percent of adolescent boys reported having sexually assaulted girls.[4] Studies such as these do not support the notion that on-campus men's groups, such as fraternities, are the cause of sexual forms of woman abuse in college dating relationships. Rather, many male undergraduates arrive at college fully prepared to abuse women with no additional learning.

One problem with Kanin's work, however, is a lack of specification. For instance, he argues that sexually aggressive men seek out friends who share and support the values they learned prior to entering college, but he does not specify the ways in which these individuals locate those who are like-minded. Of course, our own male peer support theories are also guilty of this. As well, Kanin does not particularly explain the type of pressure male peers place on their friends to have sex. There are a few other problems with Kanin's work that were overcome in research done by DeKeseredy (1988b), DeKeseredy and Kelly (1993b), and DeKeseredy and Schwartz (1998a). It is to this body of knowledge that we turn to next.

The CNS and Other Studies of Youth

Unfortunately, empirical support has sometimes been lacking in those areas where Kanin has been most specific. For example, he claims that all-male alliances do not *verbally* tell their friends to physically victimize their dating partners. However, DeKeseredy's (1988c) nonprobability survey of 308 male undergraduates found that one of the most important predictors of which men will become abusive in dating is whether they have friends who explicitly and verbally tell them to abuse women under certain conditions (e.g., challenges to patriarchal authority and sexual rejections). Thus, Kanin is completely correct in pointing to the extreme importance of indirect pro-abuse peer support, such as providing vocabularies that give men the ability to convince themselves that they are not deviant. However, direct support for this abuse (being told to do it) must also be taken into account.

The Canadian National Survey (CNS) is the first national survey to specifically examine male peer support practices and discourses in the college community. Conducted in the autumn of 1992, the sample consisted of 3,142 people, including 1,835 women and 1,307 men. A research team administered two questionnaires, one for men and another for women in ninety-five undergraduate classes across Canada, from Atlantic Canada to British Columbia on the Pacific Coast. The questionnaires were available in both French and English versions. Response rates were high, with less than 1 percent of the participants refusing to answer. A major result of this study was that having male friends who verbally encourage abuse under certain situations is a key determinant of sexual, physical, and psychological variants of woman abuse. As well, peers' patriarchal attitudes were related to all of these harms (DeKeseredy and Kelly, 1993b, 1995; DeKeseredy and Schwartz, 1998a).

Another place that the CNS expanded on Kanin's theory is that the latter neglects the importance of social bonds with abusive friends, and the amount of contact these men have with male peers, regardless of whether they are abusive. DeKeseredy's (1988b) early study and the CNS (DeKeseredy and Kelly, 1995), on the other hand, found that men who have abusive friends are more likely to engage in psychological and sexual abuse. Furthermore, research suggests that spending a large amount of time with male friends increases the probability of sexual assault (Ageton, 1983), especially in settings where alcohol consumption and patriarchal practices and discourses are routine activities (Schwartz et al., 2001), such as in fraternities and at combative sports teams' parties (Koss and Gaines, 1993; Sanday, 1990; Schwartz and DeKeseredy, 1997). Whatever the reason that it occurs, it should be noted in passing that football and basketball players based at NCAA-affiliated schools were reported to police for sexual assault 38 percent more often than the average male on campus (Burstyn, 2000; Warshaw, 1988). Overall, college and university athletes are overrepresented among students reported to campus judicial affairs boards for sexual assault (Crosset, Benedict, and McDonald, 1995; Forbes, Adams-Curtis, Pakalka, and White, 2006).

As a result of the CNS, and the many analyses that this extensive data set supported, we were eventually able to specify a modified male peer support theory, as outlined earlier. However, while we were able in a wide variety of publications to test a number of different aspects of the model, we did not test the full model. Part of the reason for that was time and money, of course, but another reason is the difficulty of specifying measures for a number of factors in the heuristic or teaching model that we developed in the early 1990s, and outlined in figure 3.2, under the title of the Modified Male Peer Support Model.

However, an attempt to test the full model was recently made by Franklin, Bouffard, and Travis (2012), evidently as part of a graduate thesis in a university in the Northwest. Here the full model was tested, although as in all empirical studies it was necessary to reduce some complex theoretical constructs to a simple thing that could be measured. Thus, they centered their piece on fraternity membership as an example of elite all-male peer groups. There is a certain logic to this, but it must always be remembered that there is no automatic reason why fraternities would be worse than other all-male peer support groups. On some campuses, researchers found that while some fraternities were, to put it bluntly, rape-prone, others were not. Mixed together, it has not been unusual for fraternity membership to fail to load (be related) in a complex formula on physical sexual coercion and aggression, or to find that while fraternity members use alcohol and verbal coercion extensively, they were not more likely than other men on campus to use physical coercion (e.g., Schwartz and Nogrady, 1996; Boeringer, Shehan, and Akers, 1991; Boeringer, 1996; Koss and Cleveland, 1996).

Franklin, Bouffard and Pratt (2012) attempted to test the entire model simultaneously, focusing in on membership in Greek male social fraternities as a proxy for male peer support. They tested whether men admitted to a wide range of illegal sexual acts with women, rather than limiting themselves to sexual intercourse or attempted sexual intercourse, as was usually done with the CNS, presumably to obtain a wider sample of admitted assaulters. Finally, they included a measure of low social control, arguing quite rightly that we had said in 1997 that men who were the least motivated to obey societal norms were the most likely to be attuned to messages from peers approving of woman abuse. Whether this would be the construct on low self-control developed by Gottfredson and Hirschi (1990) or some other construct, such as Hirschi's more rational choice model that he developed later on about how some men are willing, based on short-term interests, to break long-term social bonds (Lilly, Cullen, and Ball, 2011), is open to some question. There certainly are some problems in marrying a theory (Gottfredson and Hirschi) that suggests that peer group influence is an illusion best explained by self-selection into approving groups, and a theory (ours) that is based on the social learning effects of male peer support groups!

However, Franklin, Bouffard, and Pratt (2012) found specifically that the feminist male peer support explanation that we had outlined in figure 3.2 was a powerful one that explained much of the incidence and motivation for sexual assault on the college campus. They further found that adding a measure drawn from low self-control theory added to the model's explanatory power, and made the entire model statistically significant.

There are other North American studies of college students and adolescents that identify male peer influence as a key determinant of woman abuse in dating (e.g., Blanchard, 1959; Gwartney-Gibbs, Stockard, and Bohmer, 1987; Reitzel-Jaffe and Wolfe, 2001; Silverman and Williamson, 1997). Collectively, this body of knowledge supports the claim derived from many studies of other social problems (e.g., gang violence and soccer hooliganism) that much interpersonal violence is a product of interactions with male "reference others" (Schmitt, 1972).

The problem is that most of the studies in this area are of smaller local samples, which always raises the question of whether the problem (or lack of problem) identified is localized to one region or even one campus, or whether it is a national-level or international problem. The CNS discussed in this book, and which was the primary support for the Modified Male Peer Support Model, was a national-level, representative sample of Canadian college students. Thus, while it was national in scope, it also was limited to college students. One attempt to test the questions that dealt with these issues came from Casey and Beadnell (2010), who used an important existing data set that was a representative national study in several waves of American youth. When the youth were sixteen they were asked about peer network structures, and then five or six years later when they were about twenty-one they were asked about intimate personal violence that they had committed. Since the data already existed, they were not able to test specific models, such as the Male Peer Support Model, and they were not able to limit their study to sexual violence (as they were also studying physical violence against intimates). However, they were able to look at several types of peer groups that young men belonged to, and to compare these men by how often they admitted to engaging in intimate violence. What they found was that small, dense peer groups that were all male or essentially all male, and that engaged in a higher level of delinquent behavior, evidently produced young men who were indeed much more likely to have engaged in violence against young women. Those youth who belonged to larger, more loosely connected groups of both males and females who committed relatively fewer acts of delinquency, were themselves much less likely to engage in violence against young female intimates (Casey and Beadnell, 2010).

Male-to-Female Violence in Marriage[5]

There is relatively little empirical work on male peer support and violence against wives. Arguably, the first data on this topic were derived from Dobash and Dobash's (1979) interviews with 109 battered women in Glasgow. They, too, found that spending much time with male friends is a key factor. For example, 71 percent of the women reported that the men who hurt them spent at least one night a week with their male peers. Similarly, based on data gathered from the reports of a sample of women, Bowker (1983) found that the more contact there was between wife batterers and their male friends, the more frequent and severe the beatings of the wives would be. He explains the finding by describing a social psychological process in which males develop *standards of gratification* that dictate that they should dominate their wives and children. These standards are developed through childhood exposure to their mothers being dominated by their fathers and by the men themselves being dominated in their family of orientation. In other words, they learn that both women and children are subordinate to the male head of the household. When these men find that their patterns of domination are threatened, or even get the impression that there is a challenge to such domination, then they suffer from psychological stress. They react to this stress with a contrived rage, designed to reestablish domination patterns that meet their standards of gratification.

Standards that lead men to wife beating are fully developed in men who are heavily integrated in male peer groups that continually reinforce standards of gratification through dominance. For Bowker, these homosocial networks constitute a patriarchal subculture of violence. The more fully men are integrated into this subculture, the greater the probability that they will beat their wives. As pointed out in the introduction, Bowker also contends that this subculture is not restricted to a single class, religion, occupational category, or ethnic group, and it socializes married members to believe in both patriarchal control and the use of violence to maintain their control.

Recall from reading the introduction that Bowker's perspective certainly had an impact on us. However, the impact is still on theory, as it does not yet have strong empirical support, Bowker (1983) admits that his study did not focus directly on a male subculture of violence: "one can only guess at its broad outlines" (p. 136). His study only shows that the frequency and severity of wife beatings is positively associated with wives' reports of husbands' contacts with their male friends. Because no males were included in the sample, there were no measures of information on husbands' friends, adherence to patriarchal attitudes and beliefs, or the degree to which abuse-facilitating values and norms were actually shared by these men. Bowker is sensitive to these weaknesses and argues that interviews with wife beaters are required to adequately understand whether or not there is a relationship between wife beating and a male patriarchal subculture of violence.

Nonetheless, there is evidence from other studies, including one of wife beaters in Canada (Smith, 1990), that men who report abusing female intimates are more likely than those who do not report abusive behavior to endorse an ideology of familial patriarchy (DeKeseredy and Kelly, 1993b). Moreover, the CNS found that if these patriarchal men are supported by male peers, they are even more likely to abuse their partners (DeKeseredy and Schwartz, 1998a). As mentioned earlier, there are data showing that male peer support for female victimization is found throughout the world. Still, although Bowker is correct in claiming that the male patriarchal subculture is not limited to one specific time, or sociodemographic group, there is no evidence that it is a "universal risk factor." The problem is simple. In most cultures, most of the time, all men, most men, or at least a great many men receive male peer support for the victimization of females. Friends, jokes, asides, videos, movies, books, and other print matter, helpful relatives, local leaders, teachers, and representatives of the government such as police and soldiers are constantly giving out such messages, and all men receive them more or less.

Similarly, Smith (1991) criticized Bowker's study for failing to fill in all of the gaps. He stated, "Bowker reported positive correlations from his research on battered wives between the frequency and severity of beatings and the amount of time the batterer spent with his male friends. He provides no evidence, however, that these peers actually approved of wife beating" (p. 512). Overall, however, Smith was sympathetic to Bowker's work and used qualitative and quantitative data from his Toronto woman abuse survey[6] to try to fill in some of the gaps by trying to answer two questions: (1) "Are the male friends of abusive husbands more likely to approve of violence against wives than are the male friends of nonabusive husbands?" and (2) "To what extent and how does male peer approval of wife abuse reflect an ideology of familial patriarchy" (p. 513)?

The answer to the first of these questions is "yes." For the second question, of the 131 female respondents who stated that at least some of their husbands' male peers would approve of a husband slapping his wife, 109 offered a reason why they thought their husbands' friends would approve. Below are some of their responses:

- They have to keep women down by acting macho.
- The way they talk and the attitude they have about women.
- Their attitude about women and the way they speak to their wives. They don't respect women. (pp. 516–17)

These findings are important and address some of Bowker's limitations. Even so, Smith was still interviewing women about men. Like Bowker, Smith did not actually interview the men who abused his respondents, which raises at least some questions about the validity of his measure of peer approval. Smith was well aware of this problem and stated:

It should be noted that many of the responses are as much an explanation of why the respondent thinks that her husband's friends either do abuse, or would abuse, their own wives as they are of why her husband's friends would approve in general of a husband slapping his wife. It seems that these respondents make inferences about approval generally based on their understanding of how their husbands' male friends treated their own wives. (p. 515)

Having said this, however, Smith was, and to the best of our knowledge still is the only researcher to include a supplementary open-ended question on male peer support in a primarily quantitative survey. With this and other types of supplementary open-ended questions, Smith (1987, 1994) took steps to sensitize the woman abuse research community that such items help minimize under-reporting and contribute to the accumulation of more accurate and reliable data. Hopefully, future surveys of pro-abuse male peer influence will follow in his empirical footsteps.

Dangerous Exits: Male Peer Support for Separation/Divorce Assault[7]

As stated before, much of the work on male peer support theory is quantitative in nature and conducted on college campuses. A few researchers have both used qualitative methods and left the college campus to study the relationship between male peer support and various types of woman abuse in urban U.S. areas of concentrated disadvantage (Anderson, 1999; Bourgois, 1995; Miller, 2008; Wilson and Taub, 2006). For example, Sinclair (2002) found in a qualitative study that male peer support helped to explain the history of and attitudes toward woman abuse among socially displaced (held in custody) youth in an eastern Ontario city.[8] She studied these youths with extensive one-on-one interviews and found that their attitudes toward violence against female intimates was formed and supported by male peer groups, just as predicted in the theory. Furthermore, we (see DeKeseredy and Schwartz, 2002) offered a male peer support theory of woman abuse in public housing but that was in a theory piece, rather than a data analysis. The topic of interest in this section—sexual assault of women during and/or after separation or divorce—was a completely new one for us and all of those studying male peer support, as was for the most part the study of male peer support for abusive men in rural areas.

Funded by a grant from the National Institute of Justice of the U.S. Department of Justice, our qualitative project involved semistructured interviews with forty-three rural Ohio women who were sexually assaulted when they wanted to end, were trying to end, or had ended a relationship with a husband or live-in male partner. Our data are the first of their kind and seriously challenge the notion that rural communities are havens of serenity that are immune from violence against women and most crimes in general.

Most of these rural women had experienced different types of sexual assault at the hands of their partners or ex-partners, and virtually all experienced rape or attempted rape. Further, we confirmed that women targeted for intimate violence are rarely victimized by only one form of abuse. Instead, they typically suffer from a variety of injurious behaviors that include sexual assault, physical violence, psychological abuse, economic blackmail or denying them money (even if they earn their own wages), harm to loved animals or cherished possessions, or stalking behavior. Most (80 percent) of the women we interviewed were victimized by two or more of these forms of abuse.

Most victims of separation/divorce sexual assault are also hurt in other ways by various highly injurious acts and sometimes they are not the only ones injured by their ex-partners. For example, 19 percent of the women stated that their partners abused their children, and one woman believes that her ex-husband raped her in order to kill her unborn child. A few women in the sample said they would never be able to have children because their reproductive organs were damaged by numerous sexual assaults committed by their ex-partners.

We asked women to describe the key characteristics of the men who hurt them. It is not surprising that male peer support was a constant theme among our respondents' stories, given that it is strongly associated with other types of woman abuse, such as date rape, campus party rape, nonpartner rape in South Africa, and wife beating (Armstrong, Hamilton, and Sweeney, 2006; Bogle, 2008; Bowker, 1983; DeKeseredy and Schwartz, 1998a; Dragiewicz, 2011; Jewkes et al., 2006; Smith, 1991). Twenty-nine (67 percent) of the interviewees reported on a variety of ways in which their partner's male peers perpetuated and legitimated separation and divorce sexual assault.

Three techniques in particular stood out: frequently drinking with male friends, informational support, and attachment to abusive peers. Informational support refers to the guidance and advice that influences men to sexually, physically, and psychologically abuse their female partners, and attachment to abusive peers is defined as having male friends who also abuse women (DeKeseredy, 1988b). These factors are identical to those found to be highly significant in predicting which men on college campuses will admit to being sexual predators (DeKeseredy and Schwartz, 1998a; Schwartz et al., 2001).

As is the case with college men who sexually abuse women, "nights out drinking with the boys" were seen by many respondents as contexts that often supported patriarchal conversations about women and how to control them.[9] As Susan[10] told us: "Um, they're basically like him. They sit around, talk about women, and gossip. They're the biggest gossips there ever was. But they sit around and brag how about many times they get it and how they keep their women in line and, you know, just like crap, you know."

The social settings Susan and other respondents described are also examples of informational support, although these were not restricted to drinking events. For instance, one respondent's abusive partner spent much time with his cousin, a man who "hated women" and who often called them "fuckin' bitches" and "whore sluts." Her partner also had a married brother who "hit his wife every so often." Note, too, that although most of the participants did not explicitly label their partners' peers as patriarchal, most of them are. As Lynn put it, "And they just think women are their property and they can lay 'em anytime they want to. That's just their whole attitude about it." Moreover, 47 percent of the sample stated that they knew their partners' friends also physically or sexually abused women, which suggests that attachment to abusive peers also contributes to separation/divorce sexual assault. In fact, Betty said that *all* her ex-partners' friends hit women or sexually assault them, and several women told us that they directly watched their partners' friends abusing female intimates.

Some perpetrators also enlisted the help of their friends to sexually assault some of the interviewees. Such male peer support frequently involved forcing women to have sex with friends. This is what happened to Marie:

> Well, him and his friend got me so wasted. They took turns with me and I remembered most of it, but, um, there was also drugs involved. Not as much on my behalf as theirs. I was just drunk. And I did remember most of it, and the next morning I woke up feeling so dirty and so degraded and then it ended up getting around that I was the slut. . . . And in my eyes that was rape, due to the fact that I was so drunk. And I definitely didn't deserve that. And I was hurting. I was hurting the next day.

This violent "degradation ceremony" (Goffman, 1961) resembles what Peggy Reeves Sanday (1990) uncovered in her study of fraternity gang rape. In groups, some men do not rely on force to have sex with women but rather use alcohol or drugs to "work a yes" out of them. In other words, some perpetrators, either alone or in a group, purposely get women so drunk that they cannot resist their advances, which is a form of felony rape in most if not all states, and certainly where Marie was living.

Some of the women who were forced to have group sex were also beaten after going through vicious degradation ceremonies. Janet recalls her experience:

He ended up bringing someone into the relationship, which I didn't want, but he told me that if I didn't do it he would leave me. And I ended up staying with him. He was more into group sex and, and uh trying to be the big man. He wanted sex in a group thing or with his buddies or made me have sex with a friend of his. See one time he made me have sex with a friend of his for him to watch, and then he got mad and hit me afterwards. I mean he tied me up so I could watch him have sex with a 13-year-old girl. And then he ended up going to prison for it. So, I mean it was nasty.

The gang rapes reported to us are often referred to as "streamlining" in South Africa. According to Jewkes et al. (2006), this is

essentially a rape by two or more perpetrators. It is an unambiguously defiling and humiliating act, and is often a punishment, yet at the same time it is an act that is often regarded by its perpetrators as rooted in a sense of entitlement (Wood, 2005). A woman may be streamlined to punish her for having another partner; for behaving outside gender norms (e.g., when deeply intoxicated) (Wojcicki, 2002); for being successful, or for imagining she could be superior. Streamlining is sometimes an act of male bonding, a "favor" to the boyfriends' friends. (Niehaus, 2005; Wood, 2005)

That close to 80 percent of the men who abused the women we interviewed were reported as believing in the ideology of familial and/or societal patriarchy may also partially explain why so many perpetrators had peers who were sexist or abusive. Below is one major example of how male peers supported a respondent's husband's "right" to maintain his patriarchal control with abuse: This incident happened shortly after her husband found out that she wanted to leave him:

I remember my husband making me have sex with him one time when people were in the next room and none of them guys would come in and help me. And they knew he was hitting me, but they figured that he was my husband. If it were a stranger it would have been different.

Did male peers teach interviewees' partners to commit separation/divorce sexual assault, or did abusive men simply seek the friendship and support of violent peers? These are important empirical questions. Hopefully, future research on rural separation/divorce sexual assault will be specifically designed to do so. Furthermore, like data generated by some other studies of rural women's abusive experiences (e.g., Logan, Stevenson, Evans, and Leukefeld, 2004), our findings are based solely on women's perceptions. Whether separation and divorce sexual assault studies are conducted in rural or urban settings, we need data from men to more precisely determine what motivates them to be abusive (DeKeseredy and Schwartz, 2009; Jewkes et al., 2006). Undoubtedly, we glean rich information by interviewing the people who know these men best—the women who share or have shared their lives, who can speak extensively, for example, on men's behavior or the determinants of men's behavior. Nevertheless, such knowledge does not preclude the need for direct research on men. As Diana Scully (1990) reminds us, there are problems in depending completely on female partners to report on male sexual abusers because "they do not share the reality of sexually violent men. Such insight is acquired through invading and critically examining the social constructions of men who rape" (p. 4).

Separation/Divorce Woman Abuse in Public Housing[11]

The social and economic exclusion model of separation/divorce woman abuse in public housing (see figure 4.4) is not specifically a male peer support theory, but is partially informed by some of our work on pro-abuse all-male subcultures. Recollect from reading chapter 4 we hypothesized that separated/divorced female public housing residents are more likely to be hurt by intimate violence than their married counterparts. Again, we used the Quality of Neighborhood Life Survey (QNLS) to test it. The sites selected for this study were six public housing estates in the west end of a large eastern Ontario city. One person eighteen or older in each unit was asked to complete the QNLS questionnaire. Questionnaires were mailed out and also distributed by members of the public housing community, such as coordinators of community centers, yielding 325 useable questionnaires, of which 71 percent were filled out by women.[12]

Brownridge's (2009) review of the separation/divorce assault literature shows that separated women are thirty times more likely and divorced women nine times more likely to report violence than married women. Hence, it is not surprising that the QNLS found that separated or divorced women report higher rates (23 percent) of violence than those in marital relationships (12 percent). In a static survey such as this one, it is unclear whether these women were reporting having exited abusive relationships or whether the reported violence occurred after separation/divorce, although most researchers who have looked at large differences such as those found in this study have concluded that physical assault during separation/divorce is a serious problem. While the differences between these two groups are not statistically significant, the large differences challenge the popular belief that the most important weapon women have in the battle to end their partners' abuse is divorce or separation (DeKeseredy, 2010a; Schwartz, 1988b). One other piece of evidence to support that notion deals with welfare. When looking just at marital status, about 50 percent of all female QNLS respondents are on welfare, and both married women and estranged women had the same 50 percent level of state support. However, estranged women who reported violent victimization had a higher level of being on state support. Since the numbers are small and the percentage of all women on welfare is high, any conclusion must be tentative, but it is possible that separated/divorced women may have sought welfare and safety in public housing as a means of seeking autonomy from abusive or addictive men (Brandwien, 1999; DeKeseredy et al., 2008; Raphael, 1999; Young, 1999).

QNLS data help develop a better understanding of variations in public housing woman abuse. The data also confirm that, regardless of where they live and their economic status, separated/divorced women are at high risk of being abused. Nonetheless, several methodological improvements are necessary in future research. The most important is to isolate whether the abuse occurred before the separation, or was even a reason for the separation, or if alternatively, the abuse occurred again after separation or for the first time after separation. In general, we know that women who leave violent relationships are more likely to seek less violent relationships in the future (Carbone-Lopez, Rennison, and Macmillan, 2012), but we don't have good estimates of how many of them are abused by former intimates after separation. Of course, the best way to obtain richer information on the factors that motivate men to abuse their ex-partners is to survey or interview males in public housing communities. At the time of writing this chapter, a review of the North American public housing woman abuse literature reveals that there have been no self-report surveys administered to men, which is another major research gap that should be filled.

Male Peer Support, Fathers' Rights, and Assaults on VAWA

We live in an era characterized by a rabid antifeminist backlash. Even the best newspapers in the country are quick to take up victim blame. For just one example, in March, 2011 the *New York Times* published the story (McKinley, 2011) of an East Texas community rocked by the gang rape over months of an eleven-year-old girl that eventually resulted in twenty arrests of young men ranging in age up to twenty-seven. An effective police response gathered DNA, confessions, and a cell phone video tape of one gang rape in progress, which soon began leading to a series of convictions and long prison sentences. But the article talked about the pain to the town and the problems the young men will face in the future, and printed a series of rumors that the eleven-year-old girl had "drawn" the men into the repeated rapes by wearing makeup and acting like she was older. While the town was indeed filled with pain and remorse, other newspapers reported that by September 2012 there were still people willing to go on the record, by name, to blame the victim, or to claim that the very serious way the schools, police, prosecutors, and courts were handling the case was just the result of racism: "It's not as bad as they are saying," one named neighbor said. "Nobody tied (the girl) up" (Stebner, 2012). Meanwhile, the town has come together to try to prevent future events. The Unity Committee of Cleveland, Texas, cites as an example of this new spirit the fact that one church sponsored a conference to teach girls to respect themselves. While several churches have held prayer services for the victim, nothing has been reported from the town about teaching their men and boys not to rape eleven-year-old girls.

One easy new method of measuring the level of the backlash is to look at pretty much any newspaper story in North America on a vicious rape or other crime against women that is published in an online forum that allows for reader comments. Almost immediately anywhere responses start appearing. Sometimes dozens or even hundreds of men (and some women) will post, trying to move the blame over to the victim. Certainly there will be loud and fully appropriate protests from other posters, but any story about any victimization of a woman will probably get at least some postings about how the crime was exaggerated, not really all that bad, or the woman's fault.

Perhaps the biggest news story about the backlash recently has been the groundswell of opposition mobilized by the Republican Party and other organizations fervently resisting the Violence Against Women Act (VAWA) (Dragiewicz, 2011). VAWA was passed by the U.S. Congress in 1994, and termed by the late Senator Paul Wellstone and his wife, Sheila Wellstone (2011) "the most comprehensive anti-violence legislation to date" (p. xi). Congress reauthorized VAWA in 2000 and in 2005, but not without a partisan battle. VAWA created new penalties for gender-related violence and new grant programs to motivate states to address physical violence against women and sexual assault, including:

- law enforcement and prosecution (STOP grants)
- grants to encourage arrest

- rural domestic violence and child abuse enforcement grants
- the National Domestic Violence Hotline
- grants to battered women's shelters (Family Violence Prevention Fund, 2007, p. 1)

Ironically, crime discussion in the United States for at least two decades has been dominated by what is often termed the Crime Control Model, which has resulted in a massive increase in prison populations, usually justified in terms of protecting victims. At the same time, similar calls have resulted in some increase in various victims' rights. Yet, a strong market remains for belittling crime victims when they are women (DeKeseredy, 2011a; Schwartz and DeKeseredy, 1994). In relation to VAWA, in April, 2012, the U.S. Senate created legislation that would not only reauthorize the basic bill but also include protection for Native Americans; undocumented immigrants; and gay, lesbian, and transgender victims on top of people already protected under VAWA. The U.S. House version of the bill, though, eliminated those expansions due to Republican resistance heavily fueled by conservative fathers' rights groups. Many Americans agree with Rep. Judy Chu, who argued, "Let's call this bill what it really is. It's not the Violence Against Women Act, but the Open Season for Violence Against Women Act" (cited in Madison, 2012, p. 1). As of September 2012, the two versions of the bill had not been reconciled to allow reauthorization of the Act.

There are many other examples of the anti-feminist backlash. Molly Dragiewicz, who specializes in this area, finds a prime example in fathers' rights (FR) groups' anti-VAWA activism. She used qualitative textual analysis to examine a targeted sample of FR websites that commented on VAWA (Dragiewicz, 2008). Based on her in-depth ethnographic analysis, she concludes that:

The use of FR Web sites as places for like-minded men to seek out and receive peer support for violence-supportive attitudes is a serious concern for those interested in decreasing domestic violence, especially when we recognize their similarity to batterer accounts. The compatibility of FR commentary on VAWA with patriarchal peer support for violence should not go unnoticed. (p. 137)

Dragiewicz's study is not only a new direction in male peer support research, but it also motivated us and others (e.g., DeKeseredy, in press) to examine the relationship between new computer technologies, male peer support, and woman abuse. This will be covered in detail in chapter 6. As Vargas Martin, Garcia-Ruiz and Edwards (2011) correctly observe, "Technology is occupying an increasingly important role in everybody's life, regardless of ethnicity, social status, gender, preferences, nationality, and even technology literacy or Internet connectivity" (p. xxxi). Unfortunately, there is also a "dark side" of the Internet (DeKeseredy and Olsson, 2011) that causes considerable harm to thousands of women and children.

New Directions in Empirical and Theoretical Work[13]

Our concept of male peer support has been applied in other types of work. For example, Basile Espelage, Rivers, McMahon, and Simon (2009) developed a detailed analysis of the research literature on the relationship between bullying behavior and male sexual violence perpetration. They integrated male peer support theory into their explanation of this relationship, suggesting that male bullies learn to accept such violent behavior, up to and including sexual violence, from messages learned from their male peers in social group relationships.

Another use of male peer support theory was made by Franklin (2005), who tried to expand the theory out beyond sexual victimization to the oppression generally of women on police forces. Franklin suggests that there is a direct link between the hypermasculine social structure of modern American policing, and the problems that female police officers face in everyday experiences on the force. She sees policing as a gendered system that specifically acts in ways that build up and support an environment that is hostile to female participation, and pushes back to any female resistance to this opposition. Franklin uses the male peer support model to explain the various findings in the literature, but specifically to explain the development and maintenance of a police subculture that opposes women on the force.

Rosen, Kaminski, Parmley, Knudson, and Fancher (2003) also made use of the male peer support model as part of their attempt to explain intimate partner abuse in the U.S. Army, using it to discuss the development of a culture of hypermasculinity in Army units that mirrors the development of similar organizations such as fraternities or sports teams explained in MPS Theory (Schwartz and DeKeseredy, 1997). Earlier, Rosen and Martin (1998) used the theory as part of a similar explanation for explaining sexual harassment of female soldiers in the U.S. Army.

More recently, R. Klein (2012) used many of the findings of male peer support theory research to support her arguments on the importance of informal networks in either supporting women who are victimized or else in building and maintaining support for the opposite: the cultural values that rehearse and marshal support for the victimization of women who object to an inferior status.

We cannot exhaustively cover all uses of MPS Theory, but there have been a number of others, such as the explanation of "girlfriend abuse" committed by marginalized male youths (Totten, 2000). As mentioned earlier, Sinclair (2002) specifically tested male peer support theory on a group of institutionalized delinquent youth and found that it was an excellent fit to describe the development of their antifemale attitudes and behaviors. Where do we go from here? One answer to this question is that research on how male peer support dynamics function in public places and contribute to gender, racial, and homophobic harassment in these areas is sorely needed. Certainly, public places in many communities, regardless of their socioeconomic makeup, are "male spaces" (Miller, 2008; Renzetti, 2011). This is explained by Andrea DeKeseredy (Walter's daughter) in box 5.1. She describes an event that occurred in broad daylight in a high-income neighborhood.

Although there still are some who think that what occurred in box 5.1 is "ghetto specific" behavior (Wilson, 1996) found mainly in poor neighborhoods, the truth is that it happens throughout North America and in many other countries also. While Martin Schwartz was living in Europe similar situations happened to women he knew in urban England and Germany, and rural Spain. Such discomfiting sexual remarks reaffirm women's vulnerability in public places, and are constant reminders of "the relevance of their gender" (Gardner, 1995, p. 9). Contrary to the belief of many, public space is not "democratic," but clearly gendered: women's social behavior in public places is closely regulated (Renzetti, 2011). The harassment that Andrea endured is one mechanism of social control that perpetuates and maintains male dominance and patriarchal oppression (DeKeseredy et al., 2003; Koss, Goodman, Browne, and Fitzgerald, 1994; Lenton, Smith, Fox, and Morra, 1999; Sever, 1999). Such behavior is learned, exhibited by men, and mainly done by men in groups. It seems obvious that such behavior is subject to the approval of the entire group, and that men who engage in it achieve some sort of approval or benefit from it. Certainly, a study of such behavior from the male peer support point of view would seem to be beneficial.

An area that is beginning to gain more social scientific attention is male violence against women committed by groups of men in the military. There is already a large literature on genocidal sexual violence in countries such as Rwanda and Bosnia-Herzegovina (Kuehnast, de Jonge Oudraat, and Hernes, 2011). But, as Wood (2011) observes in her review of the theoretical literature on sexual violence and armed conflict, much of this literature simply suggests

5.1 Hurtful Comments from Ignorant Men

On a recent Saturday I stepped out of my house to meet a neighbor for coffee.

I saw a car honking its horn as it pulled around the corner from another area of houses.

Passengers in the car rolled down its windows and stopped in front of me.

I could see that there were four men in the car. They started screaming offensive sexual comments about my breasts as I tried to make my way to my neighbor's home.

When I ignored the men they then started insulting me and screaming things at me.

One man yelled: "The only good thing about you is the size of your boobs, nothing else."

The car finally drove away as the men kept calling me offensive names.

I always seem to be able to refrain from rolling down my window and screaming at men when I am driving; why couldn't they?

In a suburban town that is supposed to be a far cry from city crime, why is it that I get yelled at more walking down Rossland Road than I do walking down Bloor Street in Toronto?

Women organize marches and protests in order to "take back the night" but now we also have to take back the day.

As I walk into my surgeon's office to have breast reduction surgery done this summer, in the back of my mind I will always wonder if I truly did it for me or if deep down I did it so that all of those disgusting men would finally leave me alone.

Source: A. DeKeseredy (2012). Used by permission.

that rape is a warfare tactic, or that groups in combat find rape to be an effective weapon to use against civilian populations. However, these explanations do not account for the fact that some armies might use sexual violence extensively, while others engaged in similar warfare might not engage in sexual violence at all. Wood asks, "What might account for the observed variation in wartime sexual violence? Various potential explanations occur in the literature, at times implicitly. I argue that they are best incomplete" (2011, p. 43). This is an area where male peer support theory would be helpful. It is well documented that gang rape frequently occurs during war (Leatherman, 2011), but as Wood points out, it is also frequently absent. Our suggestion is that new empirical and theoretical work on violence against women during war could fruitfully borrow from male peer support theory because male bonding is an integral part of combatant socialization (Wood, 2011).

We know that patriarchal male peer support practices and discourses exist in a wide variety of places. However, the questions we asked fifteen years ago still remain unanswered (DeKeseredy and Schwartz, 1998b). Are white men more or less likely than African American, Native American, or Hispanic males to join and be influenced by sexist all-male collectives? Are working-class and unemployed men more or less likely than privileged male undergraduate students to receive pro-abuse male peer support? Another thing we don't know is the extent to which peer influence is related to violence within interracial couples. This, though, is not surprising, because male-to-female violence in intimate heterosexual interracial relationships of all sorts is an understudied topic (Renzetti, 2011).

Elliott Currie (2009) correctly states that "The burden of violent crime . . . is not shared equally around the globe. It is heavily concentrated in some societies, and some places and people within those societies" (p. 4). It is only logical to assume, then, that male peer support is more likely to be stronger in some societies, and some places and people within those societies. Even so, there is no conclusive evidence to support this hypothesis. Hence, male peer support studies need to move in yet another new direction: comparative research. This method produces knowledge about social problems by making qualitative and quantitative comparisons across different countries or cultures (Kraska and Neuman, 2008).

Life course theories and research are popular among mainstream criminological circles (e.g., Laub and Sampson, 2003; Sampson and Laub, 1993). Following Glen Elder (1994), the life course is defined here as "the interweave of age-graded trajectories, such as work careers and family pathways, that are subject to changing conditions and future options, and to short-term transitions ranging from leaving school to retirement" (p. 5). The life course perspective has not penetrated the realm of male peer support empirical and theoretical work, but applying it to this field of study allows for a richer understanding of joining sexist all-male networks, maintaining a membership in these peer groups, and the termination of membership across the lifespan (LeBlanc and Loeber, 1998; Piquero and Mazerolle, 2001). More specifically, by taking a life course or longitudinal approach, researchers may be able to provide answers to the following questions:

- At what age are most boys or young men most likely to join all-male pro-abuse networks?
- Do some members of a particular patriarchal male peer support group move on to join another group with similar values, beliefs, and practices?
- Do some all-male group members simply mature out of them as they get older and become employed?
- Are current or former members of sexist peer groups who get married or end up in cohabiting relationships more or less likely to be physically, sexually, and psychologically abusive?
- Do some men who join male peer groups eventually quit and then join again? (DeKeseredy and Schwartz, 1998b)

Another refreshing alternative to the cross-sectional survey research that dominates male peer support research is participant observation. In fact, two of the male peer support models we developed (DeKeseredy, 1988a; DeKeseredy and Schwartz, 1993) were heavily informed by observational studies of patriarchal pub dynamics (Hey, 1986; Whitehead, 1976), combative sports teams (K. Young, 1988), and fraternities (Sanday, 1990). More recently, Phillipe Bourgois's (1995) riveting *In Search of Respect: Selling Crack in El Barrio* continues to have a major impact on our theoretical work. His ethnographic project arose out of the tradition of critical anthropology and is still timely (Young, 2011), given that it focuses on the destructive impact of major economic transitions in North America that are still taking place at the start of this new millennium, including alarmingly high levels of unemployment plaguing metropolitan neighborhoods.

In Search of Respect also continues to assist social scientists in their attempts to develop a rich theoretical understanding of how structural determinants, such as transnational corporations moving operations to developing countries, help create criminal youth subcultures and patriarchal gangs in disenfranchised inner-city communities. In addition to being theoretically important, Bourgois's study involved spending years in East Harlem (also referred to as El Barrio) observing, tape recording, and photographing various components of the lives of roughly twenty-four Puerto Rican crack dealers.

Until recently, most empirical and theoretical work on urban gangs paid little, if any, attention to the role of gender (Miller, 2001). This cannot be said about Bourgois's contribution. Consistent with some of our own theoretical work (see DeKeseredy and Schwartz, 2002), Bourgois draws from a feminist interpretation of gender relations to explain how postindustrial factors influenced violent patriarchal practices and discourses in his research site. For example, as is the case in El Barrio and other ghettos, poor women are not simply passive victims of sexist domination and control. Rather, a growing number of them are creating autonomy for themselves and their "sisters" by participating in the paid labor force, dealing drugs, and by other means. For Bourgois, these behaviors and other examples of what he labels as "inverting patriarchy," challenge men's hegemony at home and on the streets, which in turn, motivates them to abuse women who resist domination. Moreover, they are influenced to do so by their peers.

Like the college-based hyper-erotic male subcultures identified by Kanin, Bourgois's work on gang-related woman abuse points to the fact that many inner-city all-male subcultures produce high or exaggerated levels of sexual aspiration. Some women end up being raped, and sexual relations have more to do with the gang members' need to compensate for their lack of money and their need to sustain their status among their peers than a need to satisfy their sexual urges. As well, like college-based male peer support groups, Bourgois found that the drug-dealing gang members who participated in his study provided their peers with a vocabulary that defines women as legitimate targets of abuse. Consider Primo, a young man who dealt crack in East Harlem. He told Bourgois that some of the women that he and his friends gang-raped enjoyed being targets of sexual violence and were "worthy victims." In the words of Primo, "You gotta understand Felipe, even they say no, they're loving it" (p. 210).

Ethnographic work such as Bourgois's takes us, as Young (2011) observes, into a "totally different world" from that of positivism. Undoubtedly, mainstream quantitative studies would be hard pressed to uncover information about inner-city gang rapes such as that described below by Bourgois:

> The gang rapes . . . were not the isolated brutal excesses of a fringe group of
> pathological sadists. On the contrary, they provide an insider's perspective on the
> misogyny of street culture and the violence of everyday life. A biting reminder of
> the pervasiveness of sexual violence in El Barrio was the comment made to my
> wife and me by my eleven-year-old neighbor, Angel, in the course of an otherwise
> innocuous, random conversation about how he was doing in school, and about how
> his mother's pregnancy was progressing. He told us he hoped his mother would
> give birth to a boy "because girls are too easy to rape." (p. 213)

Readers should not get the impression that we "have seen the light" and are now calling for abandoning quantitative research. However, following Claire Renzetti (1997), we have become "reformed positivists" and now embrace multiple ways of knowing. We are not wedded to any particular method, and the techniques suggested here constitute just the tip of the iceberg. Indeed, there are many more, such as archival research and observing male peer group dynamics in small-group laboratories. Regardless of which piece of the male peer support puzzle a researcher wants to study, however, ideally he or she should strive for "data triangulation" (Denzin, 1978). As Denzin and Lincoln (2005) put it, "The combination of multiple methodological practices, empirical materials, perspectives, and observers in a single study is best understood, then, as a strategy that adds rigor, breadth, complexity, richness, and depth to any inquiry" (p. 5). Like a civil engineer, using a variety of "sightings" for different angles makes it more likely that we will correctly survey the "dark side" of male peer relations (Fielding and Fielding, 1986).

Of course, it isn't only new empirical work that is needed. Theory development is also essential. What is especially needed is a male peer support perspective that emphasizes the role of race and ethnicity. Thus far, this important factor has received short shrift. And the world of adolescent males warrants more attention because peers play an integral role in the lives of these boys and many of them are at very high risk of abusing girls (Crooks et al., 2011; Klein, 2012). Perhaps, too, male peer support theory can help explain male intimate violence against older women. Roughly seventy thousand women aged fifty-five to sixty-four experience this problem each year in the United States (Basile and Black, 2011), and it is likely that many of the perpetrators receive support from their friends. Still, a study specifically designed to discern whether peer influence is a major determinant is required before attempting to chart such new theoretical terrain.

Other topics could easily be added to the list of new theoretical directions, such as gay bashing, white supremacy groups, and the "bully society" in which we live (Klein, 2012). The current condition of North American social scientific theorizing, however, is troubling because it is being undermined not only by positivism, but also by governments and university administrators intent on corporatizing institutions of higher learning (DeKeseredy, 2012a). Sadly, "academic criminology appears to becoming more marginalized and irrelevant" (Matthews, 2009, p. 341). Nonetheless, more progressive ways of thinking about social problems such as male peer support persist and scholars throughout the continent should join hands and resist ongoing efforts to turn them into "cheerful robots" (Mills, 1959). As Jock Young (2011) reminds progressive scholars:

Let us set about our task, keeping in mind the urgency of opposition, yet with an eye for irony imbued, as always, with a sense of satire at the strange meanderings of the datasaur[14] and the sad charade of science played out before us. Above all we must constantly be aware of the inherent creativity of human culture and of the rush of emotions and feelings that characterizes the human condition and the capacity for imagination that this demands and engenders. (p. 225)

Summary

Dragiewicz (2011) concluded in her brief review of the scholarly evidence of patriarchal support for violence against women that "Studies have documented the influence of patriarchal peer support for men's violence against women at the mesosystem[15] level in a variety of contexts, including studies of battered wives, dating violence, batterer narratives, campus sexual assault, separation assault, and woman abuse in representative random samples" (p. 113). Unfortunately, male peer support for woman abuse seems to be is ubiquitous and definitely has a long history. The data gathered to date tell us much, but there are still many unanswered questions and new avenues to explore. Chief among the problems in the state of male peer support theory and research is the question of how male peer support groups form or come together.

Special attention was devoted in this chapter to using multiple methods and to the importance of employing the sociological imagination. Fortunately, work in the area of male peer support has avoided falling into the trap of abstracted empiricism and continues to prioritize a gendered analysis of rape, beatings, coercive control, and the like.

6 | New Electronic Technologies and Male Peer Support

> With every technological innovation comes the potential for misuse. The law,
> however, is not particularly well-suited to the kind of quick change required to
> adapt to new technologies.
> —*Leigh Goodmark, "State, National, and International Legal Initiatives to
> Address Violence against Women"*

Count yourself very fortunate or lucky if you are reading this chapter without being periodically interrupted by electronic mail, cellular phone text messages, and/or phone calls. To be sure, we would have completed this book much sooner if it we did not have to respond to a plethora of e-mail messages every day. This is not to say, though, that new electronic technologies do not have many advantages. For example, we often use Skype to visually and verbally communicate for free with friends and relatives in other countries, states, and provinces. Like millions of people around the world, we also have quick access to information on the Internet, and we can watch movies and listen to music online. Certainly, we strongly support Adeniran's (2011) argument that "The advent of Internet technology has significantly improved the state of human existence" (p. 3). [Still, new technologies have many destructive features that harm women and children.] For instance, there has been a major increase in the number of child pornography sites. In 2006, there were nearly 100,000 such sites and now there are at least 500,000, with new ones emerging every day (Ibrahim, 2011; Law, Chow, Lai, Tse, and Tse, 2011). As well, the U.S. Center for Missing and Exploited Children receives roughly fifteen leads each day about sexual predators who troll the Internet looking for vulnerable children to have sex with. Referred to by the Federal Bureau of Investigation (FBI), as *travelers*, at least one of these offenders is arrested every day in the United States (Young, 2011). Actually, arrests for child pornography production in the United

States more than doubled from 402 in 2000–2001 to 859 in 2006 (Wolak et al., 2011).

The producers of child pornography generate much public outrage and very punitive criminal justice system responses. Societal reactions, though, are nowhere near as harsh when it comes to the "pornification" of women once they turn eighteen years of age (Nikunen, Paasonen, and Saarenmaa, 2007). In fact, Hutton and Trauntner (2011) show that media imagery in mainstream popular culture has become more sexualized for both men and women, although for women, their study showed, it was increasingly likely that such images would be "hypersexualized," along with a narrowing of the culturally acceptable ways for women to "do" femininity in mainstream popular culture. Meanwhile, thousands of legal cyberporn sites "childify" adult women, and typing "teen porn" into Google generates over nine million hits, giving users a choice of thousands of sites (Dines, 2010). Additionally, there are thousands of sites explicitly featuring women being degraded and abused in ways that few people can imagine. Actually, a routine feature of new pornographic videos is painful anal penetration, as well as men slapping or choking women and/or pulling their hair while they penetrate them orally, vaginally, and anally (Bridges et al., 2010; Dines and Jenson, 2008).

While it is beyond the scope of this chapter to graphically describe what appears on contemporary adult pornographic Internet sites, what men and boys watch (often in groups) online are not simply "dirty pictures that have little impact on anyone." Rather the images typically endorse "women as second-class citizens" and "require that women be seen as second-class citizens" (Funk, 2006, p. 165). On top of becoming increasingly more violent and normalized, Internet pornography often involves gang rapes and stereotypical racist images of "the sexually primitive black male stud," "submissive Far East nymphos," and "hot blooded Latinas" (Dines, 2010; Jensen, 2007).

Challenging the assertion that "pornography is just fantasy" are quantitative and qualitative data showing that degrading sexual images featured on the Internet and elsewhere are strongly associated with various types of violence against women. And a growing literature reveals a relationship between pornography, male peer support, and violence against women (DeKeseredy and Olsson, 2011). The main objective of this chapter is to examine this linkage and to suggest new directions in empirical work on the association between these three major social problems. Some attention, too, will be devoted to other new technologies that harm women, such as "sexting." As Klein (2012) observes, "It was bad enough when students were harassed on Facebook pages, but now they are tormented by text messages sometimes nonstop . . . in which sexual photos of them are widely distributed to embarrass and humiliate them and ruin their reputations" (p. 6).

Definition of Pornography

The term *pornography* translates from Greek to mean "writing about prostitutes" (Katz, 2006, p. 188). Pornography has certainly changed since the creation of the Internet. Today, we live in a "post-*Playboy* world" (Jensen, 2007), where defining pornography is still subject to much debate. Here, though, we are not talking about all sexually explicit media, much of which is erotica. Such material depicts sexual relations with mutuality and respect (Bridges and Jensen, 2011; Russell, 1993). Following Gail Dines (2010), pornography, on the other hand, is "gonzo"—that genre which is all over the Internet and is today one of the biggest moneymakers for the industry—which depicts hard-core, body-punishing sex in which women are demeaned and debased" (p. xi).

Pornography is "the quietest big business in the world" (Slayden, 2010), and pornographers are pioneers of new electronic technologies (Jenkins, 2007). In fact, pornographers are closely associated with the development and success of video streaming, "tweeting," DVDs, 3G mobile phones, and broadband (Barss, 2010; Maddison, 2004). Moreover, many people watch sexual images at home by themselves and this market started to drive the home entertainment industry (Jordan, 2006). It is impossible to answer just how far technology would have gone without pornography, but it is certain that many advances, including the availability of video in the home rather than theaters, were driven and sped up by the pornography industry. In other words, pornography drives technology and "sex has shaped the Internet as it currently exists" (Slayden, 2010, p. 58).

There are over four million pornography sites on the Internet (Dines, 2010), with as many as ten thousand added every week (DeKeseredy and Olsson, 2011; Funk, 2006). All of this is extremely lucrative. Estimated worldwide, pornography revenues from a variety of sources (e.g., Internet, sex shops, videos rented in hotel rooms, etc.) recently topped US$97 billion. This is more than the combined revenues of Microsoft, Google, Amazon, eBay, Yahoo, Apple, Netflix, and Earthlink (Zerbisias, 2008). More recent evidence of the growth of pornography is the emergence of "tubes," such as YouPorn, XTube, and PornoTube, all modeled after the widely used and popular YouTube. YouPorn had 15 million users after launching in 2006 and was growing at a monthly rate of 37.5 percent (Mowlabocus, 2010; Slayden, 2010).

Pornography is a widespread problem that will only get worse due to easy access offered by the Internet. For instance, a national U.S. study of undergraduate and graduate students ages eighteen to twenty-six uncovered that 69 percent of the male and 10 percent of the female participants view pornography at least once a month (Carroll et al., 2008). For whatever it is worth, and it is hardly a reliable statistic, it is still troubling to note that at least fifty out of sixty-five students in Walter DeKeseredy's 2009 Violence against Women class estimated that between 75 and 80 percent of male students enrolled at his university view Internet pornography. Slayden (2010) also provides the following claims:

- Every second, 28,258 Internet users view pornography.
- Every second, $89.00 is spent on "cyberporn."
- *Sex* is the most searched word on the Internet.
- Every day, 266 new pornography sites appear on the Internet.
- 35 percent of all Internet downloads are pornographic in nature (Slayden, 2010, p. 54).

Of course the exact accuracy of such claims is hard to ascertain, and they are sometimes contradictory. However, whether or not researchers ever obtain an absolutely accurate estimate of the percentage of males who consume adult cyberporn, most leading experts in the field agree with Robert Jensen's contention that "It's become almost as common as comic books were for you and me" (cited in Gillespie, 2008, p. A3). In fact, studies have shown that almost all boys in Northern Europe have at some point in their lives been exposed to pornography and 42 percent of Internet users ages ten to seventeen in the United States had viewed cyberporn (Hammaren and Johansson, 2007; Mossige, Ainsaar, and Svedin, 2007; Wolak, Mitchell, and Finkelhor, 2007). One study conducted in Alberta, Canada, found that one in three boys aged thirteen to fourteen had accessed sexually explicit media content on digital or satellite television, video and DVD, and the Internet. More than one-third of the boys reported viewing pornography "too many times to count" and a sizeable minority of the boys in the sample planned social time around viewing porn with their male friends (Betowski, 2007). These are not innocent users who accidentally come across sexually explicit images, voices, and texts. Nor are they constantly bombarded with such material. Rather, they make a conscious effort to locate and choose to consume and distribute pornography, and unfortunately, some of the consumers will commit criminal acts, including violently attacking intimate female partners (DeKeseredy and Schwartz, 2009).

Pornography, again, is a lucrative business, but it is a brutal one for women, and they do not last long in the industry (Bridges and Jensen, 2011). The average employment period for actors only ranges from six months to three years and they often end their careers without money saved in the bank (Calvert and Richards, 2006). It is also common for female actors to be humiliated, degraded, and abused in the process of making cyberporn and other types of pornography. For example, this is what Gail Dines (2010) read in an ad for the site Gag Me Then Fuck Me:

> "Do you know what we say to things like romance and foreplay? We say fuck off! This is not another site with half-erect weenies trying to impress bold sluts. We take gorgeous young bitches and do what every man would REALLY like to do. We make them gag till their makeup starts running, and then they get all other holes sore— vaginal, anal, double penetrations, anything brutal involving a cock and an orifice. And then we give them the sticky bath!" (p. xix)

Pornography hurts other women (Funk, 2006), including the thousands who are romantically involved with men who use it or who have left such men. For reasons provided in the section below, we couldn't agree more with Bergen and Bogle's (2000) claim that "pornography is a training manual for abuse" (p. 231). To make matters worse, boys see their first pornography site on average at eleven years of age (Dines, 2010) and an unknown but large number of them will go on to become graduates of what Lundy Bancroft (2002) refers to as "the Pornography School of Sexuality" (p. 185). Romito and Beltramini (2011) are correct in stating, "Childhood and adolescence are key periods in relation to pornography exposure" (p.1).

Pornography and Woman Abuse

Men's consumption of pornography hurts their intimate female partners on numerous levels. Many women report feeling betrayed, having lowered self-esteem, or anger from being pressured to imitate what their male partners see online, and they also suffer a range of other negative effects that aren't the result of physical force (Bridges and Jensen, 2011; Schneider, 2000). Male pornography consumption, however, is also a powerful determinant of physical and sexual violence against current and former female partners, and it is positively associated with attitudes supporting violence against women (Hald, Malamuth, and Yuen, 2010). Evidence supporting these conclusions has improved considerably over the past thirty years. For example, prior to the early 1990s, there was limited information on the extent to which graphic sexual imagery influences men's violent behavior outside artificial laboratory settings (DeKeseredy and Olsson, 2011).[1] This led critics to claim that there is little to support any connections with "real-world" behavior (Berger, Searles, and Cottle, 1991; Brannigan and Goldenberg, 1987; Schwartz and DeKeseredy, 1998). Martin Schwartz (1987), for example, published a review that argued that there was more evidence that graphic violence was the behavior being imitated than that graphic sexual images caused violence. However, as we and others have continued to study the issue, evidence has continued to amass.

Jensen (1995, 1996), for example, has used personal histories and narrative accounts of men who used pornography. Other researchers have conducted surveys of women to determine how male consumption of pornography affected them. Consider that of the 1,835 women who participated in the Canadian national survey of woman abuse in university/college dating (CNS), 1,638 both engaged in dating and also answered a quantitative question about pornography. Of these women, 8.4 percent stated that they were upset by their dating partners trying to get them to do what they had seen in pornographic media (DeKeseredy and Schwartz, 1998a). This is comparable to the 10 percent figure that Russell (1990) uncovered from asking a random sample of 930 women in the San Francisco area a similar question.

What is more salient is that the CNS found a significant relationship between being upset by men's attempt to imitate pornographic scenes and sexual victimization. Of those who were sexually abused, 22.3 percent had also been upset by attempts to get them to imitate pornographic scenarios. Only 5.8 percent of the women who were not victimized reported not being upset by pornography. The relationship also holds for physical violence of the female CNS respondents who reported being physically abused in a dating relationship; 15.4 percent also reported being upset by pornography. Only 4.5 percent of those who were not physically victimized reported being upset. The CNS data presented here, then, help us to tentatively conclude that pornography played a role in the sexual and physical abuse of Canadian women in college and university dating relationships. These statistics resemble the pornography-related abuse reported in surveys of married and formerly married women (Bergen, 1996; Bergen and Bogle, 2000; Harmen and Check, 1989).

More recently, our qualitative study of separation/divorce sexual assault in rural Ohio also found that male pornography consumption contributed to woman abuse. Of the male estranged partners of the forty-three women we interviewed, 65 percent used pornography, and 30 percent of the women stated that pornography was involved in sexually abusive events they experienced. Still, since watching or reading pornography is often a private or secret event, it is possible that other women in our sample who stated that their ex-partners did not view pornography were unaware of these men's use of pornography. The same can be said about women who participated in other studies, such as the cns (Bergen and Bogle, 2000), if the men did not specifically link the abuse to pornographic imagery.

In the most recent test that affirmed the relationship between pornography and sexual assault, Franklin, Bouffard and Pratt (2012) conducted an investigation of male peer support theory at one Northwestern university. First they found, among many other things, that viewing pornography was positively and statistically significantly associated with membership in social fraternities. In other words, men who belonged to Greek letter fraternities self-reported that they viewed more pornography than other men on campus. More importantly, the investigators included a measure of self-reported sexual assault against women, presumably intimate and dating partners. Here, in a measure that included a broader array of illegal aggressive sexual acts, up to and including forcible rape, men who admitted to watching larger amounts of pornography also admitted to performing more acts of illegal sexual aggression. This relationship was also statistically significant. Thus, at least on one university campus, there was a significant relationship between viewing pornography images (as self-defined), and admitting to committing acts of sexual aggression.

The correlation between pornography and violence against women is not only found in North America. In Italy, for example, one study of high school students uncovered strong associations between sexually harassing or raping peers and pornography consumption (Bonino, Ciairano, Rabaglietti, and Cattelino, 2006). Another Italian survey of high school students broke new ground in discovering the flip side of this: it found that females exposed to psychological violence committed by family members and to sexual violence by any type of perpetrator were significantly more likely to watch pornography, especially violent porn, than females who were not exposed to such abuse (Romito and Beltramini, 2011). The authors don't have the data to explain these findings, but they hypothesize that sexual victimization and watching pornography may be part of the same constellation of troubled youth, along with early sexual activities, parental neglect, and lack of supervision. Finally, the cns data reported above compare well with Itzin and Sweet's (1992) report of the British *Cosmopolitan* Survey, which was administered to over four thousand readers of this women's magazine and was one of the first large-scale sources of information on women's experiences with pornography in the United Kingdom.

Other studies have examined the content of today's most popular pornography. Bridges et al.'s (2010) inquiry was the most recent at the time of writing this chapter. This study of 304 scenes in fifty of the most popular pornographic DVDs argues that pornography has become more violent than before, to the point where some violence is normative. Nearly 90 percent contained physical aggression (mainly spanking, gagging, and slapping) and roughly 50 percent contained verbal aggression, primarily name-calling. Not surprisingly, males constituted most of the perpetrators and the targets were "overwhelmingly female." As well, the female targets often showed pleasure or responded neutrally to male aggression. What makes the data uncovered by Bridges et al. even more alarming is this observation by Brosi, Foubert, Bannon, and Yandell (2011):

> [A]s the pornography industry grows and seeks to satisfy its increasingly large customer base, it has continuously innovated its products and materials in a direction of more extreme, violent, "edgy," material, often featuring underage actors and scenes depicting a wide variety of dehumanizing behaviors not heretofore seen. (p. 27)

Despite a growing body of research, it is still unclear whether pornography of any sort directly causes woman abuse. A long-term and expensive longitudinal design is required to determine whether such a relationship exists (DeKeseredy and Olsson, 2011; Schwartz and DeKeseredy, 1998). Additionally, there are some important competing arguments. For example, for men who physically, psychologically, and sexually abuse women, pornography may well be just one more weapon in their arsenal. Hence, a man who cares that his partner would be scared or angry might not expose her to the lessons he learned from a pornographic video, while his abusive friend might try to force his intimate female partner to act out such scenes over her objections (DeKeseredy and Schwartz, 2009). In a somewhat related argument, the same factors that cause a man to abuse women may well also cause him to watch Internet pornography. In other words, the woman abuse came first, followed by the interest in pornography. In these scenarios, eliminating pornography might not have an effect on the amount of woman abuse, since the men are generally abusive anyway (DeKeseredy and Schwartz, 1998a). Finally, there is the argument that the problem is not the sexually graphic images at all, but the images of violence (Schwartz, 1987). In this scenario, exposure to all forms of violent behavior can be considered dangerous. In the field of graphic sexual images, this argument would not dilute our argument, which has been all along that mutually respectful sexual imagery, termed *erotica*, is not a problem. Rather, it is pornography, or the introduction and integration of violent imagery with sexually graphic scenes that is the problem.

While we might not yet understand the specific dynamics of how it operates, there is ample empirical evidence that violent pornography is a component of woman abuse (Bergen and Bogle, 2000). Perhaps, then, it would be a good idea to follow Robert Jensen's (2007) advice: "Rather than discussing simple causation, we should consider how various factors, in feminist philosopher Marilyn Frye's terms 'make something inviting.' In those terms, pornography does not cause rape but rather helps make rape inviting" (p. 103).

Further, it is still unclear where the majority of viewers of pornography obtain or access these images, and whether some forms of access facilitate male-to-female physical and sexual violence more than other types of access. In other words, are men who view, listen to, or read pornography and who abuse women more likely to seek sexually explicit material online or elsewhere? What Ferguson (1996) stated sixteen years ago is still relevant today: "Pornography (both criminal and non-criminal) does exist in Cyberspace, and can be accessed and downloaded by virtually anyone with the appropriate knowledge regarding how to go about obtaining it. In addition, sexual victimization can and has occurred" (p. 27). One certainty is that children and youth today are much more sophisticated than any earlier generation in accessing computer sites, including those with barriers to entry by youth. Still, until conclusive evidence is generated and corroborated, it is wrong to conclude that male pornography users who abuse women primarily consume Internet pornography. Nevertheless, according to Dines and Jensen (2008),

> While there are few studies on the effects of Internet pornography, past research suggest that this increase in pornography consumption is implicated in greater levels of male physical and sexual violence against women and children. (p. 366)

The Relationship between Pornography, Male Peer Support, and Woman Abuse

While the relationship between pornography and woman abuse is highly complex (Jensen, 2007), a growing body of research indicates that male peer support is a major part of the equation, especially on college campuses. In chapter 5, we discussed Kanin's notion of the "hypererotic" subculture in which members have high expectations of having sex and end up feeling disappointed or angry if women reject their advances. Such a subculture still exists today and is heavily influenced by a combination of the new "hook up culture" and pornography. What Dines (2010) notes below sounds reasonably close to Kanin's theory as described in chapter 5:

> Given the increasing prevalence of hooking up in the culture, especially on college campuses, these men's perceptions that other guys seem to have no problem finding sex is not completely inaccurate. Where they seem to lose touch with reality is in the degree to which they assume this is the norm. In the porn world of neverending sex, every interaction with a woman—be it a student, a doctor, a maid, a teacher, or just a stranger—ends up sexualized. Add to this the stories that men regale each other about their latest conquest, stories that often sound like the porn movie they just watched, and you have constructed a world of constant male access to every woman a man meets. When the real world doesn't play out like this, then disappointment and anger make sense. (p. 89)

Using pornographic videos to strengthen male "misogynist bonds" dates back to the short silent porn films of the 1890s (Slayden, 2010). Men would gather in various all-male settings, such as bachelor parties, to smoke, watch sexually explicit films, and make derogatory remarks about women (Lehman, 2006). Now let's fast forward from the 1890s to the 2005 event described by Robert Jensen in box 6.1 and try to make sense of what has happened to pornographic male bonding rituals in light of the "normalization" thesis advanced by him, Gail Dines (2010), and others (e.g., DeKeseredy, in press).

Far from the "big city," we found that separation/divorce sexual assault was fueled, in part, by male peer support and pornography (DeKeseredy and Schwartz, 2009). For example, some of the survivors we interviewed told us that their partners consumed porn with their male friends while drinking excessive amounts of alcohol. One woman who experienced this problem described this event:

> They were drinking and carrying on and they had, um, they had a bunch of porno stuff in the garage, and I had walked in and I had started to tear it up. And I was, I was, I thought it was gross. I was mad at it. I was mad at him for being around it. And he just started charging after me, and I started running to my car as fast as I could. And he got into the car and he threw me down in the seat and he just kept punching me, punching me.

We are now seeing the rapid development of online communities with members who never come into face-to-face contact with each other but who frequently exchange written, audio, and visual information with their peers. Further, some of the new cyberspace technology enables men to engage in the online victim-

6.1 Las Vegas Adult Entertainment Expo

I am at the Adult Entertainment Expo in Las Vegas in January, 2005. At one of the 300 exhibitor booths on the floor of the Sands Expo Center is Tiffany Holiday, a woman who performs in pornographic movies. She is kissing and touching another female performer, and a crowd of men gathers around. There are rules for how much actual sexual activity can take place on the convention floor, and the two women are pushing the boundary. The crowd encourages them to go further.

The other woman leaves, and Tiffany begins to simulate masturbation, all the while talking dirty to the men gathered around her. The crowd swells to 50 men. I'm stuck in the middle, holding a microphone for a documentary film crew. Emboldened by the size of the crowd, the men's chants for more explicit sex grow louder and more boisterous. Holiday responds in kind, encouraging the men to tell her what they like. The exchange continues, intensifying to the point where the men are moving as a unit—like a mob.

Men's bodies are pressed against each other as each one vies for the best view of the woman's breasts, vagina, and anus. Many of the men are using cameras, camcorders, or cell phones to record the scene. It's difficult not to notice—not to feel—that the men pressed up against me have erections. It's difficult not to conclude that if there weren't security guards on the floor, these men would likely gang-rape Tiffany Holiday.

This is an expression of the dominant masculinity in the United States today. It is the masculinity of a mob, ready to rape.

Source: Jensen (2007, p. 1).

ization of women. This involves men "virtually assaulting," "virtually raping," or "cyber stalking" women who use the Internet or female porn stars (Kendall, 2003; Southworth, Tucker, Fraser, and Shulruff, 2008). There are also "pornhorror" sites, rape sites, and video games such as RapeLay (Jones, 2010), in which players direct a man to rape a mother and her two young daughters at an underground station before raping a selection of other females (Kome, 2009).

As well, pro-abuse and antifeminist cyberspace male peer support groups are emerging (DeKeseredy and Olsson, 2011; Dragiewicz, 2011; Kendall, 2003). And, many men who never have face-to-face contact with each other share pornographic material through the Internet (DeKeseredy in press; Doring, 2009). As Attwood (2010) notes, this is where male porn users

> congregate to discuss the conventions and pleasures of their collections and more besides, amateur writers and readers engage in interactions which are at once mutually arousing and culturally appreciative, while elsewhere the sexual display of the body becomes the focus of commentary and assessment or the prelude to more material kinds of sexual encounters. (p. 242)

Although rarely discussed and studied, online communities that seek out porn that combines sex with violence not only legitimize deviant sexuality (Jones, 2010), but also include some members who commit deadly violent acts. Consider the following case described by Ferguson (1996):

> In late October, 1996, the body of a woman from Hampton, Maryland, was pulled from a shallow grave outside the trailer of her lover in Lenoir, North Carolina. The incident occurred shortly after the victim had traveled to Lenoir to meet her love for the first time following an anonymous E-mail liaison conducted using the pseudonyms "Nancy" and "Slowhand." During this liaison, the two had constructed and participated in several cyber-sexual scenarios involving sado-masochistic practices, torture, and snuff. The victim's lover was charged with murder, but claims that her death was an accident that occurred while the two were living out their sexual fantasies conceived during their E-mail liaison. (p. 17)

Since the late 1990s (see DeKeseredy and Schwartz, 1998b), we have continually argued that the sharing of cyberporn helps create and maintain patriarchal male peer support groups. This sharing reinforces attitudes that reproduce and reconstitute ideologies of male dominance by approvingly depicting women as objects to be conquered and consumed (DeKeseredy and Olsson, 2011). Such sharing also makes it difficult for users to separate sexual fantasy from reality and assists them in their attempts to initiate female victims and break down their resistance to sexual acts (Dines, 2010).

Internet Pornography Is a Reflection of Offline Environments

The organic growth of the Internet, including its hurtful elements, has consequently globalized access to pornographic materials in converged online and offline environments. Cyberporn can be distributed to millions of people around the world in only seconds due to faster means of disseminating digital media productions, as the Internet facilitates access for those seeking pornographic content, whether it is legally recognized or not. What was difficult to obtain and a secretive phenomenon is now easily accessible. It has subsequently become an "economic juggernaut" with operations all around the world (Dines, 2010). Still, before we possibly create moral panics and demand Internet restrictions, we need to understand that online environments are simply reflections of offline environments (DeKeseredy and Olsson, 2011).

The Internet not only facilitates access to previously inaccessible materials, but it has also, to a certain extent, created an environment that normalizes hurtful sexuality. The problem lies in the fact that the users and producers of violent and racist porn are contributing to the normalization of violence and degrading treatment of women to satisfy their economic needs (Jensen, 2007). As well, for the advanced user, the Internet offers anonymity while searching and accessing material. There are many ways to hide one's Internet provider (IP) address by using anonymizing services, VPN clients, and so forth, which complicates any legal intervention in cases of unlawful or criminal behavior.

The normalization and acceptance of hard-core pornography and its consumption among youth and adults also stem from harsher and more competitive broadcasting conditions where actors in the pornography and adult entertainment industry are often acknowledged as celebrities. This recent phenomenon has clearly normalized the previous ill-reputed status of the adult entertainment industry and is affecting emerging adults' perceptions of pornography (Dines, 2010). Certainly, the boundaries have been moved in a direction toward more tolerance of violence and deviant behavior than we have ever experienced before (DeKeseredy and Olsson, 2011; Jones, 2010). Moreover, the current proliferation of pornography in the lives of most people is directly linked to the changing technological context of modern society (Barss, 2010).

Manuel Castells (2001) asserts that technological systems are socially produced and that social production is culturally informed. The Internet and the online environments are in constant change and new socio-technological inventions are frequently the sources for the growth of new enterprises trying to meet the growing demands on the global market. Castells further argues that the Internet culture is a collective construction that transcends individual preferences while influencing the practices of people in the culture. The import of this, when applied to pornography and violence against women, would be our contention that the expansion of the Internet culture is strengthening men's patriarchal beliefs, attitudes, and treatment of women.

There has never been a study specifically designed to examine the linkage between adult Internet pornography, male peer support, and woman abuse. Nevertheless, preliminary evidence provided in this chapter strongly suggests that the relationship between these three factors is an emerging problem, one that will surely get worse in the near future. Still, to conclusively determine that this is actually the case much more research is necessary.

What we do know, though, is that, as Katz (2006), among others (e.g., Jensen, 2007), observes:

> Mainstream pornography has changed a lot in the past couple of decades. People of a certain age who still associated heterosexual porn with "girlie magazines" and air-brushed photos of big-breasted women shot in the soft light on luxurious beds with big pillows would be shocked by the brutality, out-right contempt for women, and racism that is common in today's product. (pp. 186–87)

Even though pornography in general is rapidly becoming more degrading, racist, and violent, many people, especially pornographers and the millions who consume their products, would argue that since an unknown but presumably large number of men who consume cyberporn and/or other types of pornography never abuse women, the assertion that porn is a key determinant of woman abuse is refuted. Yet, as Diana Russell (1998) reminds us:

> This is comparable to arguing that because some cigarette smokers don't die of lung disease, there cannot be a causal relationship between smoking and lung cancer. Only members of the tobacco industry and some seriously addicted smokers consider this a valid argument today. (p. 150)

The Dark Side of Other New Technologies

No chapter on the perils of new technological developments is complete without addressing the harms caused by some of the newest devices such as cellular phones, global positioning systems, and video cameras. Many men use these and other seemingly harmless technologies to abuse and control their current or former intimate female partners, but only a few studies have examined this problem (Pittaro, 2011). Furthermore, to the best of our knowledge, although there are descriptive reports widely available, there is no published theoretical work on how men use e-mail, texting, and other digital technologies to victimize women (DeKeseredy and Dragiewicz, 2013).

The research and publication that is available identifies many types of technological stalking, such as those listed below by Southworth and colleagues (2007, p. 843):

- Monitoring e-mail communication either directly on the victim's computer or through "sniffer" programs.
- Sending e-mail that threatens, insults, or harasses.
- Disrupting e-mail communications by flooding a victim's e-mail box with unwanted mail or by sending a virus program.
- Using the victim's e-mail identity to send false messages to others or to purchase goods and services.
- Using the Internet to seek and compile a victim's personal information for use in harassment (Finn and Banach, 2000; Kranz, 2001; Ogilvie, 2000; Spitzberg and Hoobler, 2002).

Many current and former male partners use other means of stalking or monitoring their partners, such as:

- Tapping telephone lines and intercepting calls made on cordless telephones
- Using a caller ID service to track women down
- Sender information on fax machines
- GPS devices
- Spy software and keystroke logging hardware
- Online databases and information brokers
- Hidden cameras (Southworth, Finn, Dawson, Fraser, and Tucker, 2007)

Technological means of abusing, monitoring, and terrorizing people have no time limits. Many targets of such victimization are female adolescents, and large numbers of them endure cyberbullying. Following StopCyberbullying.org (2012), this occurs "when a child, preteen or teen is tormented, threatened, harassed, humiliated, embarrassed or otherwise targeted by another child, preteen or teen using the Internet, interactive and digital technologies or mobile phones" (p. 1). Cyberbullying takes many different shapes and forms. Here are some examples:

- "Flaming," which involves posting hurtful statements or posting personal information
- Placing someone's personal information on sexual service sites

- Forwarding private e-mails to groups or posting them on social networking sites
- Blocking people from Internet social media sites
- "Sexting," which involves sharing compromising photos, videos, or written information with other people via texts or other electronic media (Klein, 2012, p. 115)

The damage caused by behaviors like "sexting" is lifelong. This warning by the National Campaign to Prevent Teen Pregnancy and Unplanned Pregnancy and CosmoGirl.Com (2012) spells out the danger:

> There is no changing your mind in cyberspace—anything you send or post will never truly go away. Something that seems fun and flirty and is done on a whim will never really die. Potential employers, college recruiters, teachers, coaches, parents, friends, enemies, strangers, and others may all be able to find your past posts, even after you delete them. And it is nearly impossible to control what other people are posting about you. Think about it: Even if you have second thoughts and delete a racy photo, there is no telling who has already copied that photo and posted it elsewhere. (p. 2)

Examine these statistics generated by a national survey conducted by the above two organizations:

- 38 percent of teen girls and 39 percent of teen boys say they have had sexually suggestive text messages or e-mails—originally meant for someone else—shared with them.
- 25 percent of teen girls and 33 percent of teen boys say they have had nude or seminude images—originally meant for someone else—shared with them.
- 37 percent of young adult women and 47 percent of young adult men have had sexually suggestive text messages or e-mails—intended for someone else—shared with them.
- 24 percent of young adult women and 40 percent of young adult men say they have had nude or seminude images—originally meant for someone else—shared with them (p. 3).

Needless to say, cyberbullying causes many physical and psychological problems, and it may result in suicide or what is now commonly termed as "cyberbullicide" (Hinduja and Patchin, 2009). In a study of 1,963 American middle schoolers, Hinduja and Patchin (2010) found that victims of cyberbullying were more likely to have suicidal thoughts and to have made suicide attempts. Of course, there is no way of knowing how many students succeeded in these attempts (since this was a survey of school students). Still, they argue that these extreme reactions suggest the need for vigilance on the part of school officials. All too often, however, this is what happens.

> A ninth grader named Mary Ellen Handy reported that she got an e-mail calling her a slut; when she ignored the comment, assuming it was a joke, her instant messages increased. One day she received word that everyone hated her; then a doctored picture of Mary Ellen with horns appeared on a photo website; then her instant messages were altered to look as if she were spreading rumors about her classmates. Friends dropped Mary Ellen to avoid becoming targets themselves. Her grades dropped and she developed an ulcer. When she and her family complained to school officials, Mary Ellen says, "they didn't take it seriously." (Klein, 2012, p. 117)

Many more examples of the brutal consequences of cyberbullying and other abusive ways of using new electronic technologies could easily be provided here. To make matters worse, many adults are completely unaware of what is going on in the dark side of the Internet and other new media (Dines, 2010). Until recently, we, too, could easily have been accused of being blind to the gender-related harms inflicted by new technologies. We agree with this observation made by Vargas Martin, Garcia-Ruiz, and Edwards (2011):

> While the future will surely bring new developments and technological applications, we, technology savvy professionals, need to continue developing new ways [and] better policies . . . to use technology for the benefit of humanity while deterring misuses and promoting best practices. (p. xxvii)

Summary

Since societal and familial patriarchy affects many aspects of our lives, we should not be surprised that these forms of inequality influence the use and abuse of new technologies. Still, as Goodmark (2011) puts it, "When the first domestic violence and stalking laws were passed, no one could have foreseen how technology would facilitate abuse, stalking, and harassment" (p. 195). As well, who could have foreseen the mainstreaming and normalization of racist and violent Internet pornography? What will the future bring? Internet and other types of porn are already so brutal that it is hard to imagine that hurtful images, as well as their negative consequences, could get worse. Even so, the future looks bleak because enormous sums of money are derived from "de-personalized, commercialized, and coercive sexuality" (Schur, 1984, p. 13). On the other hand, it is possible that the porn industry might cross a line that results in outraging most people and policy makers, leading to strict regulation and highly punitive responses (Bridges and Jensen, 2011). We don't know for sure what changes are imminent, but what we definitely know is that countless numbers of women are abused in a variety of ways by new electronic means of communication. And, as Dines (2010) notes, "What we do know is that we are surrounded by images that degrade and debase women and that for this the entire culture pays a price" (p. 163).

This is not to say, however, that new social media cannot be used to prevent woman abuse and to mobilize men to challenge patriarchy in all its shapes and forms. We suggest progressive ways of doing so informed by male peer support theories in the next chapter. It is also essential to target the mainstream media, such as MP3s, DVDs, television, and the like because they, too, promote violence against women and have become "pornified" (Paul, 2005).

7 | Policy and Practice: Where Do We Go from Here?

I'd love to change the world. But I don't know what to do. So I'll leave it up to you.   —*Alvin Lee, "I'd Love to Change the World"*[1]

What is to be done about male peer support for violence against women? Progressive answers to this question have been repeatedly provided since Walter DeKeseredy first started work in this area in the late 1980s. Unfortunately, though, while many positive changes, such as the passing of the 1994 Violence Against Women Act (VAWA), occurred over the past twenty-five years, every effort to advance women's rights is routinely "met with a counterattack seeking to undermine and reverse feminist gains" (Dragiewicz, 2011, p. 2). Furthermore, many different types of violence against women continue to devastate thousands of North American women and millions of their sisters around the world on a daily basis. Also, even in prosperous countries, economic equality is a long way off for women across the globe. In fact, as described in box 7.1, economic equality for women may be "centuries off." This has serious implications for the health and well-being of abused women and their children because they always have financial decisions to make and many who flee a "house of horrors" or who plan escaping worry about how to pay for rent, groceries, and heating bills (Davies, 2011; Sev'er, 2002). Note, too, that racial discrimination in the job market only makes matters worse for ethnic/minority women who contemplate making or who have made dangerous exits from violent households (Renzetti, 2011).

Without a doubt, things are not looking up. Added to the above problems are rabid right-wing attempts to eliminate batterers programs guided by feminism and to replace them with psychotherapy and couples counseling, approaches that degender woman abuse and portray it as a property of the individual (Gondolf, 2012). For example, the University of Montana has been rocked by

7.1 Economic Equality for Women Is Still Centuries Off

It is a common belief today that the days of economic inequality for women are the proper subject for a history lesson. What with the occasional woman showing up as a corporate CEO or a national- or regional-level politician, and constant stories about women breaking into the ranks of formerly all-male occupations, many people think that at least this one battle is over. Unfortunately, this is not the case, as women still make significantly less than men, even in the same occupations.

What is worse, according to those tracking the changes, is that in Western countries often considered by experts as models of women's economic equality, progress has been stagnant or deteriorating since the mid-1990s. Canadian law professor Kathleen Lahey is one of those experts, analyzing the gender implications of an economy held up worldwide as a model of progressive change for women (McQuigge, 2012). Lahey received a blitz of publicity when she tracked the rate of change toward complete equality for men and women in the Canadian economy and found that such equivalence was still 581 years away.

Although Canada had spent large sums transforming many government services and instituting tax and budget cuts, Lahey argued, such changes will mostly benefit men who make substantially more than women for the same work, while service cuts to programs that support women will continue to set them back. In fact, she said, there has been no progress on achieving economic parity in Canada in many years, while in recent years the gap has been increasing (Brennan 2012c).

Such stagnation is not solely a Canadian phenomenon, Lahey has argued. Despite decades of advocacy, topped by UN action and governments approving international conventions calling for changes in fiscal policy, there has been little action on this front worldwide, and in many countries current policy is undermining gains that have been made. Lahey has called for a gender-based examination and implementation of taxes, benefits, and budgets, which might sound radical if it were not for the fact that Canada has publicly agreed in international arenas to exactly such actions (Lahey 2010).

allegations and a federal investigation that the university, local police, and local prosecutors have all seemingly collaborated to refuse to investigate or prosecute as many as eighty sexual assaults in the recent past, with the most publicity going to a lengthy list of sexual assault allegations against students, and particularly members of the championship football team. Of course, as the *Huffington Post* points out, this actually might not be all that unusual an amount for a university town of this size. More unusual is the allegation that all authorities refused to even take reports, which the U.S. Department of Justice decided to investigate as possible sex discrimination by the criminal justice system. One of the university's responses has been to set up a twenty-minute mandatory set of videos; in fact, students are not allowed to register for classes until they have viewed the videos and scored 100 percent on a fairly easy quiz on the contents. Before students could even view it, however, the backlash rolled into position. National groups like the ultraconservative National Association of Scholars have received a great deal of media attention for attacking the program. The university claims that it wants to eliminate the rape culture on campus. The critics say that by forcing men who have not been legally convicted of rape to view a twenty-minute video the university is punishing the entire student body, a "severe" sanction. The NAS also disputed the information in the videos, such as the fact that women rarely lie in such allegations, and that most rapes are accomplished by coercion rather than force (Grasgreen, 2012).

While the backlash has been very powerful, having its greatest effect on legislators who are already misogynist minded, there are still many reasons for hope. Situated around the world are numerous feminist coalitions and large numbers of scholars and activists committed to ending violence against women using a variety of means. The main objective of this chapter, then, is to suggest a multipronged way of dealing with the interrelationship between broader social forces, male peer support, and woman abuse in its many shapes and forms.

The Contribution of New Technologies[2]

New electronic technologies have perils and promises, and some of the former were described in chapter 6. Much good, however, can also come from using the Internet and from joining progressive causes on social media sites. For example, launched in November, 2009 by United Nations (UN) Women, Say No—UNiTE to End Violence against Women is a feminist global organization that uses Facebook, Twitter, etc. to reach millions of people globally. With the aid of social media, Say No—UNiTE got 5,066,549 people to sign a call to make ending violence against women a top priority worldwide during its first phase (Say No—UNiTE, 2012). Say No—UNiTE is a welcome addition to the movement to end woman abuse around the world, raises awareness, and garners much support. Still, so far it is unclear whether this coalition's use of information technologies, as well as the electronic efforts of other feminist groups, actually lowers rates of male-to-female beatings, sexual assaults, coercive control, and so on. Hence, evaluation research is required.

This is not to suggest, though, that the efforts of groups like Say No—UNiTE should be abandoned if they do not greatly reduce rates of woman abuse. They definitely shouldn't and good measures of success must be broad in scope to include outcomes such as increased awareness and a growth in local educational campaigns. Even so, it would be useful to have behavioral outcome data from a wide range of groups that use new technologies to determine which of them offer the best practices that actually contribute to a reduction in the harms described in this book and elsewhere (e.g., Renzetti et al., 2011).

Whether we like it or not and whether or not we are computer savvy, communicating via social media today is vital for two key reasons. First, many people living in societies characterized by "turbo-charged capitalism" and "competitive individualism" (Luttwak, 1995; Young, 1999), especially youth, spend more time on their computers than they do in face-to-face relationships. As Jessie Klein (2012) observes, "In a culture that values independence and self-reliance to such extremes over connection, community, and interdependence, technology is more likely to be used as a means of escape from others" (p. 122). Thus, in a culture where most socializing among youth is done through electronic channels, using media outlets such as Facebook and Twitter will enable reaching a larger audience. In this way, more people can become aware of various types of patriarchal practices and discourses, and perhaps become motivated to voice their discontent with the prevailing inequitable status quo by electing politicians committed to ending woman abuse and other highly injurious symptoms of sexism (DeKeseredy, 2011b).

The other major reason for using new media is that social networking sites are now key arenas of political struggle and resistance. As Jill Walker Rettberg (2009) puts it:

Obviously, people find it easier to join a Facebook group to make a political point than to march the streets. Perhaps it's actually more effective, too. Right now, it's entirely possible that you get more press, and thus more national notice for a Facebook group with 2000 members than a demonstration of 500 people. And it's a lot easier to get 2000 people to join a Facebook group than to get 500 people to show up at a particular time and place with banners. (p. 1)

Directly related to male peer support and woman abuse, people who use social media should post the White Ribbon Campaign's (WRC) website (www .whiteribbon.ca/about_us/#1) and routinely announce this group's ongoing efforts. Spawned in 1991 shortly after Marc Lépine killed fourteen female engineering students at the University of Montreal on December 6, 1989, the WRC is the largest collective of men in the world working to get men to end woman abuse, to raise public awareness of this problem, to educate young men and boys about patriarchy and its brutal effects, and to support organizations (e.g., campus women's centers) that strive to advance women's rights. Moreover, approximately one week prior to the annual anniversary of the "Montreal Massacre," men are encouraged to wear a white ribbon symbolizing a call to all men to lay down their arms in the war against women (DeKeseredy, 2011a; Luxton, 1993). The idea caught on, attracting much attention throughout Canada, the United States, and elsewhere.

A Call to Men (ACTM) is a similar organization based in the United States and its website (www.acalltomen.com/) includes a wealth of information. Its key goals are as follows:

- To shift social norms that define manhood in our culture
- To galvanize a national movement of men committed to ending violence and discrimination against women and girls
- To influence change in men's behavior through a reeducation training process that promotes healthy manhood

An especially useful resource in the ACTM site is their "10 Things Men Can Do to Prevent Domestic and Sexual Violence." Among the ten things listed are:

- Acknowledge and understand how male dominance and aspects of unhealthy manhood are the foundation of domestic and sexual violence.
- Accept and own our responsibility that domestic and sexual violence will not end until men become part of the solution to end it. We must take an active role in creating a cultural and social shift that no longer tolerates violence and discrimination against women and girls.
- Stop supporting the notion that domestic and sexual violence is due to mental illness, lack of anger management skills, chemical dependency, stress, etc. . . . Domestic and sexual violence is rooted in male dominance and the socialization of men (A Call To Men, 2004, p. 1).

More information on the role of feminist men's formal and informal responses to woman abuse will be provided in other parts of this chapter. The most important point to consider here, however, is that there are many political actions that do not cost much time, effort, and money. Using new computer technologies to post information and exchange ideas is a prime example.

"Takin' It to the Streets"[3]

Above, Rettberg stated that large numbers of people joining a Facebook group might generate more publicity than a march in the streets. In some cases this is true, but the recent Occupy movement, which first started as the Occupy Wall Street movement on September 17, 2011, in New York City's Zuccotti Park, generated substantial mainstream media coverage around the world. Similarly, the massive 2012 Quebec university student protests that started February 13, 2012, garnered much newspaper and television attention in Canada, and eventually led to some of the changes that the students were demanding. Thus, there is good reason to argue that men's organizations need to take guidance from women's Take Back the Night rallies and "Slut Walks" (see chapter 3) in order to organize large marches and protests against woman abuse. Particularly when they are new and relatively unique such efforts can elicit considerable media attention. Mass male protests and demonstrations can be particularly newsworthy when they help spread the message that violence against women is not simply a "women's issue." Many men, regardless of whether or not they are sexist or abusive, need to be constantly reminded that "Everything that happens to women happens to men, too" (Katz, 2006, p. 18).

Caution, however, is required because some well-intentioned protests, marches, or rallies have negative consequences for women. Consider the 2012 "Walk a Mile in Her Shoes" march organized by the White Ribbon Campaign in Toronto. This event is based on the adage that to understand someone else's life and experiences it is necessary to walk a mile in their shoes. Taking a cue from research that shows that empathy-based strategies are effective (Foubert and Perry, 2007), the march requires men to walk one mile wearing women's high-heeled shoes, to raise awareness and opposition to woman abuse. Another goal is to secure donations from march sponsors to support local community organizations. "Walk a Mile in Her Shoes" marches are also organized by male university and college students across North America without the leadership of the WRC, and some men wear stereotypical women's clothes in addition to high heels.

For some people, the march is a positive event, one that sensitizes men to violence against women and other hurtful symptoms of patriarchy. For others, including us, the event is highly problematic. For example, Tristan Bridges's (2010) case study of five marches reveals that the performances of drag at marches "symbolically reproduces gender and sexual inequality despite good intentions" (p. 5). This point is well taken because cross-cultural research shows that gender inequality is the most robust correlate of sexual violence and that high heels are symbolic of societies that promote patriarchal relations (Bridges, 2010; DeKeseredy, 2012b; Sanday, 1981). According to feminist scholar Susan Brownmiller (1984), "An artificial feminine walk seems to gratify many psychological and cultural needs. The female foot and leg are turned into ornamental objects and the impractical show, which offers little protection . . . induces helplessness and dependence" (p. 184).

Of course, not all women wear high heels. As one woman stated at a march observed by Bridges (2010), "If all they have to do is walk a mile in women's shoes, why did they all pick high heels" (p. 15)? Bridges also argues that homophobia is a key element of each march: thus, "Walk a Mile in Her Shoes" marches confirm "our worst fears about acknowledging men doing feminism" (2010, p. 20). Worse yet, he argues, such marches do little, if anything, to achieve empathy. Is this the case for all marches or only those observed by Bridges? This question can only be answered with sound research. Still, it is worth mentioning that the one march Walter DeKeseredy observed near Toronto did not include a critical mass of male students who publicly identify themselves as feminist.

Boycotting Harmful Companies, Stores, Products, and Services

If hitting the streets is not a novel idea, then the same can be said about boycotting. Even so, it is a tried and true initiative. Following the Minnesota Men's Action Network: Alliance to Prevent Sexual and Domestic Violence Clean Hotel Initiative,[4] DeKeseredy (2011a, 2011b) has called for encouraging businesses and government agencies and others to only hold conferences and meetings in hotels that do not offer in-room adult pay-per-view pornography. He also calls for boycotting pornographic video stores. But this is clearly not enough. It is not unusual to find in gift shops, clothing stores, souvenir shops, and online outlets a variety of misogynistic images that promote violence against women. For example, a currently popular shirt is offered by the Toronto-based Urban Behavior chain and the trendy American online outlet Cafe Press. Called "Problem

Solved," the shirt comes in several variations, but each has two panels: "problem" and "solved." The "problem" panel obviously shows an angry woman verbally chastising a man for his behavior. In the "solution" panel the man has just delivered a mighty karate kick to the woman, literally knocking her out of the panel. Asked about the shirt, an Urban Behavior store clerk said that it was "supposed to be funny." Even more disturbing is that Urban Behavior claims that "misogyny is passé, violence against women is no longer a problem, so we can mass market a shirt with this message" (cited in Hargreaves, 2012, p. 1).

Of course, pro-woman-abuse imagery is not something that just arrived in stores. Various outlets that market "cutting-edge" slogans on signs, mugs, trinkets, hats, clothing, and even baby bibs have long found a large audience for misogynist messages. In a previous work, Schwartz and DeKeseredy (1997, pp. 75–76) discussed common artifacts that allow the representation of violent sexual and physical attacks on women because they are presented in the context of humor. When there was a fad of shirts that showed a heart from a deck of cards (as in, I "heart" my dog, I "heart" Boston), gift shops throughout North America, even in prestigious outlets such as major hotel gift shops, sold a supposedly humorous shirt with a slogan that used another image from a deck of cards to say: "I 'club' my wife." Miller and Schwartz (1992) discovered a heavy cast-iron bootjack in the shape of a naked woman lying on her back. One removed a boot by kicking the woman in the crotch.

So, like violent and racist pornography, violence against women is normalized by many parts of the private sector. When journalist Stephen Hargreaves (2012) searched the Internet for responses to Urban Behavior's shirt, he could not find one post that expressed outrage or disgust. What does that tell us? Perhaps *Guardian* columnist Ellie Mae O'Hagan (2011) has the best answer to this question:

> The normalization of misogyny is so commonplace, it's almost mundane: from Danny Dyer advising a *Zoo*[5] reader to cut his ex-girlfriend's face, to adverts for hair salons featuring battered women. The objectification and dehumanization of women is such an inescapable part of popular culture that it necessarily plays a part in the daily interactions of men and women. (pp. 1–2)

Boycotting the many products for sale with such themes, boycotting the stores that sell them, and boycotting media like *Zoo* that promote violence against women and other patriarchal practices is a vital component of the multipronged approach to curbing woman abuse. Boycotting does make a difference because of its financial impact, and boycotts are more effective when one takes the time to politely explain to clerks why one is not making a purchase. Boycotting is most effective when it is combined with social media protests. For instance, *Zoo* experienced a major fall in its circulation when condemnation for Danny Dyer and *Zoo* were trending on Twitter a few years ago (Busfield and Sweney, 2010).

Boycotting is a daunting task because sexism is all around us. Of course, too, there is never enough time in the day to monitor the myriad ways in which women are objectified, dehumanized, and exploited. Certainly it is true that given our work, family, and other commitments we must carefully pick our battles. Nonetheless, new technologies make it much easier than it was in the past to collectively expose and criticize hurtful media coverage of woman abuse and to boycott companies that profit from misogyny. If enough of us politely mention to clerks that we have chosen not to make a purchase because we are offended by dehumanizing merchandise, we may at least convince some store managers to remove items from sale.

Transforming "Well-Meaning Men" into Responders

Most men do not beat, rape, psychologically assault or abuse women in other ways. They are what Tony Porter (2006a) refers to as "well-meaning men." He defines this type of man as one

> who believes women should be respected. A well-meaning man would not assault a woman. A well-meaning man, on the surface, at least, believes in equality for women. A well-meaning man believes in women's rights. A well-meaning man honors the women in his life. A well-meaning man, for all practical purposes, is a nice guy, a good guy. (p. 1)

If most men are like this, then why is there so much woman abuse in this world? Why is there so much misogyny? Why does patriarchy still exist in societies and within families? Why do we live in an increasingly pornified society? There are three key answers to this question. First, most men are seldom asked to contribute to the struggle to overthrow patriarchy. Second, many men are reluctant to participate in antiviolence efforts (Wantland, 2008). And, third, by remaining on the sidelines praising themselves for being well-meaning, these men's silence supports abusive behavior (Bunch, 2006). Certainly, there are more men actively working to end men's violence and promote gender equity than ever before, but a key challenge raised by Jackson Katz (2006) some years ago still exists: "How to increase dramatically the number of men who make these issues a priority in their personal and professional lives" (p. 254).

A growing number of universities and colleges are responding to this challenge by creating peer education and bystander intervention initiatives. One example is Fraternity Peer Rape Education Program (FREP). This is a university class taught by Ross A. Wantland (2008) where fraternity members receive credit for training to become peer rape educators to their fraternity chapters.[6] Another, and more widely known strategy, is the Green Dot Violence Prevention Strategy developed by Dorothy Edwards. This involves interactive training to become active bystanders. This approach asks us to visualize a map with green dots spreading across a map of the United States, with each one representing an individual action. In the words, of Greendot.etcetera (2012):

> A green dot is any behavior, choice, word, or attitude that promotes safety for all our citizens and communicates utter intolerance for violence. A green dot is pulling a friend out of a high risk situation—a green dot is donating a few dollars to your local service provider—a green dot is displaying an awareness poster in your room or office—a green dot is putting a green dot message on your Facebook page—a green dot is striking up a conversation with a friend or family member about how much this issue matters to you. A green dot is simply your individual choice at any given moment to make our world safer. (p. 1)

The Green Dot strategy involves men and women from all walks of life, and can involve specific training on how to help end male violence. At the University of Kentucky's Violence Intervention and Prevention Center (2012), for example, men are trained to use the following Green Dots:

- Tell a woman in your life that power-based violence matters to you.
- Ask women in your life how power-based violence has impacted them.
- Ask a man in your life how power-based personal violence has impacted him or someone he cares about.
- Have one conversation with one male friend or relative about the Green Dot.
- Ask a woman in your life what you can do to help take a stand against violence.
- Ask one male friend or relative what he thinks about power-based violence and what men could do to help stop it.
- Visit the Jackson Katz website (www.jacksonkatz.com/) and read "10 Things Men Can Do to End Gender Violence."
- Have a conversation with a younger man or boy who looks up to you about how important it is for men to help end violence.

- Google "men against violence" and read what men around the country are doing.
- If you suspect someone you care about is a victim of violence, gently ask if you can help.
- Attend an awareness event with three male friends.
- Organize a men's event to raise money to support violence prevention.
- Text your three best guy friends that you went to Green Dot training and you want to talk to them about it (p. 1).

However, does the Green Dot program actually work? What do the data say? Green Dot is heavily informed by interdisciplinary research on violence, but so far the answer to this question is "we don't know." It is a relatively new initiative and several evaluation studies of Green Dot programs in high schools and colleges are being conducted by leading experts in the field, such as Ann Coker at the University of Kentucky and Bonnie S. Fisher at the University of Cincinnati. Needless to say, many people across the United States are anxious to see the results.[7]

One thing many campuses have tried to do over the years has been to set up various educational programs on the nature of rape. One newer advanced version of this is Personal Empowerment Through Self-Awareness (PETSA) at the University of Montana. In response to the scandals mentioned above, which resulted in an official U.S. Department of Justice investigation of the university and the local police and prosecutors on an allegation that they systematically refused to investigate any cases of sexual assault, the university is mandating that all students score 100 percent on an easy quiz about a video on sexual assault before being allowed to register for classes. The video includes several scenes of risky or dangerous behavior, or the prelude to a rape, and instructs campus men and women to intervene in these cases as bystanders to prevent sexual assault (Grasgreen, 2012). Thus, the entire program is a step beyond even bystander education programs, which also hope to change campus cultures so that other students will be willing to step forward and intercede when a woman is being, or is about to be abused (Banyard and Moynihan, 2011). Thus, while the Department of Justice investigates whether the local criminal justice system is illegally sexist and discriminatory in their actions, the university's goal is to break into the allegation that a rape culture is running rampant on the Missoula, Montana, campus. Aimed at all parties—potential male and female victims, potential offenders, and the friends and classmates of both—the video is just one part of a variety of programs designed to provide peer support for antirape efforts on campus, including bystander intervention.

While many schools for decades have run informational programs, particularly for incoming first-year students, in Montana and a few other schools with similar programs (Oklahoma, Central Florida), the difference is that the program is mandatory for all students on the campus. Once again, we look forward to seeing program evaluations, which may not be available for several years. In particular, as the *Huffington Post* points out, since so very few campus rapists nationally are ever even expelled from school, let alone prosecuted in criminal court, a major question will be whether anything more than raised awareness will take place (Kingkade, 2012; Schwartz and DeKeseredy, 1997).

Previous work published by us list many things men can do individually or collectively on campuses and elsewhere to end gendered violence, but it is beyond the scope of this book to repeat these strategies (see DeKeseredy, 2011a; DeKeseredy and Schwartz, 1998a; DeKeseredy, Schwartz, and Alvi, 2000; Schwartz and DeKeseredy, 1997). Nonetheless, it is again important to emphasize that feminist men like us recognize that people cannot eliminate one form of inequality by promoting another. Often woman abuse is simultaneously a function of economic, racial, and class inequality. Thus, feminist men consistently call for a higher minimum wage, state-sponsored childcare, and an anti-racist curriculum, among other initiatives.

Despite the progressive efforts reviewed here and elsewhere (e.g., Katz, 2006), obviously, much more ongoing work needs to be done to recruit men to join the feminist men's movement. Retaining them is another challenge, especially on university/college campuses because students eventually leave these schools. Other factors related to the problem of retention are the natural feelings that come from regular hard work without seeing a resulting major societal change: burnout, frustration, marginalization, and anger (DeKeseredy, 2012b; Gilfus et al., 1999). What we have learned from this is that it is essential for involved men to make contacts with like-minded men in other communities to broaden their social support network. Personal experiences and emotions can be shared, which helps alleviate stress and other problems associated with doing feminist work in a hostile political economic climate. As Stanko (1997) reminds us, "building alliances for social support and social change is one way to combat the feelings of isolation and frustration many of us working in the field . . . inevitably feel" (p. 84). Additionally, sharing experiences and emotions helps men reject hegemonic masculinity (DeKeseredy, 2012a). Recognizing and making explicit to others that one needs affirmation, nurturing, and support symbolizes strength and is an important step toward creating an oppositional masculinity (Connell, 1995; Thorne-Finch, 1992).

Creating an oppositional masculinity also entails developing strong, egalitarian, and meaningful alliances with women from a wide range of backgrounds. Being allies with women is as much about "liberating men from the constraints of masculinity" as it is about helping to save women's lives and supporting their inherent right to live in peace (Funk, 2006, p. 207). As has been repeatedly stated, the time has come for making men's involvement in the progressive struggle to end woman abuse a common policy (Hearn, 1998).

The Home and School

In chapter 3, we reviewed Bowker's (1983) standards of gratification thesis, which asserts that fathers teach boys that women and children are subordinate to the man of the family. It is unclear exactly how many North American fathers actually do this, but we can safely conclude that well-meaning men outnumber abusive men. Nevertheless, how many of these men actually have meaningful discussions with their sons about woman abuse and sexism? We assume the answer is "not many." This is problematic and must change. Katz's (2006) advice is warranted here:

> Clearly one of the most important roles a father—or a father figure—can play in his son's life is to teach by example. If men are always respectful toward women and never verbally or physically abuse them, their sons in all likelihood will learn to be similarly respectful. Nonetheless, every man who has a son should be constantly aware that how he treats women is not just between him and the women—there is a little set of eyes that is always watching him and picking up cues about how a man is supposed to act. If a man says demeaning and dismissive things about women, his son hears it. If he laughs at sexist jokes and makes objectifying comments about women's bodies as he watches TV, his son hears it. (p. 234)

Obviously, mothers also have a key role to play in the antiviolence and antisexism socialization process. One interesting approach that proved to be highly successful for Walter DeKeseredy's friend Darlene Murphy was to have frank, ongoing discussions with her sons about sexuality and healthy intimate relationships (something fathers should do too). She emphasized that when a woman says "No" she means "No." She also stressed that sex is a powerful source of energy, but one that can be, and should be, controlled. Darlene is a highly skilled and well-respected mediator, and boys raised by strong, assertive women like her and who have close relationships with their mothers during their teenage years grow up to be kind, successful men. They have "already seen the world through women's eyes." (Katz, 2006, p. 236)

Much has been said about preventing and controlling woman abuse on the college campus (Dragiewicz and DeKeseredy, 2012a, Schwartz and DeKeseredy, 1997). However, how can we prevent young boys from growing up to become abusive men? Elementary and high school–based educational and awareness programs, such as videos, workshops, presentations, plays, and classroom discussions are potentially effective prevention strategies. These programs help provide an atmosphere in which students show more respect for each other and can change attitudes, increase knowledge, and change behavioral intention (Bohmer and Parrot, 1993; Crooks et al., 2011; DeKeseredy and Schwartz, 1998a). Equally important is the development of school curricula that make gender, healthy relationships, and sexuality a core subject in schools (Messer-schmidt, 2012).

Part of the problem of programs that have not worked in the past is that they operated on a "haphazard, one-classroom-at-a-time approach" (Jaffe, Sunderman, Reitzel, and Killip, 1992, p. 131). The challenge is that while any single teacher or counselor may be very effective and be deeply committed to creating peaceful, equitable learning environments, it is very difficult to counteract the broad variety of influences that students encounter on a daily basis. If only one or very few teachers are engaged in programming against woman abuse, then the influence of the students in other classes, when combined with parents, new and older electronic technologies, and other broader societal influences will weaken the effectiveness of these programs. This is why "whole-school efforts" are necessary (Klein, 2012). Only when all of the teachers, counselors, and administrators at the school are in complete agreement, providing a consistent and regular message over a long period of time, supported by the parents and other members of the family, is there a hope that many of the students will begin to seriously engage with these issues.

Because of alarmingly high youth unemployment rates in the United States and Canada, it is not surprising that thousands of young people living in these countries have little hope for the future. This is one of the key reasons why many of them will end up on a "road to whatever." "Whatever" is a word that a sizeable portion of Elliott Currie's (2004) teenage respondents used to describe how they felt before committing dangerous or destructive acts. It is "an emotional place in which they no longer cared about what happened to them and that made trouble not only possible but likely" (p. 14). Cyberbullying, "sexting," and gender harassment exacerbate this problem and many schools facilitate it by promoting an environment that resembles "America's cutthroat economic culture" (Klein, 2012).

The road to whatever starts in families, which, according to Currie, "often embody the 'sink or swim' ethos of the larger culture—a neglectful and punitive individualism that sets adolescents up for feelings of failure, worthlessness, and heedlessness that can erode their capacity to care about themselves or others" (p. 14). This type of social Darwinism also guides techniques that helping professionals and teachers use to respond to troubled teenagers, and statements made by Currie's interviewees show that "there is no help out there" for many youth today. Currie is not the only scholar to uncover this widespread problem. Jessie Klein (2012) has much experience with high school guidance programs and the following statement is based on her experience working with young people: "Students are given few if any arenas to speak with responsible and compassionate adults about their questions, concerns, fears, and/or anxieties regarding their own and others' sexualities" (p. 227).

Social Darwinist environments need to be replaced with what Currie (2004) defines as a "culture of support." Klein's term for this is a "compassionate community." Regardless of what label is used, schools need to be more inclusive and offer troubled youth places to go and people to speak to in their time of need. In this day of constant demands for evidence-based practice,[8] there is considerable empirical support for such strategies (DeKeseredy, 2011b). Still, schools today make many people uncomfortable because of their strong belief in punitive strategies and opposition to open discussions of sexuality in school settings. However, defenders of the status quo need to heed Klein's (2012) warning:

> Yet in a historical moment, when, as a result of sexual slurs and related attacks, students are being killed, committing suicide, and perpetrating massacres—as well as enduring high levels of depression, anxiety, and other emotional breakdowns— we can no longer afford to keep these issues out of schools. Policies are needed to support discussion and respect among community members, especially around difficult issues related to gender and sexuality. Students don't need more punishment and criminal charges; they need guidance, support, and education. (pp. 227–28)

No discussion of school-based prevention and education programs is complete without addressing athletics because, as described in chapter 3 and elsewhere, some types of sports culture spawn homophobic and patriarchal attitudes and beliefs (Katz, 2006). First and foremost, following Jeff Benedict's (1997) advice to the National Collegiate Athletic Association (NCAA) and professional sports leagues, directors of public and private school sports programs and coaches need to publicly speak out against woman abuse, bullying, and sexual harassment, as well as strictly prohibiting these and other hurtful behaviors. Second, coaches and athletic directors should have ongoing training in gender-related issues. Of course, male student athletes should also receive anti-sexist training (Katz, 2006). These initiatives are essential because involvement in certain sports, such as football, hockey, and basketball is a strong correlate of sexually violent behavior by high school and college males. Of special relevance here is what Mike Messner (1994) uncovered in his research:

> A few of the heterosexual men whom I interviewed objected to—and eventually rejected—the sexism and homophobia of the jock subculture. But they were rare exceptions to the rule. For young men who truly wanted athletic careers, rejecting one of the key bonds to the male peer group would have ruined their chances of success. So, whether they liked the sexism and homophobia or not, most went along with these things. And when verbal sparring and bragging about sexual conquests led to actual behavior, peer group values encouraged these young men to treat females as objects of conquest. This sort of masculine peer group dynamic is at the heart of what feminists have called the "rape culture." (p. 50)

Summary

Male peer support for the abuse, objectification, domination, and dehumanization of women is part and parcel of contemporary North American society, as it is in other countries. To all the male readers of this book, how many times during high school or college have you heard "advice" given to you or others by a male friend, acquaintance, coworker, or fellow student similar to the following?

> If she wants to hear that you love her, tell her you love her. If she wants to hear that you'll marry her, tell her you'll marry her. The most important thing is to keep going. Don't stop. If she says no, keep going. If she pushes your hand away, keep going. You only stop if she hits you. (Cited in Kimmel, 2008, p. 217)

Unfortunately, for many men, unlike fine red wine, things don't get better with age and the forging of long-term, intimate relationships such as marriage. We continue to hear adult men from all walks of life make disparaging remarks about women during golf games, in bars, workplaces, and other social settings. After more than three decades of studying the topics covered in this book, we can safely say that we still have a long way to go and a lot of work to do before patriarchal male peer support disappears. Hopefully, the initiatives suggested here will contribute to making a difference.

Needless to say, there are many other strategies that could be described in this chapter, all of which have much potential and that are informed by a rich gendered understanding of woman abuse. And, it is likely that even more new approaches will be required as we encounter both new technologies and various societal changes that affect and shape gender relations. Certainly, twenty-five years ago, we would have never thought about "sexting" becoming an integral part of peer culture. What's next? In some ways, we are afraid to hear the answer, given the potential for major damage that has been mixed in with the tremendous changes for good provided by the Internet, cell phones, and other modern technology.

We are left at the end of this book with many questions. We are also left with visions and hope. In the words of Duncan (1968), "Action in the present is always problematical and we use futures, as we do pasts to create images of preferred acts, not so we can dream but so we can act" (p. 29). We are fully aware of the tremendous damage that has been done by men, and continues to be done by men today throughout the world. Yet, we are also aware that much of what is good in the world is produced by men (Bowker, 1998). While constantly reminding ourselves that the world is more than gloom and doom, every day we see and hear of more men getting involved in the struggle to end woman abuse. We definitely could use a few more of them (Katz, 2006). We need their courage to change their own lives; our social structures; our ways of living, working, loving, and playing. The long, hard journey to a truly egalitarian society is worth it, and we encourage all men to become fellow travelers.

Notes

Introduction

1. This is the subtitle of Bancroft's (2002) book.

2. See Mullins (2009), Skjelsbak (2011), and Wood (2011) for more in-depth social scientific information on rape and other forms of sexual violence during war.

1. Definitional Issues in Violence against Women

This chapter includes modified sections of work published previously by DeKeseredy (2000, 2011a), DeKeseredy and Dragiewicz (2009), DeKeseredy and Schwartz (2001, 2011), and Dragiewicz and DeKeseredy (2012b).

1. The "power and control wheel" emerged from a series of educational sessions held with abused women by the Duluth battered women's shelter in 1984 (Pence and Paymar, 1993; Ptacek, 1999).

2. See Troshynski (2012) for an in-depth review of the social scientific literature on human trafficking.

3. Statistics Canada's Violence Against Women Survey was heavily informed by feminism and garnered much international praise. See Johnson (1996) for more in-depth information on this study and the data produced by it.

4. This is the title of her book on rape and sexual assault.

5. They usually ignore same-sex victims after claiming that abuse in lesbian couples proves women are just as violent as men.

6. The Durham Regional Police Service is located in Ontario, Canada.

7. See DeKeseredy (2011a) and DeKeseredy and Schwartz (1998b) for a more in-depth critique of the CTS and the CTS-2.

8. See Archer (2000) and Straus (2011) for reviews of major studies that support the sexual symmetry of violence thesis.

2. Extent and Distribution of Violence against Women

1. See Johnson (1996) for more information on VAWS methods and the data generated by them.

2. See DeKeseredy and Schwartz (1998a), Johnson (1996), Schwartz (2000), and Smith (1987, 1994) for effective means of minimizing underreporting.

3. Conducted with the support of the National Institute of Justice and the Department of Defense.

4. This section includes revised versions of work published previously by DeKeseredy (2007a).

5. *Not a Love Story* is the title of a 1981 documentary film about pornography. It was directed by Bonnie Sherr Klein and funded by the National Film Board of Canada.

3. History of Male Peer Support Theory

1. See DeKeseredy, Ellis, and Alvi (2005), DeKeseredy and Schwartz (2011), and Jasinski (2001) for in-depth reviews of various theories of violence against women.

2. The Center for Research on Violence and Conflict Resolution was renamed the LaMarsh Centre for Child and Youth Research, and most of the original affiliates are not associated with it.

3. See Ehrmann (1959), Kanin (1967a, 1967b), and Kirkpatrick and Kanin (1957).

4. See Ellis and DeKeseredy (1989) for a detailed critique of this thesis.

5. This section includes revised versions of material published previously by DeKeseredy (1988a, 1988b) and Schwartz and DeKeseredy (1997).

6. This section includes revised parts of work published previously by DeKeseredy (2007b), DeKeseredy and Schwartz (1993), and Schwartz and DeKeseredy (1997).

7. See Schwartz and DeKeseredy (in press), DeKeseredy (2011b) and DeKeseredy and Dragiewicz (2012b) for more information on the history of critical criminology and contemporary critical criminologists' major empirical, theoretical, and political contributions.

8. See DeKeseredy and Schwartz (2012) and Renzetti (2012, 2013) for in-depth reviews of left realist and feminist perspectives on crime.

9. The DCC was granted official status by the ASC Executive Board in 1989 at the annual conference in Reno.

10. This section includes revised sections of work published previously by DeKeseredy and Schwartz (1993) and Schwartz and DeKeseredy (1997).

11. "Hooking up" is an ambiguous term and it means different things to different students. Generally, the phrase refers to a casual sexual encounter (with no promise of commitment) ranging from kissing to sexual intercourse (Bogle, 2008).

12. Basile et al. (2009) have used parts of the two male peer support models reviewed in this chapter to explain the relationship between bullying behavior and male sexual violence perpetration.

4. Contemporary Male Peer Support Theories

1. Godenzi was then at the University of Fribourg in Switzerland and is now dean of Boston College's Graduate School of Social Work.

2. A line from *The Godfather.*

3. This section includes material adapted from Godenzi, Schwartz, and DeKeseredy (2001).

4. This section includes material adapted from work published previously by DeKeseredy, Alvi, Schwartz, and Tomaszewski (2003) and DeKeseredy and Schwartz (2002).

5. See DeKeseredy et al. (2003) for a review of these studies.

6. See Renzetti, Edleson, and Bergen (2011a) for recent reviews of the literature on violence against socially and economically excluded women.

7. This section includes modified parts of work published previously by DeKeseredy, Rogness, and Schwartz (2004), DeKeseredy and Schwartz (2009), and DeKeseredy, Schwartz, Fagen, and Hall (2006).

8. See Donnermeyer (2012) for an in-depth review of critical criminological work on rural crime.

9. See DeKeseredy and Donnermeyer (2013) for a review of these contributions.

10. See Brownridge (2009), DeKeseredy et al. (2004), DeKeseredy and Schwartz (2009), and Hardesty (2002) for in-depth reviews of the literature on male-to-female physical assaults during and after separation.

11. See DeKeseredy et al. (2004), DeKeseredy and Schwartz (2009), and Rennison et al. (2012) for reviews of these studies.

12. See DeKeseredy and Schwartz (2009) for more information on such male peer support in rural southeast Ohio.

13. This section includes modified sections of work published previously by DeKeseredy, Donnermeyer, Schwartz, Tunnell, and Hall (2007).

14. This section features modified parts of work published previously by DeKeseredy, Schwartz, and Alvi (2008).

15. This section includes revised sections of work published earlier by DeKeseredy (2011b) and DeKeseredy and Schwartz (2010).

16. There are other left-realist theories, which are reviewed by DeKeseredy and Schwartz (2012).

17. See Young's (2011) book *The Criminological Imagination* for his strongest and latest critique of abstracted empiricism and positivism.

18. This label appears in their critique of Young's (1999) *The Exclusive Society.*

5. What Do the Data Say?

1. *White Collar* was published in 1951 and as George Ritzer (2008) puts it, this book is "an acid critique of the status of a growing occupational category, white-collar workers"

(p. 213). Mills argued that workers may be cheerful and well paid, but are alienated by bureaucracies into becoming near automatons.

2. Veblen was a U.S. sociologist and economist. His most widely read and cited book is *The Theory of the Leisure Class* published in 1899 (Coser, 1977).

3. This section includes revised versions of material published earlier by Schwartz and DeKeseredy (1997).

4. See Crooks, Jaffe, Wolfe, Hughes, and Chiodo (2011) and DeKeseredy (2009, 2011a) for reviews of adolescent dating violence studies.

5. This section includes revised work published previously by Schwartz and DeKeseredy (1997).

6. See Smith (1987) for more technical information about his study.

7. This section includes revised portions of work published previously by DeKeseredy (2010a); DeKeseredy and Schwartz (2009); and DeKeseredy, Schwartz, Fagan, and Hall (2006).

8. Sinclair defines socially displaced youth as "male young offenders who are taken as sharing a similar position of being socially displaced at the time of the research as they are temporarily detached from society (outside world), excluded from the economic world, and placed within custody" (p. 70).

9. See Schwartz and DeKeseredy (1997) and Schwartz et al. (2001) for more detailed information on the relationship between all-male sexist conversations, alcohol consumption, and sexual assault on the college campus.

10. Of course all names of women quoted in this chapter were changed.

11. This section includes modified parts of work published earlier (see DeKeseredy et al., 2008).

12. See DeKeseredy et al. (2003) for more detailed information on the methods used in the QNLS and the data generated by it.

13. This section includes modified parts of work published previously by DeKeseredy (2010b).

14. Also referred to by Young as "Empiricus Abstractus," Young characterizes the datasaur as "a creature with a very small head, a long neck, a huge belly, and a little tail. His head has only a smattering of theory, he knows that he must move constantly but is not sure where he is going, he rarely looks at any detail of the actual terrain on which he travels, his neck peers upwards as he moves from grant to grant, from database to database, his belly is huge and distended with the intricate intestine of regression analysis, he eats ravenously but rarely thinks about the actual process of statistical digestion, his tail is small, slight and inconclusive" (p. 15).

15. The mesosystem is a level of influence included in ecological models of violence (Carlson, 1984; Heise, 1998; World Health Organization, 2002). Other levels included are individual, interpersonal, community, and culture. Dragiewicz (2011) asserts that "the mesosystem is the most important part of the ecological model because it describes the cumulative interaction of all of the other levels upon a person. The mesosystem de-

scribes an individual's experience in context: it captures, for example, the interaction between an individual's personal history of abuse, experienced in the context of a specific relationship, in which the individual has access to particular resources in a community and cultural context that shapes his or her interpretation of events and perception of available resources (Bronfenbrenner, 1979, 1986; Edleson and Tolman, 1992)" (p. 20).

6. New Electronic Technologies and Male Peer Support

Small parts of this chapter include material adapted from DeKeseredy (in press), DeKeseredy and Dragiewicz (in press), and DeKeseredy and Olsson (2011).

1. See DeKeseredy and Olsson (2011), Schwartz and DeKeseredy (1998) and Schwartz (1997) for reviews of laboratory studies of pornography and sexual aggression.

7. Policy and Practice

1. From the album *A Space in Time* (1971), by the British rock blues band Ten Years After.

2. This section includes material adapted from work published previously by DeKeseredy and Dragiewicz (2013).

3. This section includes modified parts of work published previously by DeKeseredy (2012b).

4. Go to www.menaspeacemakers.org/programs/mnman/hotels for more information on the Clean Hotel Initiative.

5. *Zoo* is a magazine published in the United Kingdom and it features Danny Dyer's "advice" column.

6. Ross Wantland teaches this course at the University of Illinois at Urbana-Champaign.

7. For more information on these studies, go to www.livethegreendot.com/gd_eva lasses.html.

8. See Clegg (2005), DeKeseredy and Dragiewicz (2013), Gondolf (2012), and Goldenberg (2006) for critiques of the conceptualization and implementation of evidence-based practice.

References

A Call To Men. (2004). 10 things men can do to prevent domestic and sexual violence. Retrieved July 23, 2012, from www.acalltomen.com/page.php?id=51.

ACWS. (2013). Men's attitudes and behaviours toward violence against women. Retrieved May 19, 2013, from www.acws.ca/sites/default/files/documents/ PresentationACWSMensAttitudesBehaviorsTowardViolenceAgainstWomen releasedCalgaryBWTG.pdf.

Adams, A. E., Sullivan, C. M., Bybee, D., and Greeson, M. R. (2008). Development of the scale of economic abuse. *Violence Against Women, 15,* 563–88.

Adams, D. (2007). *Why do they kill? Men who murder their intimate partners.* Nashville: Vanderbilt University Press.

Adeniran, A. (2011). Cafe culture and heresy of Yahooboyism in Nigeria. In K. Jaishankar (Ed.), *Cyber criminology: Exploring Internet crimes and criminal behavior* (pp. 3–12). New York: CRC Press.

Ageton, S. (1983). *Sexual assault among adolescents.* Lexington, MA: D.C. Heath.

Agnew, R. (2011). *Toward a unified criminology: Integrating assumptions about crime, people, and society.* New York: New York University Press.

Akers, R. L., and Sellers, C. S. (2004). *Criminological theories: Introduction, evaluation, and application* (4th ed). Los Angeles, CA: Roxbury.

———. (2009). *Criminological theories: Introduction, evaluation, and application* (5th ed.). New York: Oxford University Press.

Aldarondo, E., and Castro-Fernandez, M. (2011). Risk and protective factors for intimate partner violence. In J. W. White, M. P. Koss, and A. E. Kazdin (Eds.), *Violence against women and children* (pp. 221–42). Washington, DC: American Psychological Association.

Aldarondo, E., Kaufman-Kantor, G. K., and Jasinski, J. L. (2002). Risk marker analysis for wife assault in Latino families. *Violence Against Women, 8,* 429–54.

Anderson, E. (1999). *Code of the street: Decency, violence, and the moral life of the inner city.* New York: W.W. Norton.

Archer, J. (2000). Sex differences in aggression between heterosexual partners: A meta-analytic review. *Psychological Bulletin, 126,* 651–80.

Armbruster, B. (2012, February 13). Fox pundit says women in the military should "expect" to be raped. *ThinkProgress.org*. Retrieved February 23, 2012, from http://thinkprogress.org/security/2012/02/13/424239/fox-women-military-expect-raped.

Armstrong, E. A., Hamilton, L., and Sweeney, B. (2006). Sexual assault on campus: A multilevel integrative approach to party rape. *Social Problems, 53*, 483–99.

Attwood, F. (2010). Conclusion: Toward the study of online porn cultures and practices. In F. Attwood (Ed.), *Porn.com: Making sense of online pornography* (pp. 236–43). New York: Peter Lang.

Auchter, B. (2010). Men who murder their families: What the research tells us. *NIJ Journal, 266*. Retrieved February 12, 2012, from www.nij.gov/journals/266/murderfamilies.htm.

Bancroft, L. (2002). *Why does he do that? Inside the minds of angry and controlling men.* New York: Penguin.

Banyard, V. L., Plante, E. G., and Moynihan, M. M. (2004). Bystander education: Bringing a broader community perspective to sexual violence prevention. *Journal of Community Psychology, 32*, 61–79.

Banyard, V. L. and Moynihan, M. M. (2011). Variations in bystander behavior related to sexual and intimate partner violence prevention: Correlates in a sample of college students. *Psychology of Violence, 1*, 287–301.

Barak, G. (2007). Doing newsmaking criminology from within the academy. *Theoretical Criminology, 11*, 191–207.

———. (2009). *Criminology: An integrated approach.* Lanham, MD: Roman and Littlefield.

Barrett, M. (1985). *Women's oppression today: Problems in Marxist feminist analysis.* London: Verso.

Barss, P. (2010). *The erotic engine: How pornography has powered mass communication, from Gutenberg to Google.* Toronto: Random House.

Basile, K. C., and Black, M. C. (2011). Intimate partner violence against women. In C. M. Renzetti, J. L. Edleson, and R. Kennedy Bergen (Eds.), *Sourcebook on violence against women* (2nd ed., pp. 111–32). Thousand Oaks, CA: Sage.

Basile, K. C., Espelage, D. L., Rivers, I., McMahon, P. M., and Simon, T. R. (2009). The theoretical and empirical links between bullying behavior and male sexual violence perpetration. *Aggression and Violent Behavior, 14*, 336–47.

Basile, K. C., Swahn, M. H., Chen, J., and Saltzman, L. E. (2006). Stalking in the United States: Recent national prevalence estimates. *American Journal of Preventive Medicine, 31*, 172–75.

Baum, K., Catalano, S., Rand, M., and Rose, K. (2009). *Stalking victimization in the United States.* Washington, DC: U.S. Department of Justice.

Becker, H. S. (1967). Whose side are we on? *Social Problems, 14*, 239–47.

Belknap, J. (2006). *The invisible woman: Gender, crime and justice.* 3rd ed. Belmont, CA: Wadsworth Publishing.

Benedict, J. (1997). *Public heroes, private felons: Athletes and crimes against women.* Boston: Northeastern University Press.

———. (1998). *Athletes and acquaintance rape.* Thousand Oaks, CA: Sage.

Bergen, R. K. (1996). Wife rape: Understanding the response of survivors and service providers. Thousand Oaks, CA: Sage.

———. (2006). Marital rape: New research and directions. *VAWnet,* February, 1–13.

Bergen, R. K., and Bogle, K. A. (2000). Exploring the connection between pornography and sexual violence. *Violence and Victims, 15,* 227–234.

Berger, R. J. Searles, P., and Cottle, C. E. (1991). *Feminism and pornography.* New York: Praeger.

Betowski, B. (2007). 1 in 3 boys heavy porn users, study shows. Retrieved February 23, 2007, from www.eurekalert.org/pub_releases/2007–02/uoa-oit022307.php.

Bierstedt, R. (1957). *The social order.* New York: McGraw-Hill.

Bindel, J. (2012, January 19). Ellen Pence obituary: Pioneer of innovative strategies to deal with domestic abuse. *Guardian.* Retrieved January 26, 2012, from www .guardian.co.uk/coiety/2012/jan/19/ellen-pence.

Black, M. C., Basile, K. C., Breiding, M. J., et al. (2011). *The National Intimate Partner and Sexual Violence Survey (*nisvs*): 2010 Summary Report.* Atlanta, GA: National Center for Injury Prevention and Control, Centers for Disease Control and Prevention.

Blanchard, W. H. (1959). The group process in gang rape. *Journal of Social Psychology, 49,* 259–66.

Block, C. R., and DeKeseredy, W. S. (2007). Forced sex and leaving intimate relationships: Results of the Chicago women's health risk study. *Women's Health and Urban Life 6,* 6–24.

Block, C. R., Devitt, C. O., Fonda, D., et al. (2000). *The Chicago women's health risk study, risk of serious injury or death in intimate violence: A collaborative research project.* Washington, D.C.: Department of Justice.

Boeringer, S. D. (1996). Influences of fraternity membership, athletics, and male living arrangements on sexual aggression. *Violence Against Women, 2,* 134–47.

Boeringer, S. D., Shehan, C. L., and Akers, R. L. (1991). Social contexts and social learning in sexual coercion and aggression: Assessing the contribution of fraternity membership. *Family Relations, 40,* 58–64.

Bogle, K. A. (2008). *Hooking up: Sex, dating, and relationships on campus.* New York: New York University Press.

Bohmer, A., and Parrot, A. (1993). *Sexual assault on the college campus: The problem and the solution.* New York: Lexington.

Bonino, S., Ciairano, S., Rabaglietti, E., and Cattelino, E. (2006). Use of pornography and self-reported engagement in sexual violence among adolescents. *European Journal of Developmental Psychology, 3,* 265–88.

Bonisteel, M., and Green, L. (2005). Implications of the shrinking space for feminist anti-violence advocacy. Retrieved March 11, 2012, from www.crvawc.ca/documents/ ShrinkingFeministSpace_AntiViolenceAdvocacy_OCT2005.pdf.

Bourgois, P. (1995). *In search of respect: Selling crack in el barrio*. New York: Cambridge University Press.

Bowker, L. H. (1983). *Beating wife-beating*. Lexington, MA: Lexington Books.

———. (1998). Introduction. In L. H. Bowker (Ed.), *Masculinities and violence* (pp. xi–xviii). Thousand Oaks, CA: Sage.

Branch, K. A., Sellers, C. S., and Cochran, J. K. (2001). Social learning and self-control: An integrated model of intimate violence. Paper presented at the annual meetings of the Academy of Criminal Justice Sciences, Washington, D.C.

Brandwein, R. A. (1999). Family violence, women, and welfare. In R. A. Brandwein (Ed.), *Battered women, children, and welfare reform: The ties that bind* (pp. 3–16). Thousand Oaks, CA: Sage.

Brannigan, A., and Goldenberg, S. (1987). The study of aggressive pornography: The vicissitudes of relevance. *Critical Studies in Mass Communication, 4,* 289–304.

Brennan, R. J. (2012a, March 5). Nearly 1 in 10 Alberta men say hitting women is okay. *Toronto Star,* A13.

———. (2012b, March 14). Some Alberta men believe violence against women is okay. *Toronto Star*. Retrieved from www.thestar.com/news/canada/2012/03/14/poll_some_alberta_men_believe_violence_against_women_is_okay.html.

———. (2012c, May 22). Economic equality for women is centuries away, professor says. *Toronto Star*. Retrieved from: www.thestar.com/news/canada/2012/05/22/economic_equality_for_women_is_centuries_away_professor_says.html.

Bridges, A. J., and Jensen, R. (2011). Pornography. In C. M. Renzetti, J. L. Edleson, and R. Kennedy Bergen (Eds.), *Sourcebook on violence against women* (2nd ed., pp. 133–48). Thousand Oaks, CA: Sage.

Bridges, A. J., Wosnitzer, R., Scharrer, E., Sun, C., and Liberman, R. (2010). Aggression and sexual behavior in best-selling pornography videos: A content analysis. *Violence Against Women, 16,* 1065–85.

Bridges, T. S. (2010). Men were just not made to do this: Performances of drag at Walk a Mile in her Shoes marches. *Violence Against Women, 24,* 5–30.

Briere, J., and Malamuth, N. (1983). Self-reported likelihood of sexually aggressive behavior: Attitudinal versus sexual explanations. *Journal of Research in Personality, 17,* 315–23.

Bronfenbrenner, U. (1979). *The ecology of human development: Experiments by nature and design*. Cambridge, MA: Harvard University Press.

———. (1986). Ecology of the family as a context for human development: Research perspectives. *Developmental Psychology, 22,* 723–42.

Brosi M., Foubert, J. D., Bannon, R. S., and Yandell, G. (2011). Effects of sorority members' pornography use on bystander intervention in a sexual assault situation and rape myth acceptance. *Oracle, 6,* 26–35.

Brotherton, D. (2008). Beyond social reproduction: Bringing resistance back into gang theory. *Theoretical Criminology, 12,* 55–77.

Brownmiller, S. (1984). *Femininity.* New York: Linden Press.

Brownridge, D. A., (2009). *Violence against women: Vulnerable populations.* New York: Routledge.

Brownridge, D. A., and Halli, S. S. (2001). *Explaining violence against women in Canada.* Lanham, MD: Lexington Books.

Bunch, T. (2006). *Ending men's violence against women.* New York: A Call to Men: National Association of Men and Women Committed to Ending Violence Against Women.

Burawoy, M. (2008). Open letter to C. Wright Mills. *Antipode, 40,* 365–75.

Burstyn, V. (2000). *The rites of men: Manhood, politics, and the culture of sport.* Toronto: University of Toronto Press.

Busfield, S., and Sweney, M. (2010, May 5). Danny Dyer letter-writer seeks apology from *Zoo. Guardian.* Retrieved July 23, 2012, from www.guardian.co.uk/media /2010/may/05/danny-dyer-zoo-magazine.

Calvert, C., and Richards, R. D. (2006). Porn in their words: Female leaders in the adult entertainment industry address free speech, censorship, feminism, culture, and the mainstreaming of adult content. *Vanderbilt Journal of Entertainment and Technology Law, 9,* 255–99.

Campbell, H. (2000). The glass phallus: Pub(lic) masculinity and drinking in rural New Zealand. *Rural Sociology, 65,* 532–36.

———. (2006). Real men, real locals, and real workers: Realizing masculinity in small-town New Zealand. In H. Campbell, M. Mayerfeld Bell, and M. Finney (Eds.), *Country boys: Masculinity and rural life* (pp. 87–104). University Park: Pennsylvania State University Press.

Campbell, J. C. (2007). *Assessing dangerousness: Violence by batterers and child abusers* (2nd ed.). New York: Springer.

———. (2008). Femicide. In C. M. Renzetti and J. L. Edleson (Eds.), *Encyclopedia of interpersonal violence* (pp. 265–67). Thousand Oaks, CA: Sage.

Campbell, J. C., Webster, D., Koziol-McLain, J., et al. (2003). Risk factors for femicide in abusive relationships: Results from a multisite case control study. *American Journal of Public Health, 93,* 1089–97.

Campbell, R., and Townsend, S. M. (2011). Defining the scope of sexual violence against women. In C. M. Renzetti, J. L. Edleson, and R. K. Bergen (Eds.), *Sourcebook on violence against women* (2nd. ed., pp. 95–108). Thousand Oaks, CA: Sage.

Caplan, G. (1974). *Social systems and community mental health.* New York: Behavioral Publications.

Carbone-Lopez, K., Rennison, C. M., and Macmillan, R. (2012). The transcendence of violence across relationships: New methods for understanding men's and women's experiences of intimate partner violence across the life course. *Journal of Quantitative Criminology, 28,* 319–46.

Cardarelli, A. P. (1997). Confronting intimate violence: Looking toward the twenty-first century. In A. P. Cardarelli (Ed.), *Violence between intimate partners: Patterns, causes, and effects* (pp. 178–85). Boston: Allyn and Bacon.

Carlson, B. E. (1984). Causes and maintenance of domestic violence: An ecological analysis. *Social Services Review, 58,* 569–87.

Carringella, S. (2009). *Addressing rape reform in law and practice.* New York: Columbia University Press.

Carroll, J. S., Padilla-Walker, L. M., Nelson, L. J., Olson, C. D., Barry, C. M., and Madsen, S. D. (2008). Generation XXX: Pornography acceptance and use among emerging adults. *Journal of Adolescent Research, 23,* 6–30.

Casey, E. A., and Beadnell, B. (2010). The structure of male adolescent peer networks and risk for intimate partner violence perpetration: Findings from a national sample. *Journal of Youth Adolescence, 39,* 620–33.

Cassell, J. C. (1976). The contribution of the social environment to host resistance. *American Journal of Epidemiology, 104,* 107–23.

Castells, M. (2001). *The Internet galaxy: Reflections on the Internet, business, and society.* New York: Oxford University Press.

CBC News. (2011, April 3). Toronto "slut walk" takes to city streets. Retrieved March 19, 2012, from www.cbc.ca/news/canada/toronto/story/2011/04/03/slut-walk-toronto .html.

Chia, S., and Lee, W. (2008). Pluralistic ignorance about sex: The direct and the indirect effects of media consumption on college students' misperception of sex-related peer norms. *International Journal of Public Opinion Research, 20,* 52–73.

Clegg, S. (2005). Evidence-based practice in educational research: A critical realist critique of systematic review. *British Journal of Sociology of Education, 26,* 415–28.

Cohen, A. (1955). *Delinquent boys: The culture of the gang.* New York: Free Press.

Cohen, L. E., and Felson, M. (1979). Social change and crime rate trends: A routine activities approach. *American Sociological Review, 44,* 588–608.

Cohen, S., and Hoberman, H. M. (1983). Positive events and social support as buffers of life events stress. *Journal of Applied Social Psychology, 13,* 95–125.

Cohen, S., and Wills, T. A. (1985). Stress, social support, and the buffering hypothesis. *Psychological Bulletin, 98,* 310–57.

Connell, R. W. (1995). *Masculinities.* Berkeley: University of California Press.

Cooper, A., and Smith, E. L. (2011). *Homicide trends in the United States, 1980–2008: Annual rates for 2009 and 2010.* Washington, DC: U.S. Department of Justice.

Coser, L. A. (1977). *Masters of sociological thought: Ideas in historical and social context* (2nd ed.). New York: Harcourt Brace Jovanovich.

Crawford, B. (2011, May 23). SlutWalks all over the world. Feminist Law Professors blog. Retrieved from www.feminstlawprofessors.com/2011/05/slutwalks-all-over -the-world.

Crooks, C. V., Jaffe, P. G., Wolfe, D. A., Hughes, R., and Chiodo, D. (2011). School-based dating violence prevention: From single events to evaluated, integrated programming. In C. M. Renzetti, J. L. Edleson, and R. K. Bergen (Eds.), *Sourcebook on violence against women* (2nd ed.) (pp. 327–46). Thousand Oaks, CA: Sage.

Cross, P. (2007, July 6). Femicide: Violent partners create war zone for women. *Toronto Star*, A8.

Crosset, T. W., Benedict, J. R., and McDonald, M. A. (1995). Male student-athletes reported for sexual assault: A survey of campus police departments and judicial affairs offices. *Journal of Sport & Social Issues, 19*, 126–40.

Cullen, F. T. (1994). Social support as an organizing concept for criminology: Presidential address to the Academy of Criminal Justice Sciences. *Justice Quarterly, 11*, 527–59.

———. (2009). Preface. In A. Walsh and K. M. Beaver (Eds.), *Biosocial criminology: New directions in theory and research* (pp. xv–xvii). London: Routledge.

Currie, E. (1985). *Confronting crime: An American challenge.* New York: Pantheon.

———. (1993). *Reckoning: Drugs, the cities and the American future.* New York: Hill and Wang.

———. (2004). *The road to whatever: Middle-class culture and the crisis of adolescence.* New York: Metropolitan Books.

———. (2009) *The roots of danger: Violent crime in global perspective.* Upper Saddle River, NJ: Prentice Hall.

———. (2012). Violence and social policy. In W. S. DeKeseredy and M. Dragiewicz (Eds.), *Routledge handbook of critical criminology* (pp. 465–75). London: Routledge.

Dalton, M. (2012, January 29). Shafia jury finds all guilty of 1st-degree murder. CBC News Montreal. Retrieved February 16, 2012, from www.cbc.ca/news/canada/montreal/story/2012/01/29/shafia-sunday.html.

Dasgupta, S. D. (2002). A framework for understanding women's use of nonlethal violence in intimate relationships. *Violence Against Women, 8*, 1364–89.

Davies, J. (2011). Personal reflection. In C. M. Renzetti, J. L. Edleson, and R. K. Bergen (Eds.), *Sourcebook on violence against women* (p. 188). Thousand Oaks, CA: Sage.

DeKeseredy, A. (2012, May 18). Hurtful comments from ignorant men. *Whitby This Week*, 4.

DeKeseredy, W. S. (1988a). Woman abuse in dating relationships: The relevance of social support theory. *Journal of Family Violence, 3*, 1–13.

———. (1988b). *Woman abuse in dating relationships: The role of male peer support.* Toronto: Canadian Scholars' Press.

———. (1988c). Woman abuse in dating: A critical evaluation of research and theory. *International Journal of Sociology of the Family, 18*, 79–96.

———. (2000). Current controversies in defining nonlethal violence against women in intimate heterosexual relationships: Empirical implications. *Violence Against Women, 6*, 728–46.

———. (2007a). Factoids that challenge efforts to curb violence against women. *Domestic Violence Report, 12*, 81–82, 92–95.

———. (2007b). Changing my life, among others: Reflections on the life and work of a feminist man. In S. Miller (Ed.), *Criminal justice research and practice: Diverse voices from the field* (pp. 127–45). Boston: Northeastern University Press.

———. (2009). Girls and women as victims of crime. In J. Barker (Eds.), *Women and the criminal justice system* (pp. 313–45). Toronto: Emond Montgomery.

———. (2010a). Dangerous exits in the heartland: Separation/divorce sexual assault in rural America. *Sexual Violence Report, 13,* 49, 60–63.

———. (2010b). Bourgois, Phillippe: In search of respect. In F. T. Cullen and P. Wilcox (Eds.), *Encyclopedia of criminological theory, volume 1* (pp. 103–5). Thousand Oaks, CA: Sage.

———. (2011a). *Violence against women: Myths, facts, controversies.* Toronto: University of Toronto Press.

———. (2011b). *Contemporary critical criminology.* London: Routledge.

———. (2011c). Feminist contributions to understanding woman abuse: Myths, controversies, and realities. *Aggression and Violent Behavior, 16,* 297–302.

———. (2012a). The current condition of criminological theory in North America. In S. Hall and S. Winlow (Eds.), *New directions in criminological theory* (pp. 66–80). London: Routledge.

———. (2012b). Ending woman abuse on Canadian university and community college campuses: The role of feminist men. In J. Laker (Ed.), *Men & masculinities: An interdisciplinary reader* (pp. 69–89). Toronto: Oxford University Press.

———. (in press). Patriarchy.com: Adult Internet pornography and the abuse of women. In C. M. Renzetti and R. K. Bergen (Eds.), *Understanding diversity: Celebrating difference, challenging inequality.* Boston: Allyn and Bacon.

DeKeseredy, W. S., Alvi, S., and Schwartz, M. D. (2006). An Economic Exclusion/Male Peer Support Model Looks at 'Wedfare' and Woman Abuse. *Critical Criminology, 14,* 23–41.

DeKeseredy, W. S., Alvi, S., Schwartz, M. D., and Perry, B. (1999). Violence against and the harassment of women in Canadian public housing. *Canadian Review of Sociology and Anthropology, 36,* 499–516.

DeKeseredy, W. S., Alvi, S. Schwartz, M. D., and Tomaszewski, E. A. (2003). *Under siege: Poverty and crime in a public housing community.* Lanham, MD: Lexington Books.

DeKeseredy, W. S., and Donnermeyer, J. F. (2013). Thinking critically about rural crime: Toward the development of a new left realist perspective. In R. Atkinson and S. Winlow (Eds.), *New directions in crime and deviance: Papers from the York Deviancy Conference 2011.* London: Routledge.

DeKeseredy, W. S., Donnermeyer, J. F., Schwartz, M. D., Tunnell, K. D., and Hall, M. (2007). Thinking critically about rural gender relations: Toward a rural masculinity crisis/male peer support model of separation/divorce sexual assault. *Critical Criminology, 15,* 295–311.

DeKeseredy, W. S., and Dragiewicz, M. (2007). Understanding the complexities of feminist perspectives on woman abuse: A commentary on Donald G. Dutton's Rethinking domestic violence. *Violence Against Women, 13,* 874–84.

———. (2009). *Shifting public policy direction: Gender-focused versus bidirectional intimate partner violence.* Report prepared for the Ontario Women's Directorate. Toronto: Ontario Women's Directorate.

———. (2012a). Introduction: Critical criminology: Past, present and future. In W. S. DeKeseredy and M. Dragiewicz (Eds.), *Routledge handbook of critical criminology* (pp. 1–8). London: Routledge.

———. (Eds.). (2012b). *Routledge handbook of critical criminology.* London: Routledge.

———. (2013). Gaps in knowledge and emerging areas in gender and crime studies. In C. M. Renzetti, S. L. Miller, and A. R. Gover (Eds.), *Routledge international handbook of crime and gender studies* (pp. 297–307). London: Routledge.

———. (in press). Woman abuse in Canada: Sociological reflections on the past suggestions for the future. *Violence Against Women.*

DeKeseredy, W. S., Dragiewicz, M., and Rennison, C. (2012). Racial/ethnic variations in violence against women: Urban, suburban and rural differences. *International Journal of Rural Criminology, 1,* 184–202.

DeKeseredy, W. S., Ellis, D., and Alvi, S. (2005). *Deviance and crime: Theory, research and policy.* Cincinnati: Anderson.

DeKeseredy, W. S., and Flack, W. F. (2007). Sexual assault in colleges and universities. In G. Barak (Ed.), *Battleground: Criminal justice* (693–97). Westport, CT: Greenwood.

DeKeseredy, W. S., and Joseph, C. (2006). Separation/divorce sexual assault in rural Ohio: Preliminary results from an exploratory study. *Violence Against Women, 12,* 301–11.

DeKeseredy, W. S., and Kelly, K. (1993a). The incidence and prevalence of woman abuse in Canadian university and college dating relationships. *Canadian Journal of Sociology, 18,* 157–59.

———. (1993b). Woman abuse in university and college dating relationships: The contribution of the ideology of familial patriarchy. *Journal of Human Justice, 4,* 25–52.

———. (1995). Sexual abuse in Canadian university and college dating relationships: The contribution of male peer support. *Journal of Family Violence, 10,* 41–53.

DeKeseredy, W. S., and MacLeod, L. (1997). *Woman abuse: A sociological story.* Toronto: Harcourt Brace.

DeKeseredy, W. S., and Olsson, P. (2011). Adult pornography, male peer support, and violence against women: The contribution of the "dark side" of the Internet. In M. Vargas Martin, M. Garcia-Ruiz, and A. Edwards (Eds.), *Technology for facilitating humanity and combating social deviations: Interdisciplinary perspectives* (pp. 34–50). Hershey, PA: IGI Global.

DeKeseredy, W. S., Rogness, M., and Schwartz, M. D. (2004) Separation/divorce sexual assault: The current state of social scientific knowledge. *Aggression and Violent Behavior, 9,* 675–91.

DeKeseredy, W. S., and Schwartz, M. D. (1993). Male peer support and woman abuse: An expansion of DeKeseredy's model. *Sociological Spectrum, 13,* 394–414.

———. (1998a). *Woman abuse on campus: Results from the Canadian national survey.* Thousand Oaks, CA: Sage.

———. (1998b). Male peer support and woman abuse in postsecondary school courtship: Suggestions for new directions in sociological research. In R. K. Bergen (Ed.), *Issues in intimate violence* (pp. 83–96). Thousand Oaks, CA: Sage.

———. (2001). Definitional issues. In C. M. Renzetti, J. L. Edleson, and R. K. Bergen (Eds.), *Sourcebook on violence against women* (pp. 23–34). Thousand Oaks, CA: Sage.

———. (2002). Theorizing public housing woman abuse as a function of economic exclusion and male peer support. *Women's Health and Urban Life, 1,* 26–45.

———. (2003). Backlash and whiplash: A critique of Statistics Canada's 1999 general social survey on victimization. *Online Journal of Justice Studies, 1.* Retrieved July 12, 2012, from http://sisyphe.org/article.php3?id_article=1689.

———. (2005). Masculinities and interpersonal violence. In M. S. Kimmel, J. Hearn, and R. W. Connell (Eds.), *Handbook of studies on men & masculinities* (pp. 353–66). Thousand Oaks, CA: Sage.

———. (2009). *Dangerous exits: Escaping abusive relationships in rural America.* New Brunswick, NJ: Rutgers University Press.

———. (2010). Friedman economic policies, social exclusion, and crime: Toward a gendered left realist subcultural theory. *Crime, Law and Social Change, 54,* 159–70.

———. (2011). Theoretical and definitional issues in violence against women. In C. M. Renzetti, J. L. Edleson, and R. K. Bergen (Eds.), *Sourcebook on violence against women* (2nd. ed.) (pp. 3–20). Thousand Oaks, CA: Sage.

———. (2012). Left realism. In W. S. DeKeseredy and M. Dragiewicz (Eds.), *Routledge handbook of critical criminology* (pp. 105–16). London: Routledge.

DeKeseredy, W. S., Schwartz, M. D., and Alvi, S. (2000). The role of profeminist men in dealing with woman abuse on the Canadian college campus. *Violence Against Women, 9,* 918–35.

———. (2008). Which women are more likely to be abused? Public housing, cohabitation, and separated/divorced women. *Criminal Justice Studies, 21,* 283–93.

DeKeseredy, W. S., Schwartz, M. D., Fagen, D., and Hall, M. (2006). Separation/divorce sexual assault: The contribution of male support. *Feminist Criminology, 1,* 228–50.

Denham, D., and Gillespie, J. (1999). *Two steps forward . . . one step back: An overview of Canadian initiatives and resources to end woman abuse 1989–1997.* Ottawa, ON: Family Violence Prevention Unit, Health Canada.

Denzin, N. (1978). *The research act.* New York: McGraw-Hill.

Denzin, N., and Lincoln, Y. S. (2005). Introduction. In N. Denzin and Y. S. Lincoln (Eds.), *The Sage handbook of qualitative research* (3rd ed.) (pp. 1–32). Thousand Oaks, CA: Sage.

Dilorio, J. A. (1989). Being and becoming coupled: The emergence of female subordination in heterosexual relationships. In B. J. Risman and P. Schwartz (Eds.), *Gender in intimate relationships: A microstructural approach* (pp. 94–108). Belmont, CA: Wadsworth.

Dines, G. (2010). *Pornland: How porn has hijacked our sexuality.* Boston: Beacon Press.

Dines, G., and Jensen, R. (2008). Internet pornography. In C. M. Renzetti and J. L. Edleson (Eds.), *Encyclopedia of interpersonal violence* (pp. 365–66). Thousand Oaks, CA: Sage.

Dobash, R. E., and Dobash, R. (1979). *Violence against wives: A case against the patriarchy.* New York: Free Press.

Dobash, R. P., and Dobash, R. E. (1995). Reflections on findings from the Violence Against Women Survey. *Canadian Journal of Criminology, 37,* 457–84.

———. (1998). Cross-border encounters: Challenges and opportunities. In R. E. Dobash and R. P. Dobash (Eds.), *Rethinking violence against women* (pp. 1–22). Thousand Oaks, CA: Sage.

Dobash, R. E., Dobash, R. P., Cavanagh, K., and Medina-Ariza, J. (2007). Lethal and nonlethal violence against an intimate female partner: Comparing male murderers to nonlethal abusers. *Violence Against Women, 13,* 329–53.

Donnermeyer, J. F. (2012). Rural crime and critical criminology. In W. S. DeKeseredy and M. Dragiewicz (Eds.), *Routledge handbook of critical criminology* (pp. 290–302). London: Routledge.

Donnermeyer, J. F., DeKeseredy, W. S., and Dragiewicz, M. (2011). Policing rural Canada and the United States. In R. I. Mawby and R. Yarwood (Eds.), *Rural policing and policing the rural: A constable countryside?* (pp. 23–32). Burlington, VT: Ashgate.

Donnermeyer, J. F., Jobes, P., and Barclay, E. (2006). Rural crime, poverty, and community. In W. S. DeKeseredy and B. Perry (Eds.), *Advancing critical criminology: Theory and application* (pp. 199–218). Lanham, MD: Lexington Books.

Doring, N. (2009). The Internet's impact on sexuality: A critical review of 15 years of research. *Computers in Human Behavior, 25,* 1089–1101.

Dragiewicz, M. (2008). Patriarchy reasserted: Fathers' rights and anti-VAWA activism. *Feminist Criminology, 3,* 121–44.

———. (2011). *Equality with a vengeance: Men's rights groups, battered women, and antifeminist backlash.* Boston: Northeastern University Press.

Dragiewicz, M., and DeKeseredy, W. S. (2012a). Confronting campus sexual assault. In W. S. DeKeseredy and M. Dragiewicz (Eds.), *Routledge handbook of critical criminology* (pp. 454–64). London: Routledge.

———. (2012b). Claims about women's use of non-fatal force in intimate relationships:

A contextual review of the Canadian research. *Violence Against Women, 18,* 1008–26.

Duffy, A., and J. Momirov. (1997). *Family violence: A Canadian introduction.* Toronto: Lorimer.

Duncan, H. D. (1968). *Symbols in society.* New York: Oxford University Press.

Durkheim, E. (1951). *Suicide: A study in sociology.* Glencoe, IL: Free Press.

Dutton, D. G. (2006). *Rethinking domestic violence.* Vancouver, BC: University of British Columbia Press.

———. (2010). The gender paradigm and the architecture of antiscience. *Partner Abuse, 1,* 5–25.

Dutton, M. A., Orloff, L., and Hass, G. A. (2000). Characteristics of help-seeking behaviors, resources, and services seeds of battered immigrant Latinas: Legal and policy implications. *Georgetown Journal on Poverty Law and Policy, 7,* 247–305.

Dvorak, P. (July 17, 2012). Why D.C.'s bicycle groper must be found. *Washington Post,* Retrieved July 20, 2012, from www.washingtonpost.com/local/why-dcs-bicycle -groper-must-be-found/2012/07/16/gJQAbOuSpW_allComments.html?ctab=all _and.

Eckhardt, C. I., Holtzworth-Munroe, A., Norlander, B., Sibley, A., and Cahill, M. (2008). Readiness to change, partner violence subtypes, and treatment outcomes among men in treatment for partner assault. *Violence and Victims, 23,* 446–77.

Edin, K. (2000). What do low-income single mothers say about marriage? *Social Problems, 47,* 112–33.

Edleson, J. L., and Tolman, R. M. (1992). *Intervention for men who batter: An ecological approach.* Newbury Park, CA: Sage.

Ehrmann, W. (1959). *Premarital dating behavior.* New York: Holt.

Eisenstein, Z. (1980). *Capitalist patriarchy and the case for socialist feminism.* New York: Monthly Review Press.

Elder, G. H. (1994). Time, human agency, and social change: Perspectives on the life course. *Social Psychology Quarterly, 57,* 4–15.

Ellis, D. (1987). *The wrong stuff: An introduction to the sociological study of deviance.* Toronto: Collier Macmillan.

———. (1988). Post-separation woman abuse: The contribution of social support. *Victimology, 13,* 439–50.

———. (1989). Male abuse of a married or cohabiting female partner: The application of sociological theory to research findings. *Violence and Victims, 4,* 235–55.

Ellis, D., and DeKeseredy, W. S. (1996). *The wrong stuff: An introduction to the sociological study of deviance* (2nd ed.). Toronto: Allyn and Bacon.

———. (1997). Rethinking estrangement, interventions and intimate femicide. *Violence Against Women, 3,* 590–609.

Ellis, D., and Wight, L. (1987). Post-separation woman abuse: The contribution of lawyers. *Victimology, 13,* 420–29.

Family Violence Prevention Fund. (2007). *History of the Violence Against Women Act*. San Francisco, CA: Author.

Federal Bureau of Investigation. (2010). *Crime in the United States 2010*. Retrieved February 16, 2012, from www.fbi.gov/about-us/cjis/ucr/crime-in-the-u.s/2010 /crime-in-the-u.s.-2010/tables/

Ferguson, I. (1996). *A preliminary investigation into offensive and illegal content on the Internet: Deviant criminal pornography*. Ottawa: Department of Justice Canada.

Fielding, N., and Fielding, J. (1986). *Linking data*. Beverly Hills, CA: Sage.

Fine, M. (1985). Unearthing contradictions: An essay inspired by women and male violence. *Feminist Studies, 11*, 397.

Finn, J., and Banach, M. (2000). Victimization online: The downside of seeking human services for women on the Internet. *CyberPsychology & Behavior, 3*, 785–96.

Fisher, B. (2009). The effects of survey question wording on rape estimates: Evidence from a quasi-experimental design. *Violence Against Women, 15*, 133–147.

Fisher, B. S., Cullen, F. T., and Turner, M. G. (2000). *The sexual victimization of college women*. Washington, DC: U.S. Department of Justice.

Fisher, B. S., Daigle, L. E., and Cullen, F. T. (2010). Unsafe in the ivory tower: The sexual victimization of college women. Los Angeles, CA: Sage.

Fisher, B.S., Sloan, J.J., Cullen, F.T., and Lu, C. (1998). Crime in the ivory tower: The level and sources of student victimization. *Criminology, 36*, 671–710.

Flack, D. (2011, March 22). The origins of Slutwalk Toronto. BlogTO. Retrieved from www.blogto.com/city/2011/03/the_orgins_of_slutwalk_toronto.

Flack, W. F. Jr., Daubman, K. A., Caron, M. L., et al. (2007). Risk factors and consequences of unwanted sex among university students: Hooking up, alcohol, and stress responses. *Journal of Interpersonal Violence, 22*, 139–57.

Follingstad, D. R., Rutledge, L. L., Berg, B. J., Hause, E. S., and Polek, D. S. (1990). The role of emotional abuse in physically abusive relationships. *Journal of Family Violence, 5*, 107–20.

Fong, J. (2010). Introduction. In J. Fong (Ed.), *Out of the shadows: Woman abuse in ethnic, immigrant, and Aboriginal communities* (pp. 2–7). Toronto: Women's Press.

Fontes, L. A., and McCloskey, K. A. (2011). Cultural issues in violence against women. In C. M. Renzetti, J. L. Edleson, and R. Kennedy Bergen (Eds.), *Sourcebook on violence against women* (2nd ed.) (pp. 151–67). Thousand Oaks, CA: Sage.

Forbes, G. B., Adams-Curtis, L. E., Pakalka, A., and White, K. B. (2006). Dating aggression, sexual coercion, and aggression-supporting attitudes among college men as a function of participation in aggressive high school sports. *Violence Against Women, 15*, 441–55.

Foss, K. (2002, June 27). Men as likely to face abuse from partner, Statscan says. *Globe and Mail*, A8.

Foubert, J., and Perry, B. (2007). Creating lasting attitude and behavior change in fraternity members and male student athletes. *Violence Against Women, 13*, 1–17.

Fox, B. J. (1993). On violent men and female victims: A comment on DeKeseredy and Kelly. *Canadian Journal of Sociology, 18,* 320–24.

Franklin, C. A. (2005). Male peer support and the police culture: Understanding the resistance and opposition of women in policing. *Women & Criminal Justice, 16,* 1–25.

Franklin, C. A., Bouffard, L. A. and Pratt, T. C. (2012). Sexual assault on the college campus: Fraternity affiliation, male peer support, and low self-control. *Criminal Justice and Behavior, 39,* 1457–80.

Fraser, N. (1989). Talking about needs: Interpretive contests as political conflicts in welfare-state societies. *Ethics, 99,* 291–313.

Friedman, M. (1962). *Capitalism and freedom.* Chicago: University of Chicago Press.

Friedrichs, D. O. (2010). *Trusted criminals: White collar crime in contemporary society* (4th ed.). Belmont, CA: Wadsworth.

Funk, R. E. (1993). *Stopping rape: A challenge for men.* Philadelphia: New Society Publishers.

———. (2006). *Reaching men: Strategies for preventing sexist attitudes, behaviors, and violence.* Indianapolis, IN: Jist Life.

Gagne, P. L. (1992). Appalachian women: Violence and social control. *Journal of Contemporary Ethnography, 20,* 387–415.

———. (1996). Identity, strategy, and identity politics: Clemency for battered women who kill. *Social Problems, 43,* 77–93.

Gallup Wellbeing. (2010). *U.S. drinking rate edges up slightly to 25-year high.* Princeton, NJ: Gallup, July 30.

Gallup-Black, A. (2005). Twenty years of rural and urban trends in family and intimate partner homicide. *Homicide Studies, 9,* 149–73.

Garcia-Moreno, C., Jansen, A. F. M. H., Ellsberg, M., Heise, L., and Watts, C. (2005). *WHO multi-country study on women's health and domestic violence against women: Initial results on prevalence, health outcomes, and women's responses.* Geneva: World Health Organization.

———. (2006). Prevalence of intimate partner violence: Findings from the WHO multi-country study on women's health and domestic violence. *The Lancet, 368,* 1260–69.

Gardner, C. B. (1995). *Passing by: Gender and public harassment.* Berkeley: University of California Press.

Gelles, R. J. (1982). Domestic criminal violence. In M. E. Wolfgang and N. E. Weiner (Eds.), *Criminal violence* (pp. 201–29). Beverly Hills: Sage.

Gelles, R. J., and Cavanaugh, M. M. (2005). Association is not causation: Alcohol and other drugs do not cause violence. In D. R. Loseke, R. J. Gelles, and M. M. Cavanaugh (Eds.), *Current controversies on family violence* (2nd ed., pp. 175–89). Thousand Oaks, CA: Sage.

Gelles, R. J., and Cornell, C. P. (1985). Intimate violence in families. Beverly Hills: Sage.

Gelles, R. J., and Straus, M. A. (1988). *Intimate violence: The causes and consequences of abuse in the American family.* New York: Simon and Schuster.

Gilbert, N. (1991). The phantom epidemic of sexual assault. *The Public Interest, 103,* 54–65.

Gilfus, M. E., Fineran, S., Cohan, D. J., Jensen, S. A., Hartwick, L., and Spath, R. (1999). Research on violence against women: Creating survivor-informed collaborations. *Violence Against Women, 10,* 1194–1212.

Gillespie, I. (2008, June 11). Nowadays, it's brutal, accessible: Pornography. *London Free Press,* A3.

Gillum, T. L., and Tarrezz Nash, S. (2011). Faith-based programs and interventions. In C. M. Renzetti, J. L. Edleson, and R. K. Bergen (Eds.), *Sourcebook on violence against women* (2nd ed., pp. 309–23). Thousand Oaks, CA: Sage.

Girard, A. (2009). Backlash or equality? The influence of men's and women's rights discourses on domestic violence legislation in Ontario. *Violence Against Women, 15,* 5–23.

Godenzi, A., Schwartz, M. D., and DeKeseredy, W. S. (2001). Toward a gendered social bond/male peer support theory of university woman abuse. *Critical Criminology, 10,* 1–16.

Goffman, E. (1961). *Asylums.* Garden City, NY: Doubleday Anchor Books.

Goldenberg, M. J. (2006). On evidence and evidence-based medicine: Lessons from the philosophy of science. *Social Science & Medicine, 62,* 2621–32.

Gondolf, E. W. (1999). MCMI results for batterer program participants in four cities: Less "pathological" than expected. *Journal of Family Violence, 14,* 1–17.

———. (2012). *The future of batterer programs: Reassessing evidence-based practice.* Boston: Northeastern University Press.

Goode, E. (1989). *Drugs in American society* (3rd ed.). New York: Knopf.

Goodmark, L. (2011). State, national, and international legal initiatives to address violence against women: A survey. In C. M. Renzetti, J. L. Edleson, and R. K. Bergen (Eds.), *Sourcebook on violence against women* (2nd ed.) (pp. 191–208). Thousand Oaks, CA: Sage.

Gottfredson, M. R., and Hirschi, T. (1990). *A general theory of crime.* Stanford, CA: Stanford University Press.

Grasgreen, A. (2012). Counter-rape culture. *Inside Higher Ed.* Retrieved February 15, 2012, www.insidehighered.com/news/2012/08/29/amid-rape-investigations -university-montana-requires-all-students-take-tutorial.

Greendot.ecetera. (2012). The green dot overview. Retrieved June 21, 2012, from www.livethegreendot.com/gd_overview.html.

Gwartney-Gibbs, P. A., Stockard, J., and Bohmer, S. (1987). Learning courtship aggression: The influence of parents, peers, and personal experiences. *Family Relations, 36,* 276–82.

Hald, G. M., Malamuth, N., and Yuen, C. (2010). Pornography and attitudes supporting violence against women: Revisiting the relationship in nonexperimental studies. *Aggressive Behavior, 36,* 545–53.

Hall, R. (1985). *Ask any woman: A London inquiry into rape and sexual assault.* London: Falling Wall Press.

Hamby, S. L. (2004). Sexual victimization in Indian country. *VAWnet.* Retrieved July 11, 2012 from www.vawnet.org.

Hammaren, N., and Johansson, T. (2007). Hegemonic masculinity and pornography: Young people's attitudes toward and relations to pornography. *Journal of Men's Studies, 15,* 57–71.

Hammer, R. (2002). *Antifeminism and family terrorism: A critical feminist perspective.* Lanham, MD: Roman and Littlefield.

Hardesty, J. J. (2002) Separation assault in the context of postdivorce parenting: An integrative review of the literature. *Violence Against Women, 8,* pp. 597–621.

Hargreaves, S. (2012, June 15). Urban (mis) behavior's misogynistic summer wear markets on violence against women. *Canadian University Press Newswire.* Retrieved June 19, 2012, from http://cupwire.hotlink.net/articles/52847.

Harmon, P. A., and Check, J. V. P. (1989). *The role of pornography in woman abuse.* Toronto: LaMarsh Research Program on Violence and Conflict Resolution, York University.

Hashimi, S. (2013, January 29). Opinion: Crimes against women know no religion. *The Montreal Gazette.* Retrieved from www.montrealgazette.com/news/Opinion +Crimes+against+women+know+religion/7883779/story.html#ixzz2TvbLs6Ze.

Hatton, E., and Trautner, M. N. (2011). Equal opportunity objectification? The sexualisation of men and women on the cover of the *Rolling Stone. Sexuality & Culture, 15,* 256–78.

Haynie, D. L. and Osgood, D. W. (2005). Reconsidering peers and delinquency: How do peers matter? *Social Forces, 84,* 1109–30.

Hayward, K. J. (2010). Jock Young. In K. J. Hayward, S. Maruna, and J. Mooney (Eds.), *Fifty key thinkers in criminology* (pp. 260–66). London: Routledge.

Hearn, J. R. (1998). *The violences of men: How men talk about and how agencies respond to men's violence to women.* London, UK: Sage.

Heise, L. L. (1998). Violence against women: An integrated, ecological framework. *Violence Against Women, 4,* 262–90.

Heller, K., and Swindle, R. W. (1983). Social networks, perceived social support and coping with stress. In R. E. Feiner, L. A. Jason, J. N. Moritsugu, and S. S. Farber (Eds.), *Preventive psychology: Theory, research and practice* (pp. 87–103). New York: Pergamon.

Hey, V. (1986). *Patriarchy and pub culture.* London: Tavistock.

Hill, C. A. (2008). *Human sexuality: Personality and social psychological perspectives.* Thousand Oaks, CA: Sage.

Hinduja, S., and Patchin, J. W. (2009). *Bullying beyond the schoolyard: Preventing and responding to cyberbullying.* Thousand Oaks, CA: Sage.

———. (2010). Bullying, cyberbullying and suicide. *Archives of Suicide Research, 14,* 206–21.

Hirschi, T. (1969). *Causes of delinquency.* Berkeley: University of California Press.

Hobbes, T. (1651/1963). *Leviathan.* New York: Meridian Books.

Hoff, L. A. (1990). *Battered women as survivors.* New York: Routledge.

Hogg, R., and Carrington, K. (2006). *Policing the rural crisis.* Sydney: Federation Press.

Holtzworth-Munroe, A. Meehan, J. C., Herron, K., Rehman, U., and Stuart, G. L. (2000). Testing the Holtzworth-Munroe and Stuart (1994) batterer typology. *Journal of Consulting and Clinical Psychology, 68,* 1000–1019.

Holzman, H. R., Hyatt, R. A., and Dempster, J. M. (2001). Patterns of aggravated assault in public housing. Mapping the nexus of offense, place, gender, and race. *Violence Against Women, 6,* 662–84.

Hunnicutt, G. (2009). Varieties of patriarchy and violence against women: Resurrecting "patriarchy" as a theoretical tool. *Violence Against Women, 15,* 553–73.

Ibrahim, A. (2011). Child pornography and IT. In M. Vargas Martin, M. A. Garcia Ruiz, and A. Edwards (Eds.), *Technology for facilitating humanity and combating social deviations: Interdisciplinary perspectives* (pp. 20–32). Hershey PA: Information Science Reference.

Independent Women's Forum. (2002, March 12). Pfotenhauer, Margot Hill Appointed to the VAWA Advisory Committee. Retrieved March 13, 2002, from www.iwf.org /media/media_list.asp?page=1andfType=37.

Itzin, C., and Sweet, C. (1992). Women's experience of pornography: UK magazine survey evidence. In C. Itzin (Ed.), *Pornography: Women, violence and civil liberties* (pp. 222–35). New York: Oxford University Press.

Jacobs, J. (2005). *Dark age ahead.* Toronto: Vintage.

Jacquier, V., Johnson, H., and Fisher, B. (2011). Research methods, measures, and ethics. In C. M. Renzetti, J. L. Edleson, and R. K. Bergen (Eds.), *Sourcebook on violence against women* (2nd ed., pp. 23–45). Thousand Oaks, CA: Sage.

Jaffe, P., Sundermann, M., Reitzel, D., and Killip, S. (1992). An evaluation of a secondary school primary prevention program on violence in intimate relationships. *Violence and Victims, 7,* 129–46.

Jahnke, A. (2012, September 5). Hockey task force finds oversight deficiencies, culture of entitlement. *BU Today.* Retrieved from: www.bu.edu/today/2012/hockey-task-force-finds-oversight-deficiencies-culture-of-entitlement.

Jasinski, J. L. (2001). Theoretical explanations for violence against women. In C. M Renzetti, J. L. Edleson, and R. K. Bergen (Eds.), *Sourcebook on violence against women* (pp. 5–22). Thousand Oaks, CA: Sage.

Jasinski, J. L., Wesely, J. K., Wright, J. D., and Mustaine, E. E. (2010). *Hard lives, mean* streets: Violence in the lives of homeless women. Boston: Northeastern University Press.

Jenkins, H. (2007). Porn 2.0. Retrieved July 19, 2012, from http://henryjenkins.org /2007/10/porn_20.html.

Jensen, L. (2006). At the razor's edge: Building hope for America's rural poor. *Rural Realities, 1*, 1–8.

Jensen, R. (1995). Pornographic lives. *Violence Against Women, 1*, 32–54.

———. (1996). Knowing pornography. *Violence Against Women, 2*, 82–102.

———. (2007). *Getting off: Pornography and the end of masculinity*. Cambridge, MA: South End Press.

Jewkes, R., Dunkle, K., Koss, M. P., et al. (2006). Rape perpetration by young rural South African men: Prevalence, patterns, and risk factors. *Social Science and Medicine, 63*, 2949–61.

Johnson, H. (1996). *Dangerous domains: Violence against women in Canada*. Toronto, ON: Nelson.

Johnson, H., and Dawson, M. (2011). *Violence against women in Canada: Research and policy perspectives*. Toronto, ON: Oxford University Press.

Johnson, H. Ollus, N., and Nevala, S. (2008). *Violence against women: An international perspective*. New York: Springer.

Johnson, M. P. (2008). *A typology of domestic violence: Intimate terrorism, violent resistance, and situational couple violence*. Boston: Northeastern University Press.

Johnson, M. P. and Ferraro, K. (2000). Research on domestic violence in the 1990s: Making distinctions. *Journal of Marriage and the Family, 62*, 948–63.

Jones, A. (1980). *Women who kill*. Holt, Reinhart and Winston.

Jones, S. (2010). Horrorporn/pornhorror: The problematic communities and contexts of online shock imagery. In F. Attwood (Eds.), *Porn.com: Making sense of online pornography* (pp. 123–37). New York: Peter Lang.

Jordan, Z. (2006). A view at cyberporn and its influence on aggression against women. Unpublished manuscript. Ames, Iowa: Iowa State University.

Kanin, E. J. (1967a). An examination of sexual aggression as a response to sexual frustration. *Journal of Marriage and the Family, 29*, 428–33.

———. (1967b). Reference groups and sex conduct norm violations. *The Sociological Quarterly, 8*, 1504–1695.

———. (1985). Date rapists: Differential sexual socialization and relative deprivation. *Archives of Sexual Behavior, 14*, 219–31.

Katz, J. (2006). *The macho paradox: Why some men hurt women and how all men can help*. Naperville, IL: Sourcebooks.

Kaufman-Kantor, G., Jasinski, J. L., and Aldarondo, E. (1994). Sociocultural status and incidence of violence against women. *Violence and Victims, 9*, 207–22.

Kelly, K. (1994). The politics of data. *Canadian Journal of Sociology, 19*, 81–85.

Kelly, L. (1988). *Surviving sexual violence*. Minneapolis: University of Minnesota Press.

Kelly, L., and Radford, J. (1998). Sexual violence against women and girls: An approach to an international overview. In R. E. Dobash and R. P. Dobash (Eds.), *Rethinking violence against women* (pp. 53–76). Thousand Oaks, CA: Sage.

Kendall, L. (2003). Cyberporn. In M. S. Kimmel and A. Aronson (Eds.), *Men and masculinities: A social, cultural, and historical encyclopedia, volume 1* (p. 193). Santa Barbara, CA: ABC-CLIO.

Kernsmith, P. (2008). Coercive control. In C. M. Renzetti and J. L. Edleson (Eds.), *Encyclopedia of interpersonal violence* (pp. 133–34). Thousand Oaks, CA: Sage.

Kettani, A. (2009). Out from the shadows: Women's studies programs have changed how we view violence against women. *University Affairs,* June–July, 19.

Kidd, B. (1990). The men's cultural center: Sports and the dynamic of women's oppression/men's repression. In M. A. Messner and D. A. Sabo (Eds.), *Sport, men, and the gender order: Critical feminist perspectives* (pp. 31–44). Champaign, IL: Human Kinetics Books.

Kilpatrick, D. G. (2004). What is violence against women? Defining and measuring the problem. *Journal of Interpersonal Violence, 19,* 1209–34.

Kimmel, M. (2008). *Guyland: The perilous world where boys become men.* New York: Harper.

Kingkade, T. (2012). Sexual assaults on campus prompt heightened security, required courses on prevention. *Huffington Post* (September 1). www.huffingtonpost.com /2012/09/01/sexual-assaults-on-campus_n_1847736.html.

Kirkpatrick, C., and Kanin, E. J. (1957). Male sexual aggression on a university campus. *American Sociological Review, 22,* 52–58.

Kirkwood, C. (1993). *Leaving abusive partners.* Newbury Park, CA: Sage.

Klein, A., and Hart, B. (2012). *Practical implications of current domestic violence research for victim advocates and service providers.* Washington, DC: U.S. Department of Justice.

Klein, J. (2012). *The bully society: School shootings and the crisis of bullying in America's schools.* New York: New York University Press.

Klein, R. (2012). *Responding to intimate violence against women: The role of informal networks.* New York: Cambridge University Press.

Knight, R. A., and Sims-Knight, J. (2011). Risk factors for sexual violence. In J. W. White, M. P. Koss, and A. E. Kazdin (Eds.), *Violence against women and children: Mapping the terrain* (pp. 125–50). Washington, DC: American Psychological Association.

Kome, P. J. (2009). Amazon declines to sell "Rapelay" video game. Retrieved February 16, 2009, from www.telegraph.co.uk/scienceandtechnology/technology/46I11161 /rapelay-virtual-rape-game-banned-by-Amazon.html.

Koss, M. P. (1996). The measurement of rape victimization in crime surveys. *Criminal Justice and Behavior, 23,* 55–69.

Koss, M. P. and Cleveland, H. H. (1996). Athletic participation, fraternity membership, and date rape: The question remains—self-selection, or different causal processes. *Violence Against Women, 2,* 180–90.

Koss, M. P., and Gaines, J. A. (1993). The prediction of sexual aggression by alcohol use, athletic participation, and fraternity affiliation. *Journal of Interpersonal Violence, 8,* 94–108.

Koss, M. P., Gidycz, C. A., and Wisniewski, N. (1987). The scope of rape: Incidence and prevalence of sexual aggression and victimization in a national sample of higher education students. *Journal of Consulting and Clinical Psychology, 55,* 162–70.

Koss, M. P., Goodman, L. A., Browne, A., and Fitzgerald, L. F. (1994). *Male violence against women at home, at work, and in the community.* Washington, DC: American Psychological Association.

Kranz, A. (2001). *Helpful or harmful? How innovative communication technology affects survivors of intimate violence.* Retrieved July 23, 2012, from www.vaw.umn.edu /documents/5survivortech/5survivortech.html.

Kraska, P. B., and Neuman, W. L. (2008). *Criminal justice and criminology research methods.* Boston: Pearson.

Kreager, D. A., Rulison, K., and Moody, J. (2011). Delinquency and the structure of adolescent peer groups. *Criminology, 49,* 95–127.

Krug, E., Dahlberg, E. L., Mercy, J., et al. (2002). *World report on violence and health.* Geneva: World Health Organization.

Kuehnast, K., de jonge Oudraat, C., and Hernes, H. (Eds.). (2011). *Women and war: Power and protection in the 21st century.* Washington, DC: United States Institute of Peace.

Lahey, K. A. (2010). Women, substantive equality, and fiscal policy: Gender-based analysis of taxes, benefits, and budgets. *Canadian Journal of Women and the Law 22,* 27–106.

Lamanna, M. A., and Riedmann, A. C. (1985). *Marriages and families.* Belmont, CA: Wadsworth.

Laner, M. R., and Thompson, J. (1982). Abuse and aggression in courting couples. *Deviant Behavior, 3,* 229–44.

Laub, J. H., and Sampson, R. J. (2003). *Shared beginnings, divergent lives: Delinquent boys to age 70.* Cambridge, MA: Harvard University Press.

Law, F. Y. W., Chow, K. P., Lai, P. K. Y., Tse, H. K. S., and Tse, K. W. H. (2011). Digital child pornography. In M. Vargas Martin, M. A. Garcia Ruiz, and A. Edwards (Eds.), *Technology for facilitating humanity and combating social deviations: Interdisciplinary perspectives* (pp. 1–19). Hershey PA: Information Science Reference.

Lea, J., and Young, J. (1984). *What is to be done about law and order?* New York: Penguin.

Leatherman, J. L. (2011). *Sexual violence and armed conflict.* Malden, MA: Polity Press.

LeBlanc, M., and Loeber, R. (1998). Developmental criminology updated. In M. Tonry (Ed.), *Crime and justice: A review of research* (pp. 115–98). Chicago: University of Chicago Press.

Lehman, P. (2006). Introduction: "A dirty little secret"—Why teach and study pornography? In P. Lehman (Ed.), *Pornography: Film and culture* (pp. 1–24). New Brunswick, NJ: Rutgers University Press.

Lenton, R., Smith, M. D., Fox, J., and Morra, N. (1999). Sexual harassment in public places: Experiences of Canadian women. *Canadian Review of Sociology & Anthropology, 36,* 517–40.

Leone, J. M., Johnson, M. P., and Cohan, C. M. (2007). Victim help-seeking: Differences between intimate terrorism and situational couple violence. *Family Relations, 56,* 427–39.

Levinson, D. (1989). *Family violence in cross-cultural perspective.* Newbury Park, CA: Sage.

Lewin, K. (1951). *Field theory in social science; selected theoretical papers.* New York: Harper and Row.

Lilly, J. R., Cullen, F. T., and Ball, R. A. (2011). *Criminological theory: Context and consequences, 5th ed.* Thousand Oaks, CA: Sage.

Liska. A. E. (1987). A critical examination of macro perspectives on crime control. *Annual Review of Sociology, 13,* 67–88.

Lloyd, S. (1991). The dark side of courtship: Violence and sexual exploitation. *Family Relations, 40,* 14–20.

Lobao, L. (2006). Gendered places and place-based gender identities: Reflections and refractions. In H. Campbell, M. Mayerfeld Bell, and M. Finney (Eds.), *Country boys: Masculinity and rural life* (pp. 267–76). University Park: Pennsylvania State University Press.

Lobao, L., and Meyer, K. (2001). The great agricultural transition: Crisis, change, and social consequences of twentieth-century U.S. farming. *Annual Review of Sociology, 27,* 103–24.

Logan, T. K., Cole, J., Shannon, L., and Walker, R. (2006). *Partner stalking: How women respond, cope, and survive.* New York: Springer.

Logan, T. K., Stevenson, E., Evans, L., and Leukefeld, C. (2004) Rural and urban women's perceptions of barriers to health, mental health, and criminal justice services: Implications for victim services. *Violence and Victims, 19,* 37–62.

Luttwak, E. (1995, November). Turbo-charged capitalism and its consequences. *London Review of Books,* pp. 6–7.

Luxton, M. (1993). Dreams and dilemmas: Feminist musing on the men question. In T. Haddad (Ed.), *Men and masculinities* (pp. 347–74). Toronto, ON: Canadian Scholars' Press.

Machado, C., Dias, A. R., and Coelho, C. (2010). Culture and wife abuse: An overview of theory, research, and practice. In S. G. Shoham, P. Kneper, and M. Kett (Eds.), *International handbook of victimology* (pp. 639–68). New York: CRC Press.

Madison, L. (2012, May 16). Violence Against Women Act passes in House, but partisan battle looms. *CBS News.* Retrieved May 31, 2012, from www.cbsnews.com.

Maddison, S. (2004). From porno-topia to total information awareness, or what forces really govern access to porn? *New Formations, 52,* 35–57.

Madigan, L., and Gamble, N. (1989). *The second rape: Society's continued betrayal of the victim*. New York: Lexington Books.

Mahoney, P., and Williams, L. M. (1998). Sexual assault in marriage: Prevalence, consequences, and treatment of wife rape. In J. L. Jasinski and L. M. Williams (Eds.), *Partner violence: A comprehensive review of 20 years of research* (pp. 113–62). Thousand Oaks, CA: Sage.

Maier, S. L., and Bergen, R. (2012). Critical issues in intimate partner violence. In W. S. DeKeseredy and M. Dragiewicz (Eds.), *Routledge handbook of critical criminology* (pp. 329–41). London: Routledge.

Makepeace, J. M. (1981). Courtship violence among college students. *Family Relations, 30*, 97–102.

Matthews, R. (2009). Beyond "so what?" criminology. *Theoretical Criminology, 13*, 341–62.

Massey, D. R. (2007). *Categorically unequal: The American stratification system*. New York: Russell Sage Foundation.

May, P. (2012, March 10). BU hockey culture under investigation: Two ex-players facing sexual assault charges prompt puck probe. *Toronto Star*, S3.

McFarlane, J., and Malecha, A. (2005). *Sexual assault among intimates: Frequency, consequences, and treatments*. Washington, DC: U.S. Department of Justice.

McGloin, J. M. (2009). Self-control and deviant peer network structure. *Journal of Research in Crime and Delinquency, 46*, 35–72.

McGloin, J. M. and Stickle, W. P. (2011). Influence or convenience? Rethinking the role of peers for chronic offenders. *Journal of Research in Crime and Delinquency, 48*, 419–47.

McGregor, J. (2012). The legal heritage of the crime of rape. In J. M. Brown and S. L. Walklate (Eds.), *Handbook on sexual violence* (pp. 69–89). London: Routledge.

McKinley, J. D. Jr. (March 8, 2011). Vicious assault shakes Texas town. *New York Times*, downloaded February 12, 2012.

McIvor, S., and Nahanee, T. (1998). Aboriginal women: Invisible victims of violence. In K. Bonnycastle and G. Rigakos (Eds.), *Unsettling truths: Battered women, policy, politics and contemporary research in Canada* (pp. 63–70). Vancouver: Collective Press.

McQuigge, M. (2012, June 13). Canada tops for women, ranked 20th for UN gender inequality: Survey. Others say different. *Child Care Canada*. Retrieved from: www.childcarecanada.org/documents/child-care-news/12/06/canada-tops-women-ranked-20th-un-gender-inequality-survey-others-say.

Mead, G. H. (1934). *Mind, self, and society*. Chicago: University of Chicago Press.

Mechanic, M. B., Uhlmansick, M. H., Weaver, T. L., and Resick, P. A. (2000). The impact of severe stalking experienced by acutely battered women: An examination of violence, psychological symptoms, and strategic responses. *Violence and Victims, 15*, 443–58.

Mechanic, M. B., Weaver, T. L., and Resick, P. A. (2000). Intimate partner violence and stalking behaviors: Exploration of patterns and correlates in a sample of acutely battered women. *Violence and Victims, 15,* 55–72.

Meloy, M. L., and Miller, S. L. (2011). *The victimization of women: Law, policies, and politics.* New York: Oxford University Press.

Melton, H. C. (2007a). Predicting the occurrence of stalking in relationships characterized by domestic violence. *Journal of Interpersonal Violence, 22,* 3–25.

———. (2007b). Stalking in the context of intimate partner abuse: In the victim's words. *Feminist Criminology, 2,* 347–63.

Menard, A. (2001). Domestic violence and housing: Key policy and program challenges. *Violence Against Women, 7,* 707–21.

Mercer, S. L. (1988). Not a pretty picture: An exploratory study of violence against women in high school dating. *Resources for feminist research, 17,* 15–22.

Merton, R. K. (1965). *On the shoulders of giants.* Chicago: University of Chicago Press.

Messerschmidt, J. W. (1986). *Capitalism, patriarchy, and crime: Toward a socialist feminist criminology.* Totowa, NJ: Roman and Littlefield.

———. (1993). *Masculinities and crime: Critique and reconceptualization.* Lanham, MD: Roman and Littlefield.

———. (2012). *Gender, heterosexuality, and youth violence: The struggle for recognition.* Lanham, MD: Roman and Littlefield.

Messman-Moore, T. L., Coates, A. A., Gaffey, K. J., and Johnson, C. E. (2008). Sexuality, substance use, and susceptibility to victimization: Risk for rape and sexual coercion in a prospective study of college women. *Journal of Interpersonal Violence, 23,* 1730–46.

Messner, M. A. (1994). Women in the men's locker room? In M. A. Messner and D. F. Sabo (Eds.), *Sex, violence and power in sports* (pp. 42–52). Freedom, CA: The Crossing Press.

Mihalic, S. W., and Elliot, D. (1997). If violence is domestic, does it really count? *Journal of Family Violence, 12,* 293–311.

Millar, E. (2009). Protecting our kids on campus. *Reader's Digest,* October, 42–53.

Miller, H. V. (2010). If your friends jumped off of a bridge, would you do it too? Delinquent peers and susceptibility to peer influence. *Justice Quarterly 27,* 473–91.

Miller, J. (2001). *One of the guys: Girls, gangs, and gender.* New York: Oxford University Press.

———. (2008). *Getting played: African-American girls, urban inequality, and gendered violence.* New York: New York University Press.

Miller, J., and Brunson, R. K. (2000). Gender dynamics in youth gangs. *Justice Quarterly, 17,* 419–48.

Miller, J., and Schwartz, M. D. (1992). Lewd lighters and dick-ee darts: The commodification of women through sexual objects. Paper presented at the annual meetings of the American Society of Criminology, New Orleans, November.

Miller, S. L., and Burack, C. (1993). A critique of Gottfredson and Hirschi's general theory of crime: Selective (in)attention to gender and power positions. *Women & Criminal Justice, 4,* 115–33.

Miller, S. L., and Wellford, C. F. (1997). Patterns and correlates of interpersonal violence. In A. P. Cardarelli (Ed.), *Violence between intimate partners: Patterns, causes, and effects* (pp. 16–28). Boston: Allyn and Bacon.

Mills, C. W. (1951). *White collar.* New York: Oxford University Press.

———. (1959). *The sociological imagination.* New York: Oxford University Press.

Minaker, J. C., and Snider, L. (2006). Husband abuse: Equality with a vengeance? Canadian *Journal of Criminology and Criminal Justice, 48,* 753–80.

Mooney, J. (1996). Violence, space and gender. In N. Jewson and S. MacGregor (Eds.), *Transforming cities* (pp. 100–15). London: Routledge.

Mossige, S., Ainsaar, M., and Svedin, C. (Eds.). (2007). *The Baltic Sea regional study on adolescent sexuality* (NOVA Rapport 18/07). Oslo, Norway: Norwegian Social Research.

Mowlabocus, S. (2010). Porn 2.0? Technology, social practice, and the new online porn industry. In F. Attwood (Eds.), *Porn.com: Making sense of online pornography* (pp. 69–87). New York: Peter Lang.

Mujica, A., and Ayala, A. I. U. (2008). Femicide in Morelos: An issue on public health. Paper presented at the World Health Organization's 9th World Conference on Injury Prevention and Safety Promotion, Yucatan, Mexico, March 18.

Mullins, C. W. (2009). "He would kill me with his penis": Genocidal rape in Rwanda as a state crime. *Critical Criminology, 17,* 15–34.

Nash Chang, V. (1996). *I just lost myself: Psychological abuse of women in marriage.* London: Praeger.

National Campaign to Prevent Teen and Unplanned Pregnancy and CosmoGirl.Com. (2012). *Sex and tech: Results from a survey of teens and young adults.* Retrieved July 23, 2012, from www.thenationalcampaign.org/sextech/PDF/SexTech_Summary.pdf,

National Coalition Against Domestic Violence. (2007). Violence Against Women Act appropriations. Retrieved July 9, 2009, from www.naesv.org/Resources/2007VAWAApprops.pdf.

National Institute of Justice. (1996). *Domestic violence, stalking, and antistalking legislation: An annual report to Congress under the Violence Against Women Act.* Washington, DC: Author.

———. (2000). Workshop on gender symmetry. Retrieved July 9, 2012, from www.ojp .usdoj.gov/nij/topics/crime/violence-against-women/workshops/gender-symmetry .htm#future2.

National Organization of Women. (2004, August 26). Stop the Bush/right-wing attacks on women. Retrieved August 27, 2006, from www.now.org/issues/right/082604right .html.

Niehaus, I. (2005). Masculine dominance in sexual violence: Interpreting accounts of three cases of rape in the South Africa Lowveld. In G. Reid and L. Walker (Eds.), *Men behaving differently* (pp. 65–83). Cape Town: Juta.

Nikunen, K., Paasonen, S. and Saarenmaa, L. (Eds.). (2007). *Pornification: Sex and sexuality in media culture.* Oxford, UK: Berg Publishers.

Ni Laoire, C., and Fielding, S. (2006). Rooted and routed masculinities among the rural youth of North Cork and Upper Swaledale. In H. Campbell, M. Mayerfeld Bell, and M. Finney (Eds.), *Country boys: Masculinity and rural life* (pp. 105–20). University Park: Pennsylvania State University Press.

Ogilvie, E. (2000). *Cyber stalking.* Retrieved July 23, 2012, from www.aic.gov.au/docu ments/4/7/A/%7B47A7FA60–8EBF-498A-BB9E-D61BC512C053%7Dti166.pdf.

O'Hagan, E. M. (2011, September 15). As the Topman T-shirts show, misogyny is now so commonplace it's mundane. *Guardian.* Retrieved June 20, 2012, from www .guardian.co.uk.

Osthoff, S. (2002). But, Gertrude, I beg to differ, a hit is not a hit is not a hit: When battered women are arrested for assaulting their partners. *Violence Against Women, 8,* 1521–44.

Paul, P. (2005). *Pornified: How pornography is damaging our lives, our relationships, and our families.* New York: Owl Books.

Pearce, F. (1989). *The radical Durkheim.* Boston: Unwin Hyman.

Pence, E. L., and Shepard, M. F. (1999). An introduction: Developing a coordinated community response. In M. F. Shepard and E. L. Pence (Eds.), *Coordinating community responses to domestic violence: Lessons from Duluth and beyond* (pp. 3–25). Thousand Oaks, CA: Sage.

Pence, E., and Dasgupta, S. D. (2006). *Re-examining "battering": Are all acts of violence against intimate partners the same? Duluth: Praxis International.* Retrieved July 9, 2012, from www.praxisinternational.org/pages/library/files/pdf/Reexamining Battering.pdf.

Pence, E., and Paymar, M. (1993). *Education groups for men who batter: The Duluth model.* New York: Springer.

Perilla, J. L., Lippy, C., Rosales, A., and Serrata, J. V. (2011). Prevalence of domestic violence. In J. W. White, M. P. Koss, and A. E. Kazdin (Eds.), *Violence against women and children* (pp. 199–220). Washington, DC: American Psychological Association.

Peterson del Mar, D. (1996). *What trouble I have seen: A history of violence against women.* Cambridge, MA: Harvard University Press.

Piquero, A., and Mazerolle, P. (Eds.). (2001). *Life-course criminology: Contemporary and classic readings.* Belmont, CA: Wadsworth.

Pittaro, M. L. (2011). Cyber stalking: Typology, etiology, and victims. In K. Jaishankar (Ed.), *Cyber criminology: Exploring Internet crimes and criminal behavior* (pp. 277–98). New York: CRC Press.

Pitts, V. L., and Schwartz, M. D. (1993). Promoting self-blame among hidden rape survivors. *Humanity & Society 17*, 383–98.

Platt, A. (1978). Street crime: A view from the left. *Crime and Social Justice, 9*, 26–34.

Polk, K. (2003). Masculinities, femininities and homicide: Competing explanations for male violence. In M. D. Schwartz and S. E. Hatty (Eds.), *Controversies in critical criminology* (pp. 133–46). Cincinnati, OH: Anderson.

Porter, T. (2006a). *Well meaning men: Breaking out of the man box*. Charlotte, NC: A Call to Men: National Association of Men and Women Committed to Ending Violence Against Women.

———. (2006b). *Becoming part of the solution*. Charlotte, NC: A Call to Men: National Association of Men and Women Committed to Ending Violence Against Women.

Potter, H. (2008). *Battle cries: Black women and intimate partner abuse*. New York: New York University Press.

Powell, B., and Brown, L. (2007, October 5). 8 boys charged with sex assault on school grounds: 12- and 13-year-old students accused of restraining and groping girls; parents fear charges overblown. *Toronto Star*, A1, A27.

Proudfoot, S. (2009, July 23). "Honor killings" of females on rise in Canada: Expert. *(Saskatoon) Star Pheonix*, 1.

Ptacek, J. (1999). *Battered women in the courtroom: The power of judicial responses*. Boston: Northeastern University Press.

Rae, C. (1995). That macho thing: Social supports of violence against women. Unpublished doctoral dissertation, Ohio University.

Raphael, J. (1999). Keeping women poor: How domestic violence prevents women from leaving welfare and entering the world of work. In R. A. Brandwein (Ed.), *Battered women, children, and welfare reform: The ties that bind* (pp. 31–44). Thousand Oaks, CA: Sage.

———. (2001a). Public housing and domestic violence. *Violence Against Women, 7*, 699–706.

———. (2001b). Domestic violence as a welfare-to-work barrier: Research and theoretical issues. In C. M. Renzetti, J. L. Edleson, and R. K. Bergen (Eds.), *Sourcebook on violence against women* (pp. 443–56). Thousand Oaks, CA: Sage.

Ray, L. (2011). *Violence & society*. London: Sage.

Reitzel-Jaffe, D., and Wolfe, D. A. (2001). Predictors of relationship abuse among young men. *Journal of Interpersonal Violence, 16*, 99–115.

Rennison, C. M., DeKeseredy, W. S., and Dragiewicz, M. (2012). Urban, suburban, and rural variations in separation/divorce rape/sexual assault: Results from the national crime victimization survey. *Feminist Criminology*. Online version available at http://fcz.sagepub.com/content/early/2012/02/15/1557085111435660.

———. (in press). Intimate relationship status variations in violence against women: Urban, suburban, and rural differences. *Violence Against Women*.

Renzetti, C. M. (1995). Editor's introduction. *Violence Against Women, 1*, 3–5.

———. (1997). Confessions of a reformed positivist: Feminist participatory research as good social science. In M. D. Schwartz (Ed.), *Researching sexual violence against women* (pp. 131–43). Thousand Oaks, CA: Sage.

———. (2008). Psychological/emotional abuse. In C. M. Renzetti and J. L. Edleson (Eds.), *Encyclopedia of interpersonal violence* (pp. 570–71). Thousand Oaks, CA: Sage.

———. (2011). Economic issues and intimate partner violence. In C. M. Renzetti, J. L. Edleson, and R. K. Bergen (Eds.), *Sourcebook on violence against women* (2nd ed., pp. 171–87). Thousand Oaks, CA: Sage.

———. (2012). Feminist perspectives in criminology. In W. S. DeKeseredy and M. Dragiewicz (Eds.), *Routledge handbook of critical criminology* (pp. 129–37). London: Routeldge.

———. (2013). *Feminist criminology.* London: Routledge.

Renzetti, C. M., Edleson, J. L., and Bergen, R. K. (Eds.). (2011a). *Sourcebook on violence against women* (2nd ed.). Thousand Oaks, CA: Sage.

———. (2011b). Theoretical and methodological issues in researching violence against women. In C. M. Renzetti, J. L. Edleson, and R. K. Bergen (Eds.), *Sourcebook on violence against women* (2nd. ed., pp. 1–2). Thousand Oaks, CA: Sage.

Renzetti, C. M., and Maier, S. L. (2002). Private crime in public housing: Fear of crime and violent victimization among women public housing residents. *Women's Health and Urban Life, 1,* 46–65.

Rettberg, J. W. (2009). Joining a Facebook group as political action. jill/txt. Retrieved January 20, 2010, from http://jilltxt.net/?p=2367.

Riggs, D. S., and O'Leary, K. D. (1989). A theoretical model of courtship aggression. In M. A. Pirog-Good and J. E. Stets (Eds.), *Violence in dating relationships: Emerging social issues* (pp. 53–71). New York: Praeger.

Ritzer, G. (2008). *Sociological theory* (7th ed.). Boston: McGraw-Hill.

Roberts, A., and Dziegielewski, S. (1996). Assessment typology and intervention with the survivors of stalking. Aggression and Violent Behavior, 1, 359–68.

Rock, P. (1992). The criminology that came in from the cold. In J. Lowman and B. D. MacLean (Eds.), *Realist criminology: Crime control and policing in the 1990s* (pp. ix–xiv). Toronto: University of Toronto Press.

Rogness, M. (2002). Toward an integrated male peer support model of marital rape in the United States. MA thesis. Department of Sociology and Anthropology, Ohio University. Athens, Ohio.

Roiphe, K. 1993. *The morning after: Sex, fear and feminism on campus.* Boston: Little, Brown.

Romita, P., and Beltramini, L. (2011). Watching pornography: Gender differences, violence and victimization. An exploratory study in Italy. *Violence Against Women.* Online version retrieved October 13, 2011, from http://vaw.sagepub.com/content /early/2011/10/11/1077801211424555.

Rosen, L. N., and Martin, L. (1998). Predictors of tolerance of sexual harassment among male U.S. army soldiers. *Violence Against Women, 4,* 491–504.

Rosen, L. N., Kaminski, R. J., Parmley, A. M., Knudson, K. H., and Fancher, P. (2003). The effects of peer group climate on intimate partner violence among married male U.S. army soldiers. *Violence Against Women, 9,* 1072–1092.

Russell, D. E. H. (1990). *Rape in marriage* (Rev. ed.). Bloomington: Indiana University Press.

———. (1993). *Against pornography: The evidence of harm.* Berkeley, CA: Russell Publications.

———. (1998). *Dangerous relationships: Pornography, misogyny, and rape.* Thousand Oaks, CA: Sage.

———. (2001). Defining femicide and related concepts. In D. E. H. Russell and R. A. Harmes (Eds.), *Femicide in global perspective* (pp. 12–28). New York: Teachers College Press.

Ryan, A. (2001). *Feminist ways of knowing: Towards theorising the person for radical adult education.* Leicester, UK: NIACE.

Salter, M. (2013). *Organised sexual abuse.* London: Routledge.

Sampson, R. J. (2000). Whither the sociological study of crime? *Annual Review of Sociology, 26,* 711–14.

Sampson, R. J., and Laub, J. H. (1993). *Crime in the making: Pathways and turning points through life.* Cambridge, MA: Harvard University Press.

Sanday, P. R. (1981). The socio-cultural context of rape. *Journal of Social Issues, 37,* 5–27.

———. (1990). *Fraternity gang rape.* New York: New York University Press.

Sarason, I. G., and Sarason, B. R. (1985). *Social support: Theory, research, and applications.* The Hague, The Netherlands: Martinus Nijhof.

Sartre, J. P. (1964). *The words.* London: Penguin.

Say No—Unite to End Violence Against Women. (2012.). About Say No. Retrieved March 15, 2012, from http://saynotoviolence.org/about-say-no.

Schmitt, R. L. (1972). *The reference other orientation.* Carbondale, IL: Southern Illinois University Press.

Schneider, J. P. (2000). Effects of cybersex addiction on the family: Results of a survey. *Sexual Addiction and Compulsivity, 7,* 31–58.

Schur, E. M. (1984). *Labeling women deviant.* New York: Random House.

Schwartz, M. D. (1987). Censorship of sexual violence: Is the problem sex or violence? *Humanity & Society 11,* 212-43.

———. (1988a). Ain't got no class: Universal risk theories of battering. *Contemporary Crises, 12,* 373–92.

———. (1988b). Marital status and woman abuse theory. *Journal of Family Violence, 3,* 239–48.

———. (1989). The undercutting edge in critical criminology. *The Critical Criminologist 1(2),* 1-5.

———. (2000). Methodological issues in the use of survey data for measuring and characterizing violence against women. *Violence Against Women, 8*, 815–38.

Schwartz, M. D., and DeKeseredy, W. S. (1988). Liberal feminism on violence against women. *Social Justice, 15*, 213–21.

———. (1993). The return of the "battered husband syndrome" through the typification of women as violent. *Crime, Law and Social Change, 20*, 249–65.

———. (1994). People without data attacking rape: The Gilbertizing of Mary Koss. *Violence Update, 5*, 5, 8, 11.

———. (1997). *Sexual assault on the college campus: The role of male peer support.* Thousand Oaks, CA: Sage.

———. (1998). Pornography and the abuse of Canadian women in dating relationships. *Humanity & Society, 22*, 137–54.

———. (in press). Critical theory. In Albanese, J. (Ed.). *The encyclopedia of criminology and criminal justice.* New York: Wiley-Blackwell.

Schwartz, M. D., DeKeseredy, W. S., Tait, D., and Alvi, S. (2001). Male peer support and routine activities theory: Understanding sexual assault on the college campus. *Justice Quarterly, 18*, 701–27.

Schwartz, M. D. and Leggett, M. S. (1999). Bad dates or emotional trauma? The aftermath of campus sexual assault. *Violence Against Women 5.* 251–71.

Schwartz, M. D. and Nogrady, C. (1996). Fraternity membership, rape myths, and sexual aggression on a college campus. *Violence Against Women, 2*, 148–62.

Schwartz, M. D., and Pitts, V. L. (1995). Exploring a feminist routine activities approach to explaining sexual assault. *Justice Quarterly, 12*, 9–31.

Scully, D. (1990). *Understanding sexual violence.* Boston, MA: Unwin Hyman.

Sernau, S. (2001). *Worlds apart: Social inequalities in a new century.* Thousand Oaks, CA: Pine Forge Press.

———. (2006). *Global problems: The search for equity, peace, and sustainability.* Boston: Pearson.

Sev'er, A. (1999). Sexual harassment: Where we were, where we are and prospects for the new millennium. *Canadian Review of Sociology and Anthropology, 36*, 469–98.

———. (2002). *Fleeing the house of horrors: Women who have left abusive partners.* Toronto: University of Toronto Press.

———. (2008). Discarded daughters: The patriarchal grip, dowry deaths, sex ratio imbalances and foeticide in India. *Women's Health and Urban Life, 7*, 56–75.

Sherman, J. (2005). *Men without sawmills: Masculinity, rural poverty, and family stability.* Columbia, MO: Rural Poverty Research Center.

Silverman, J. G., and Williamson, G. M. (1997). Social ecology and entitlements involved in battering by heterosexual college males: Contributions of family and peers. *Violence and Victims, 12*, 147–64.

Silvestri, M., and Crowther-Dowey, C. (2008). *Gender and crime.* London: Sage.

Sinclair, D. (2003). Overcoming the backlash: Telling the truth about power, privilege, and oppression. Retrieved March 4, 2011, from www.crvawc.ca/documents/over comingthebacklash.pdf.

Sinclair, R. L. (2002). Male peer support and male-to-female dating abuse committed by socially displaced male youth: An exploratory study. Doctoral dissertation. Ottawa: Carleton University.

Skjelsbak, I. (2011). Sexual violence in the post-Yugoslav wars. In K. Kuehnast, C. de Jonge Oudraat, and H. Hernes (Eds.), *Women & war: Power and protection in the 21st century* (65–84). Washington, DC: United States Institute of Peace.

Slayden, D. (2010). Debbie does Dallas again and again: Pornography, technology, and market innovation. In F. Attwood (Ed.), *Porn.com: Making sense of online pornography* (pp. 54–68). New York: Peter Lang.

Sloan, J. J., and Fisher, B. S. (2011). *The dark side of the ivory tower: Campus crime as a social problem.* New York: Cambridge University Press.

Smith, M. D. (1979). Hockey violence: A test of the violent subculture thesis. *Social Problems, 27,* 235–47.

———. (1983). *Violence and sport.* Toronto: Butterworths.

———. (1987). The incidence and prevalence of woman abuse in Toronto. *Violence and Victims, 2,* 173–87.

———. (1990). Patriarchal ideology and wife beating: A test of a feminist hypothesis. *Violence and Victims, 5,* 257–73.

———. (1991). Male peer support of wife abuse: An exploratory study. *Journal of Interpersonal Violence, 6,* 512–19.

———. (1994). Enhancing the quality of survey data on violence against women: A feminist approach. *Gender and Society, 8,* 109–27.

Sokoloff, N. J. (Ed.). (2005). *Domestic violence at the margins: Readings on race, class, gender, and culture.* New Brunswick, NJ: Rutgers University Press.

Sokoloff, N. J., and Dupont, I. (2005). Domestic violence: Examining the intersections of race, class, and gender—An introduction. In N. J. Sokoloff (Ed.), *Domestic violence at the margins: Readings on race, class, gender, and culture* (pp. 1–13). New Brunswick, NJ: Rutgers University Press.

Southworth, C., Finn, J., Dawson, S., Fraser, C., and Tucker, S. (2007). Intimate partner violence, technology and stalking. *Violence Against Women, 13,* 842–56.

Southworth, C., Tucker, S., Fraser, C., and Shulruff, T. (2008). High-tech violence against women. In In C. M. Renzetti and J. L. Edleson (Eds.), *Encyclopedia of interpersonal violence* (pp. 329–30). Thousand Oaks, CA: Sage.

Spitzberg, B. H., and Hoobler, G. (2002). Cyberstalking and the technologies of interpersonal terrorism. *New Media & Society, 4,* 71–92.

Stanko, E. A. (1985). *Intimate intrusions: Women's experience of male violence.* London: Routledge and Kegan Paul.

———. (1997). I second that emotion: Reflections on feminism, emotionality, and research on sexual violence. In M. D. Schwartz (Ed.), *Researching sexual violence against women: Methodological and personal perspectives* (pp. 74–85). Thousand Oaks, CA: Sage.

Stark, E. (2006). Commentary on Johnson's conflict and control: Gender symmetry and asymmetry in domestic violence. *Violence Against Women, 12,* 1019–25.

———. (2007). *Coercive control: How men entrap women in personal life.* New York: Oxford University Press.

Statistics Canada. (1993). *Violence against women Survey.* Ottawa: Author.

———. (2002, June 26). Family violence: Impacts and consequences of spousal violence. *The Daily.* Retrieved March 15, 2012, from www.statcan.gc.ca/daily -quotidien/020626/tdq020626-eng.htm

———. (2005, July 14). Family violence in Canada: A statistical profile. *The Daily.* Retrieved March 15, 2012, from www.statcan.gc.ca/daily-quotidien/050714/dq05 0714a-eng.htm

———. (2011). *Family violence in Canada: A statistical profile.* Ottawa: Author.

Stebner, B., and Associated Press. (September 1, 2012). "It's not as bad as what they are saying. Nobody tied her up." *DailyMailOnline.* www.dailymail.co.uk.

Stephenson, A. (2013, March 12). One in ten men say it's OK to hit a woman if she makes him angry: Alberta survey. National Post. Retrieved from: http://news .nationalpost.com/2012/03/13/1-in-10-men-says-its-ok-to-hit-a-woman-if-she -makes-him-angry-alberta-survey.

Stevens, A. (2011). *Drugs, crime and public health: The political economy of drug policy.* London: Routledge.

StopCyberbullying.org (2012). What is it? Retrieved July 23, 2012, from www.stopcyber bullying.org/what_is_cyberbullying_exactly.html.

Stosny, S. (2008, December 17). Are you dating an abuser? *Psychology Today.* Retrieved February 24, 2012, from www.psychologytoday.com/blog/anger-in-the-age -entitement/200812/are-you-dati . . .

Stout, K. D. (2001). Intimate femicide: A national demographic overview. In D. E. H. Russell and R. A. Harmes (Eds.), *Femicide in global perspective* (pp. 41–49). New York: Teacher's College Press.

Straus, M. A. (1979). Measuring intrafamily conflict and violence: The Conflict Tactics (CT) Scales. *Journal of Marriage and the Family, 41,* 75–88.

———. (2011). Gender symmetry and mutuality in perpetation of clinical-level partner violence: Empirical evidence and implications for prevention and treatment. *Aggression and Violent Behavior, 16,* 279–88.

Straus, M. A., Gelles, R. J., and Steinmetz, S. K. (1981). *Behind closed doors: Violence in the American family.* New York: Anchor.

Straus, M. A., Hamby, S. L., Boney-McCoy, S., and Sugarman, D. B. (1996). The revised Conflict Tactics Scales (CTS2): Development and preliminary psychometric data. *Journal of Family Issues, 17,* 283–316.

Suris, A., and Lind, L. (2008). Military sexual trauma: A review of prevalence and associated health consequences in veterans. *Trauma, Violence, & Abuse, 9,* 250–69.

Sutherland, E. H. (1939). *Principles of criminology*. Philadelphia: J. B. Lippincott.

Tanha, M., Beck, C. J. A., Figueredo, A. J., and Raghavan, C. (2010). Sex differences in intimate partner violence and the use of coercive control as a motivational factor for intimate partner violence. *Journal of Interpersonal Violence, 10,* 1836–54.

Tanner, J. (2012). The contemporary youth gang: Critical perspectives. In W. S. DeKeseredy and M. Dragiewicz (Eds.), *Routledge handbook of critical criminology* (pp. 387–400). London: Routledge.

Taylor, I. (1981). *Law and order: Arguments for socialism*. London: Macmillan.

Taylor, I., Walton, P., and Young, J. (1973). *The new criminology*. London: Routledge and Kegan Paul.

Thoits, P. A. (1983). Dimensions of life events that influence psychological distress: An evaluation and synthesis of the literature. In H. B. Kaplan (Ed.), *Psychosocial stress: Trends in theory and research* (pp. 33–103). New York: Academic Press.

Thorne-Finch, R. (1992). *Ending the silence: The origins and treatment of male violence against men*. Toronto: University of Toronto Press.

Tjaden, P., and Thoennes, N. (2000). *Extent, nature, and consequences of intimate partner violence: Findings from the National Violence Against Women Survey*. Washington, DC: U.S. Department of Justice.

Toews, J. C. (2010, June 10). The disappearing family farm. *Real Truth*. Retrieved May 15, 2012, from http://realtruth.org/articles/100607-006-family.html?print_view=yes.

Totten, M. D. (2000). *Guys, gangs, and girlfriend abuse*. Peterborough, ON: Broadview Press.

Troshynski, E. (2012). Human trafficking. In W. S. DeKeseredy and M. Dragiewicz (Eds.), *Routledge handbook of critical criminology* (pp. 342–60). London: Routledge.

Ulloa, E. C., Dyson, R. B., and Wynes, D. D. (2012). Inter-partner violence in the context of gangs: A review. *Aggression and Violent Behavior, 17,* 397–404.

United States Department of Agriculture. (2011). *Rural America at a glance 2011 edition*. Washington, DC: Author.

University of Kentucky Violence Intervention and Prevention Center. (2012). Green dots for men. Retrieved July 23, 2012, from www.uky.edu/StudentAffairs/VIP Center/learn_greendot.php.

Ursel, E. (1986). The state and maintenance of patriarchy: A case study of family and welfare legislation. In J. Dickinsin and B. Russell (Eds.), *Family, economy and state* (pp. 150–91). Toronto: Garamond.

Vallee, B. (2007). *The war on women*. Toronto: Key Porter.

Vander Ven, T. (2011). *Getting wasted: Why college students drink so much and party so hard*. New York: New York University Press.

Vargas Martin, M., Garcia-Ruiz, M. A., and Edwards, A. (2011). Preface. In M. Vargas Martin, M. A. Garcia Ruiz, and A. Edwards (Eds.), *Technology for facilitating humanity and combating social deviations: Interdisciplinary perspectives* (pp. xxii–xxvii). Hershey PA: Information Science Reference.

Vaux, A. (1985). Variations in social support associated with gender, ethnicity, and age. *Journal of Social Issues, 41,* 89–110.

Veblen, T. (1899/1934). *The theory of the leisure class.* New York: Modern Library.

Venkatesh, S. A. (2000). *American project: The rise and fall of a modern ghetto.* Cambridge, MA: Harvard University Press.

Villalon, R. (2010). *Violence against Latina immigrants: Citizenship, inequality, and community.* New York: New York University Press.

Wacquant, L. (2008). *Urban outcasts: A comparative sociology of advanced marginality.* Malden, MA: Polity.

Walby, S., and Myhill, A. (2001). New survey methodologies in researching violence against women. *British Journal of Criminology, 41,* 502–22.

Walker, L. E. (1977–78). Battered women and learned helplessness. *Victimology, 3–4,* 525–34.

———. (1979). *The battered woman.* New York: Harper and Row.

———. (1983). The battered women syndrome study. In D. Finkelhor, R. J. Gelles, G. T. Hotaling, and M. A. Straus (Eds.), *The dark side of families* (pp. 31–48). Beverly Hills, CA: Sage.

Wantland, R. A. (2008). Our brotherhood and your sister: Building anti-rape community in the fraternity. *Journal of Preventions & Interventions in the Community, 36,* 57–74.

Ward, S., Chapman K., Cohen, E., White, S., and Williams, K. (1991). Acquaintance rape and the college social science. *Family relations, 40,* 65–71.

Warr, M. (2002). *Companions in crime: The social aspects of criminal conduct.* Cambridge, UK: Cambridge University Press.

Warshaw, R. (1988). *I never called it rape.* New York: Harper and Row.

Watts, C., and Zimmerman, C. (2002). Violence against women: Global scope and magnitude. *Lancet,* April 6, 359.

Websdale, N. (1998). *Rural woman battering and the justice system: An ethnography.* Thousand Oaks, CA: Sage.

———. (1999). *Understanding domestic homicide.* Boston: Northeastern University Press.

———. (2010). *Familicidal hearts: The emotional styles of 211 killers.* New York: Oxford University Press.

Weerman, F. M. (2011). Delinquent peers in context: A longitudinal network analysis of selection and influence effects. *Criminology, 49,* 253–86.

Wellstone, P. D., and Wellstone, S. (2011). Foreword to the first edition. In C. M. Renzetti, J. L. Edleson, and R. K. Bergen (Eds.), *Sourcebook on violence against women* (2nd ed., pp. xi–xii). Thousand Oaks, CA: Sage.

Wheeler, S. (1976). Trends and problems in the sociological study of crime. *Social Problems, 23,* 525–34.

Whitehead, A. (1976). Sexual antagonisms in Herefordshire. In D. Barker and S. Allen (Eds.), *Dependence and exploitation in work and marriage* (pp. 169–203). London: Longman.

Wilcox, B. L. (1981). Social support, life events stress, and psychological adjustment: A test of the buffering hypothesis. *American Journal of Community Psychology, 9,* 371–86.

Wills, T. A. (1985). Supportive functions in interpersonal relationships. In S. Cohen and S. Syme (Eds.), *Social support and health* (pp. 61–78). Toronto: Academic Press.

Wilson, M., and Daly, M. (1992). Til death do us part. In J. Radford and D. E. H. Russell (Eds.), *Femicide: The politics of women killing* (pp. 83–98). New York: Twayne.

Wilson, W. J. (1987). *The truly disadvantaged: The inner-city, the underclass and public policy.* Chicago: University of Chicago Press.

———. (1996). *When work disappears: The world of the new urban poor.* New York: Knopf.

Wilson, W. J., and Taub, R. P. (2006). *There goes the neighborhood: Racial, ethnic, and class tensions in four Chicago neighborhoods and their meaning for America.* New York: Knopf.

Winstok, Z. (2011). The paradigmatic cleavage on gender differences in partner violence perpetration and victimization. *Aggression and Violent Behavior, 16,* 303–11.

Wojcicki, J. (2002). "She drank his money": Survival sex and the problem of violence in taverns in Gauteng Province, South Africa. *Medical Anthropology, 16,* 267–93.

Wolak, J., Finkelhor, D., Mitchell, K. J., and Jones, L. M. (2011). Arrests for child pornography production: Data at two time points from a national sample of U.S. law enforcement agencies. *Child Maltreatment,* July 22, 1–12.

Wolak, J., Mitchell, K., and Finkelhor, D. (2007). Unwanted and wanted exposure to online pornography in a national sample of youth Internet users. *Pediatrics, 119,* 247–55.

Wolfe, D., and Jaffe, P. (2001). Prevention of domestic violence: Emerging initiatives. In S. Graham-Bermann and J. Edleson (Eds.), *Domestic violence in the lives of children* (pp. 283–98). Washington, DC: American Psychological Association.

Wolff, A. (2012). Is this the end for Penn State? *Sports Illustrated, 117* (July 30), 38–41.

Wolfgang, M. E., and Ferracuti, F. (1967). *The subculture of violence: Toward an integrated theory in criminology.* London: Tavistock.

Woliver, L. (1993). *From outrage to action: The politics of grassroots dissent.* Chicago: University of Illinois Press.

Wood, D., Myrstol, B., Rosay, A., Rivera, M., and TePas, K. (2011). Intimate partner violence against Alaska native and non-native women: Estimates from the Alaska victimization survey. Paper presented at the annual meetings of the American Society of Criminology, November.

Wood, E. J. (2011). Rape is not inevitable in war. In K. Kuehnast, C. de Jonge Oudraat, and H. Hernes (Eds.), *Women and war: Power and protection in the 21st century* (37–64). Washington, DC: United States Institute of Peace.

Wood, K. (2005). Contextualizing group rape in post-apartheid South Africa. *Culture, Health, and Sexuality, 7,* 303–17.

World Health Organization. (2002). *World report on violence and health: Summary.* Geneva: Author.

Wykes, M., and Welsh, K. (2009). *Violence, gender and Justice.* London: Sage.

Yar, M., and Penna, S. (2004). Between positivism and post-modernity? Critical reflections on Jock Young's *The exclusive society. British Journal of Criminology, 44,* 533–49.

Yllo, K. (1983). Sexual equality and violence against wives in American states. *Journal of Comparative Family Studies, 1,* 1–29.

Young, J. (1975). Working class criminology. In I. Taylor, P. Walton, and J. Young (Eds.), *Critical criminology* (pp. 63–94). London: Routledge and Kegan Paul.

———. (1988). Radical criminology in Britain: The emergence of a competing paradigm. *British Journal of Criminology, 28,* 159–83.

———. (1999). *The exclusive society.* London: Sage.

———. (2011). *The criminological imagination.* Malden, MA: Polity Press.

Young, J. T. N., Barnes, J. C., Meldrum, R. C. and Weerman, F. M. (2011). Assessing and explaining misperception of peer delinquency. *Criminology, 49,* 599–630.

Young, K. (1988). Performance, control, and public image of behavior in a deviant subculture: The case of rugby. *Deviant Behavior, 9,* 275–93.

———. (2011). Virtual sex offenders: A clinical perspective. In K. Jaishankar (Ed.), *Cyber criminology: Exploring internet crimes and criminal behavior* (pp. 53–64). New York: CRC Press.

Zerbisias, A. (2008, January 26). Packaging abuse of women as entertainment for adults: Cruel, degrading scenes "normalized" for generation brought up in dot-com world. *Toronto Star,* L3.

Index

Page numbers in *italics* refer to illustrations

Bouffard, L. A., 98, 99, 125
Bourgois, P., 88, 115–16
Bowker, L., 46–47, 49
Brownridge, D., 24, 107
bullying, 68, 111, 156n12
Burawoy, M., 93–94

campus sexual assault, 63, 118. *See also*
sexual assault; woman abuse
Canada, 4, 8, 19, 24, 26, 29, 34, 37, *58*, 75,
96, 97, *138*, 141, 142; and alcohol, 57;
and male peer support theories, 45;
and pornography, 122; rural, 79, 84;
urban, 75; wife beaters in, 101; and
youth unemployment, 150. *See also*
North America
Canadian national survey of woman abuse
in university/college dating (CNS), 24,
31, 36, 96–101, 124–25
Centers for Disease Control's National
Intimate Partner and Sexual Violence
Survey (NISVS). *See* NISVS
coercive control, 14, 41, 20, 21, 33, 118, 140.
See also blackmail
cohabiting women: and blackmail, 12; risks
of, 33
Cohen, A., 50, 59, 71, 89, 91, 94
college women, 25, 47, 61, 62, 73
conformity, 72–74
Conflict Tactics Scale (CTS), 17–18, 19, 33,
155n7
crime, xv, 4, 5, 7, 9, 37, 47, 62, 64, 66, 91,
93, 109, *113*; and campuses, 35, 62;
Control Model, 110; corporate, 73; and
critical criminology, 51–52; gender-blind
theory, 71–72; gender-neutral, 16; and
left realism, 89; and masculinities, 68;
organized, 65, 69; in public housing, 75;
rural, 78–79, 104, 157n8; survey, 7, 23, 24,
30; violent, 114. *See also* Hirschi; sexual
assault
critical criminology, 51–52, 92, 156n7; and
left realism, 89; research, 79
Currie, E., 87, 89, 114, 150, 151

cyberbullying, 133–35, 150
cyberporn, xviv, 120, 122, 123, 131, 132; and
male peer support groups, 130

DeKeseredy, A., 112
DeKeseredy, W., xiv, xv, xvii, xix, 13, 15–17,
20, 32, 34, 36; and boycotting, 143–44,
149; and LaMarsh Center, 45–47; and
modified male peer support model,
53, *54*, 74, 75, 78, 86, 97, 98, 122, 137;
and original male peer support model,
49–51, *50*, 52, 53; and social support
theory, 48, 49
deterrence: absence of, 53, *55*, 61–64
deviance. *See* conformity
Dines, G., 121, 123, 127, 128, 136
Dobash, R. and Dobash, R. E., 6, 54, 100
domestic violence, 1, 2, 3, 16, 29, 57, 110,
135, 141; and Canada, 29; Intervention
Program, 3; in public housing, 76; rural,
110
Donnermeyer, J., 79
Dragiewicz, M., 20, 79, 110, 118
drugs, *36*, 37, 87, 88, 105; dealing, 116; by
perpetrator, 28; and rural crime, 79; and
sexual assault, 35, 69; and urban areas,
87; use by women, 62
Durkheim, E., 47–48, 91
Dyer, D., 144, 145, 159n5

economic exclusion/male peer support
model, 74, *77*, 78; and woman abuse
data, 75
Edwards, A., 110, 135
Ellis, D., 18, 45, 46, 70; and social support
theory, 47–49, 51. *See also* LaMarsh
Center
emotional separation, 81, 82
empiricism, 93; abstracted, 27, 46, 91–93, 118,
157n17. *See also* Mills, C. W.
Empiricus Abstractus, 158n2
ethnicity, 33, 37; of males, 32, 117; and
technology, 111; and violence against
women, 32. *See also* race

111–18; patriarchal, 35, 37, 80, 82, 90, 114; and pornography, xix, 120, 127; research, 94, 110, 111, 112, 115, 118; and sexual assault, 105; studies of, 103, 104; and technologies, 119; for victimization, 101, 102; and violence against wives, 100–103. *See also* deterrence; feminist/male peer support model of separation and divorce sexual assault; gendered; rural masculinity crisis/male peer support model of separation/divorce sexual assault

male peer support groups, 96, 98, 99; and antifeminist cyberspace, 129–30; patriarchal, 78, 130

male peer support model, xviii, 35, 45, 69, 76, 78; DeKeseredy's original, 49, 50, 52; modified, xv, 53, 65, 67, 68, 99. *See also* feminist/male peer support model of separation and divorce sexual assault; rural masculinity crisis/male peer support model of separation/divorce sexual assault; social groups; violence

male peer support theory, xv, xvi, xviii, xix, 26, 55, 72, 74, 75, 85, 86, 94, 96; history of, 44–68; and pornography, 125; of wife abuse, 46–47. *See also* feminist/male peer support model of separation and divorce sexual assault; gendered social bond/male peer support theory of university woman abuse; pro-abuse

male-to-female violence, xv, xvii, 2, 7, 23, 46, 72, 87, 90, 114; marriage, 100–103; and pornography, 127. *See also* beatings

male violence, 15, 23, 26, 81; as patriarchal control, 18; end, 146

married women, 28, 33, 45, 107, 108, 124

Martin, V., 110, 135, 135

masculinity, 44, 49, 55, 65, 81, 82, 90, 129; hegemonic, 148; narrow conception of, 55, 64; oppositional, 149; patriarchal, 78, 82; rural, xviii, 83, 84, 85

Matthews, R., 89, 91

Mead, G., 47–48

mesosytem, 118, 158n15

military, 35, 38, 68, 111, 112

Miller, J., 69, 71, 74, 144

Miller, S., 29, 70, 71

Mills, C. W., xiii, 91–94

misogyny, 116, 144, 145

Modified Male Peer Support Model, 98, 100

murder, 24, 25, 26, 28, 130; US rates of, 27. *See also* femicide

Murphy, D., 149

National Violence Against Women Survey (VAWS), 7, 31, 33; Canada, 23–24, 30–31

Native American women, 9, 28, 37, 110

Native women in Canada, 37

new technologies, xix, 30, 119, 120, 140, 142, 150, 153; contributions, 139–42; and cyberbullying, 135; harms of, 132–35; and male peer support, 110, 119–36; and pornographers, 121

National Intimate Partner and Sexual Violence Survey (NISVS), 15–16, 31, 32, 35, 36, 39, 41

North America, 4, 21, 25, 32, 64, 80, 86, 109, 112, 142; boycotting in, 143–45; and deterrence, 61; and gender-neutral, 16; and left realists, 89–90; and woman abuse, xv, 24. *See also* Canada; United States

offenders, male, 1, 16, 29, 30, 72, 78, 91, 119, 147

Ohio, 62; rural, xiv, 9, 10, 11, 13, 15, 79, 81, 83, 85, 103, 124

patriarchal subculture of violence, xiv, 47, 101

patriarchy, xv, 8, 54, 56, 64; courtship, 53, 55, 56; familial, 53, 54, 56, 84, 88, 90, 101, 102, 106, 135; invert, 77, 88, 116, 136, 141, 143, 145; social, 54, 55, 56; societal, 81, 106, 135. *See also* male dominance; social support theory

Pence, E., 1, 3, 20. *See also* power and control wheel

penetration, xix, 4, 12, 34, 36, 120
Penn State, 59, 64, 65, 66, 67
physical assault, 7, 11, 24, 31, 32, 57, 11, 107.
     See also physical force
physical force, 6, 12, 69, 96, 123. *See also*
     physical violence
physical violence, xix, 5, 6, 11, 13, 15, 24, 45,
     79, 100, 104; CNS rate of, 31; marital/
     cohabiting, 31; nonlethal, 29–34, 35, 79;
     and pornography, 123, 124, 127; research,
     29, 34
Pitts, V., 7, 35, 71
pluralistic ignorance, 65
pornography, xiv, xx, 83, 121, 123, 124, 125,
     127, 131, 132; child, 119–20; definition
     of, 121; growth, 121–22; Internet, xix,
     120, 121, 122, 126, 127, 130, 135; and male
     peer support system, xix, 120, 127–30;
     research, 126, 127; and rural Ohio,
     124–25; and woman abuse, 123–27. *See
     also* cyberporn; fraternities; penetration
Porter, T., 53, 145
positivism, 91, 92, 93, 116, 117
poverty, xvii, 34, 76, 89, 90; rural, 84; urban,
     75, 77
power and control wheel, 1, 3, 5, 155n1. *See
     also* violence
Pratt, T. C., 99, 125
pro-abuse, 60, 97, 103, 107; male peer sup-
     port, xiv, 56, 59, 74, 78, 97, 114, 129–30;
     and peer groups, xix, 56, 59, 67, 115. *See
     also* social groups
psychological abuse, xii, 11, 13, 15, 17, 39,
     40–41, 47, 49, 53, 98, 104; definition of,
     42. *See also* aggression

race, 32, 33, 37, 51, 64, 65, 73, 76. *See also*
     ethnicity
rape, xviii, xx, 6, 8, 10, 23, 31, 35, 36, 37, *38,*
     39, 43, *57,* *60,* 61, 63, 69, 73, 82, 105, 106,
     107, 109, *129,* 147, 155n2; on campus,
     34–35, 64, 65, 67, 139, 147; forcible, 7, 62,
     64, 125; and male peer support, 118, 152;
     marital, 9, 12, 80; and new technologies

129; rural, 104; and warfare, 113–14.
     See also gang rape; penetration; sex;
     victimization
reference group theory. *See* Kanin, E
Renzetti, C., 2, 32, 75, 76, 116
Rettberg, J. W., 140, 142
rural masculinity crisis/male peer support
     model of separation/divorce sexual
     assault, 83, *84.*
Russell, D. E. H., 12, 28, 124, 132

Sanday, P. R., 67, 105
Say NO-UNiTE, 139–40
Schwartz, M. D., 7, 32, 35, 36, 52, 62, 65, 71,
     97, 112, 124, 144
separation/divorce sexual assault, xviii,
     10, 18, 53, 80, 82, 83, 85, 103, 104, 105,
     106, 128; and male peer support and
     pornography, 128–30; and pornography,
     125–26; rural study of, 104, 106, 124. *See
     also* rural masculinity crisis/male peer
     support model of separation/divorce
     sexual assault; woman abuse
separation/divorce woman abuse in public
     housing, 107–8. *See also* assault
Sernau, S., 86; and web of exclusion model,
     76, 83
sex, 9, 10, 12, 46, 49, 59, 65, 95, 97, 105,
     106, 119, 122, 127, 128, 130, 149; body-
     punishing, 121; forced, 62, 71, 96; group,
     60, 105, 106; objects, 96; unwanted, 12,
     34. *See also* military
sexting, 120, 134, 150, 153
sexual abuse, 15, 31, 46, 47, 49, 50, 81–82,
     98, 104; and college men, 96, 104; in
     military, 38; and pornography, 124
sexual aggression, 36, 59, 60, 61, 64, 125;
     history of, 94
sexual assault, xvii, 4, 6, 7, 9, 12, 13, 18, 23,
     31, 36, 53, 56, 58, 65, 79, 98, 109; on
     college campus, 34–35, 62, 63, 64, 67,
     71, 99, 118, 147; and male peer support
     theories, 69, 74; and pornography, 125;
     by race/ethnicity, 37; and sports, *60,*

66, 98, 139; survey of, 24, 45. *See also* intimate partner; military; Penn State; separation/divorce sexual assault; victimization

sexual coercion, *36*, 99

sexual harassment, 6, 69, 73, 75, 111, 152; in military, 68, 111. *See also* harassment

sexual intercourse, 56, 63, 64, 95, 96, 99; consensual, 95; forced, 7

sexuality, 36, 59, 123, 130, 131, 136, 149, 150, 151

sexual objectification of women, xiv, *55*, 66, 94

sexual symmetry, 18, 155n8

sexual violence, 5, 15, 24, 34–35, 68, 100, 113, 116, 141, 142, 155n2; and bullying, 111; CNS rates of, 31; distribution of, 35–37; genocidal, 112–14; NISVS rates of, *36*; and pornography, 123, 125, 127. *See also* crime

Sinclair, R., 103, 112

Slut Walk, 56, *58*

Smith, M. D., 10, 45–46; and familial patriarchy, 56; and male peer support, 102–3

social and economic exclusion model of separation/divorce woman abuse in public housing, xviii, 86–89, 103, 107

social control, 56, 61, 99, 112; informal, 61, 85; rural, 79; theory, 74

social groups, 32, 36, 53, 58, 66, 67, 95; all-male, 68

socially displaced youth, 103, 158n8

social support, xviii, 10, 47, 48, 51, 56, 68; lawyering, 48–49; network, 148; and unemployment, 84

social support theory, xviii, 45, 47, 51; definition of, 47–48; and woman abuse, 48–51. *See also* Ellis, D.

sports, 60, 64–66; culture, 59, 151, 152; teams, 50, 53, 59, 98, 111, 115. *See also* fraternities

stalking, xvii, 6, 7, 15–16, 18, 31, 39–40, 135; behavior, 13, 28, 104; cyber, 129; definition of, 39; technical, 133

standards of gratification, xviii, 100, 101, 149

Stark, E., 14, 20

Statistics Canada's Violence Against Women Survey (VAWS), 23, 30, 155n3

Straus, M., 1, 17, 45–46, 76

suicide, *5*, 15, 28, 47, 134, 151

survivor, xvi, 3, 10, 13, 128; rural, 82; of sexual assault, 37, 39

technology, xvi, 30, 110–11, 119, 121, 129, 135, 140, 153. *See also* new technologies

Travis, C., 98

Trotta, L., *38*, 39

Twitter, xix, 139, 140, 145

underreporting, 9, 10, 29, 30, 35, 103, 158n2

United Kingdom, 4, 58, 126; and critical criminology, 52, 89; rural, 79

United States (U.S.), 23, 25, 26, 28, 35, 41, *58*, 80, 96, 129, 141; and alcohol, 57; and Crime Control Model in, 110; cyberporn, 122; and Green Dot Program, 146–47; and left realism, 89; and pornography, 119, 121; rural, 34, 79, 83, 84; and sexual violence, 35, 37; stalking in, 39; urban, 75, 103; youth unemployment, 150

Urban Behavior, 143–44

Veblon, T., 94, 158n2

victim, 28, 40, 130, 147; blame, *58*, 108, 109

victimization, xvii, 5, 7, 8, 30, 42, 49, 51, 79, 109, 112; and male peer support, 101-102; rape, 65, 73; risk factors of, 35–36; sexual, 34, 47, 111, 124, 125, 127; violent, 32, 108. *See also* male-to-female violence; violence

violence, xix, 10, 14, 18, 23, 44, 54, *57*, 76, 82, 84, 90, 116, 141, 146, 147; and all-male subcultures, xiv, 10; anti-, 21, 145, 148; and antifeminists, 6, 8; broad definition of, 10–16, 21; continuum, 21–22; CTS, 17–19; family, 1, 2, 33; gendered, 24, 73, 79, 109, 148; interpersonal, 2, 99; intimate, 8, 19, 21, 32, 43, 75, 86, *88*, 100,

104, 107, 117; male, 8, 9, 26, 28, 81; and male gangs, 65, 99; marital, 8, 30, 31; motivation, 20–21; narrow definition of, 6–7, 19; pornography, 123, 126, 130, 131; in same-sex relationships, 16, 31–32, 43; and VAWS, 24–25. *See also* domestic violence; gender-neutral; gender-specific; intimate partner; male-to-female violence; physical violence; power and control wheel; separation/divorce woman abuse in public housing; sexual violence; violence against women

violence against women, 3, 4, 19, 23, 29, 43, 44, 57, 64, 75, 119, 127, 136, 142; boycotting, 143–44; broad definition of, 10–16; class, 41–42, 122; ending, 139–40; male peer support for, 37, 56; march, 142–43; in military, 112–14; and narrow definition of, 4–10; new technologies, 131–32; and pornography, 120, 123, 125; in rural areas, 34, 104; surveys of, 31–32. *See also* male peer support model; social support theory

Violence Against Women (journal), 75

Violence Against Women Act (VAWA), 8–9, 108, 109–11, 137

violent resistance, 19

vocabulary of adjustment, 59, 96

vulnerable populations, 33, 43

Warr, M., 91, 92

Water Torturer, 42

Websdale, N., 27, 79

Wellford, C. S., 70

"well-meaning men", 145–49

Whitehead, A., 50, 59

White Ribbon Campaign (WRC), 141, 142

wife beating, 46, 78, 101, 102, 104

Wilson, W. J., 74–75, 76, 78

woman abuse, 1, 2, 13, 15, 19, 23, 29, 41, 43, 50, 52, 55, 56, 58, 72, 76, 77, 86, 89, 104; and alcohol consumption, 57, 58; boycotting, 143–45; in Canadian public housing, 52, 76; CNS, 24, 31, 96, 124; feminist men, 142, 148; and gang, 71, 116; history of, 45–47; male peer support, 45, 53, 55, 75, 90, 103, 118, 152; and pornography, 123–27; and pornography and male peer support, 127–30, 132; research, 68, 97, 103; rural, 79, 85; separation/divorce, 88, 107, 108; and social groups, 67, 72, 74, 78; and social support theory, 48–51; and technologies, 110, 136, 140, 141; theories of, 68, 69, 70, 78, 80, 139; university/college, 53, 73, 74, 96–97, 97–100. *See also* economic exclusion/male peer support model; feminist/male peer support model of separation and divorce sexual assault; gendered social bond/male peer support theory of university woman abuse; pro-abuse; separation/divorce woman abuse in public housing; social and economic exclusion model of separation/divorce woman abuse in public housing

Wood, E. J., 112–14

Young, J., 70, 76, 89, 91, 92, 93, 116, 117

Zoo, 144–45, 159n5